Memoirs of the Warrior

KUMAGAI

A Historical Novel

by

Donald Richie

❖

Charles E. Tuttle Company
Rutland, Vermont & Tokyo, Japan

Published by Charles E. Tuttle Publishing,
an imprint of Periplus Editions (HK) Ltd.

LCC Card No. 98-88195
ISBN 0-8048-2126-7

First edition, 1999

Printed in Singapore

Distributed by:
USA **Charles E. Tuttle Co., Inc.**
     Airport Industrial Park
     RR1 Box 231-5
     North Clarendon, VT 05759
     Tel: (802) 773-8930
     Fax: (802) 773-6993

Japan **Tuttle Shokai Ltd.**
     1-21-13 Seki
     Tama-ku, Kawasaki-shi
     Kanagawa-ken 214-0022, Japan
     Tel: (81) (44) 833-0225
     Fax: (81) (44) 822-0413

Southeast Asia
     Berkeley Books Pte Ltd.
     5 Little Road #08-01
     Singapore 536983
     Tel: (65) 280 3320
     Fax: (65) 280 6290

Tokyo Editorial Office:
2-6, Suido 1-chome,
Bunkyo-ku, Tokyo 112-0005, Japan

Boston Editorial Office:
153 Milk Street, 5th Floor
Boston, MA 02109, USA

Singapore Editorial Office:
5 Little Road #08-01
Singapore 536983

for
Richard Hayes

To become a man,
a true and worthwhile man,
that was all I wanted

— from the *kowaka-mai*
Atsumori

Excerpt from the deposition of the Priest Rensei

On the thirteenth day of the first month in the first year of the Genkyū era [1204] I, the lay priest Rensei, declare the following:

It was in the fourth year of the Kenkyū era [1193], now eleven years past, that I began to pray for my rebirth in the highest paradise of the Pure Land.

I well know that to be reborn among the lower would bring an afterlife of bliss. But I also know that he who is reborn into the highest paradise may then lead the dying into the Pure Land.

It is for the sake of these others that I, Rensei, wish to be reborn into the highest paradise. Otherwise, I would refuse to be reborn into any of the other eight.

MS.
Seiryōji, Kyoto

Untitled MS.

On the fifteenth day of the fifth month in the first year of the Genkyū era [1204], I, the monk Rensei, formerly the Minamoto officer Kumagai no Jirō Naozane, take up my brush.

I am sixty-five years of age and, having written my deposition and thus prepared for my death, I now wish to turn to my life. It has been full and I now wish to transcribe what I have experienced.

In this I am different from other men only in that I have the leisure and disposition to do so. A priest with few tasks, I am free to sit here and contemplate the past in my chamber at Seiryōji.

It is old, this temple—built long before I was born. Just outside my porch lies a small garden of which I have grown fond. It does not consist of much—a few rocks, a tree, some moss—but it is pleasing. The winter sun reaches it in the afternoon.

Here I sit and remember and write. I have a library here and an archive, including some of the military lists of my time. Nonetheless, my account will be as badly written as my deposition probably is, and in my usual execrable hand. Like so many of my station and generation I never properly learned calligraphy.

I cast an eye upon this deposition, a copy lying here before me. An official statement, it seems certain, dignified—particularly the part about leading in the dying.

That part about my refusing any paradise except for the highest is, however, quite true. Having aspired to a position in this life, I see no reason for relinquishing it in the next.

TO BEGIN AT THE BEGINNING, NOW SIXTY-FIVE YEARS AGO, I WAS born in the sixth year of the Hōen era [1140] on the plains of Musashi, a flat land of marshes and meadows two weeks' march east of the capital. Back then many of the forests were still standing and none of the fens had been drained. There were consequently many animals—rabbits, badgers, bears. It was one of these last that my father killed, an act through which I came to carry the name that I do.

It happened in the following manner. One of these bears was ravaging Ōsata on the Musashi plain. After my father had killed the animal he was given an amount of land. Since the place was fittingly called Kumagaya—Bear Valley—he took its name for his own.

A name was needed. Though we were a Taira family and though my grandfather had held high office, exile to Musashi left us unknown. This was interpreted as punishment, since my grandfather had received an imperial order to kill himself. He loyally did so and my infant father would doubtless have died as well had not his nurse carried him off from the capital. Eventually brought to Musashi, he was adopted as a son by a local magnate, Nariki Tayu, of the Hisashita family, and upon attaining sufficient years married the daughter of the house.

Kumagai Naosada he was called. The name must have had a new and raw sound to it. If so, it fitted us well, living out there on the plains in a clump of huts dignified by the title of manor, surrounded by peasants and by soldiers no longer allowed to fight.

Perhaps that is the reason my father killed the bear. He desired to distinguish himself, to rise in the world. Killing bears was, to be sure, no especial feat in Bear Valley, but some notice was given this deed, perhaps because he was only sixteen at the time. Thus my parent received the right to the lands that became known as the family estate, and upon his death two years later much was made of the bear story and he was mourned as a great hunter.

Though I was only two at the time, I remember something of the ceremony—the long speeches, the great funeral pyre, and the invocation to the spirit of my disgraced grandparent. Later, when appropriately older, I was more fully informed about this person. He, a true Taira, had been loyal to the imperial cause and his enforced suicide was the result of slander. The emperor had been misled by the Fujiwara family, always meddling in government, and by the Minamoto clan, always maneuvering for power.

One result was that my father, who otherwise should have achieved fame as a great warrior, became known only as a local hunter. Another was that, after my elder brother had died— soon after our father's funeral, some childhood ailment—I was left with few prospects. Upon my mother's death, when I was six or so, I was given as a deserving orphan to one of the sons of old Nariki, a man named Hisashita Naomitsu.

My father had lived his short life lying always in the shadow of his family's history, and so initially did I. Though I swam in the river, climbed the old quince tree, trapped rabbits, caught fish, and snared pheasant like any country boy, in the evenings I would sit around the hearth with my adoptive relatives and listen to stories of the old days in the capital when my family had prospects and when my grandfather was still a great man.

It was during these long summer evenings, far from the capital, that I made my resolve to better myself. Having now no father, no elder brother, no one at all to assist me, I realized early that my future lay entirely in my own hands and that I must make my own success.

To this end, I, alone among these rustic children, attempted to educate myself. Old Nariki Tayu also believed that this would assist me in prospering and discovered a priest in a distant temple who would cheaply enough teach me my letters.

So I eagerly trudged through the winter cold and the summer heat to where the yawning priest attempted to inculcate *sodoku,* my reading of Chinese characters. In this he was not successful—to this day I cannot properly read, or write, a page. Fortunately, *katakana* was also taught as a help to reading the *kanji,* and this I successfully made mine. This simplified script still remains my main means of written communication. Nonetheless, despite my lack of aptitude, I remain grateful to old Nariki for thus beginning an education. Not, however, to his son.

Already I had learned that I could not look to this adoptive uncle of mine, Hisashita Naomitsu, for assistance. He had taught me to ride and to use the spear and the short sword but would take no further responsibility for my future. A cold man—avaricious too, as I was later to learn—he told me one evening that he would feed me until I was eighteen, the age at which my father had died, and that I must then look after myself.

* * *

And so I did, and here I sit, nearly forty years later, brush in hand, contemplating my past. I left Musashi, journeyed to distant Heiankyō [Kyoto] to become a warrior, and now sit here in that capital, at Seiryōji in Kurodani, a lay priest preparing for a somewhat longer journey.

A pleasant place, this temple. The paneling is seasoned, the lintels are worn, and the carved grill over the door is nicely fashioned. It reminds me of that country temple where I first learned to read and to write while the priest fell asleep and the fat summer flies buzzed.

The resemblance is all the stronger in that I am still learning. Occasionally an acolyte comes and helps me with my Chinese characters: late learning, necessary if I am to make my success-

ful way in what is left of this world. I am fond of my temple. It
has, like myself, seen much life.

It continues to—it is even lively. Now that Hōnen is in exile
and no one is any longer in charge of church affairs, a number
of young people have been moved in. Really they are laymen
who have taken to wearing the robes and are given leave to stay.
I do not know why—perhaps because they draw a congregation.

They are really no better than itinerant entertainers. Mostly
they improvise ballads, accompanying themselves on their lutes.
They have few duties, none of them devotional, and how they
expect to rise in the church I do not know.

I can hear them now, strumming away, testing this verse or
that—so typical of our youth these days: callow, feckless. They
are so confident too. Listen to them singing away:

> While yet governor of Aki, on a pilgrimage from Ise
> to Kumano, he was much surprised when a great sea
> bass jumped into his boat. Remembering that just
> such a fish had jumped in ancient days into the vessel
> of King Wu, he declared an auspicious event, and
> though it was a time of abstinence and observance of
> the ten prohibitions, they all partook of this felicitous
> fish. Perhaps that is why he was blessed with luck and
> why he and his sons and grandsons rose in office
> faster than a dragon mounts the clouds.

Commander Kiyomori—that is their subject this morning. As
usual, they have it wrong. That large sea bass jumped into his
boat, if it did, much later. Also, though it was eaten on a day
when such was prohibited, this did not result—as the young
know-nothings have it—in one stroke of luck after the other.
Rather, as I know, having served under Kiyomori, it would have
seemed rather to presage the end of all good fortune.

But, no. Glory is what the young want. Just listen to them.
Sons and grandsons rose to office more swiftly than dragons to

the clouds. This is what they sing—maybe because now the ambitious young have difficulty rising in the world. Perhaps that is why they come to out-of-the-way temples and sing about it. In my day, so unlike now, there was a need for ambitious youths, particularly those of us who had no parents, no money, and no prospects. We felt this, even in far Musashi. The times were unsettled, a change was upon us.

Long before I was born, the rapacity of Heiankyō was infamous. Local administrators appeared, always with soldiers, and carted off whatever they could find in lieu of taxes. Punishments and fines were much dispensed and many landowners were ruined. We daily heard of more and more land seized upon one pretext or another.

Manors were taken, along with livestock and the peasants themselves—whole families turned from the fields they had once tilled. Then the newly confiscated lands were deemed imperial, hence tax free. Whether the royal coffers received much of the money is doubtful. Our oppressors were the administrative officials who had gained independence from the court itself. And as more fields were freed from tax, those left were taxed the higher. Such greed seemed to fill the entire country.

We saw this happening. A neighboring farmer was ruined and his children were sold, a manor house was seized along with the owner and his wife, both still hanging from its eaves. Things could not continue as they were. Something must change. Something did—provincial families turned to the military for protection, and this meant work for local warriors from local clans, either Taira, from my part of the country, or from Minamoto soldiery. It was wiser to hire this protection than to lose everything to administrative agents.

Consequently, this patronage eventually turned straggling groups of soldiers into standing armies. I can only tell what I saw in Musashi among the Taira, but I presume the same thing occurred in Minamoto lands as well. Though units of both families had traditionally served as guards in the capital—my grandfather was one of them—and though troops were kept both in and around the city to ensure order, there had been until then no actual armies, nothing like the one we have now, as I write.

When I was fifteen or so, however, I saw them forming, these armies. I would run to the gate to watch a group of soldiers marching somewhere or other. Often a traveling platoon would present itself at the door and demand to be fed. While eating our millet, they would sometimes tell us of the great things going on in the capital.

I was, of course, wild to join these youthful troops. Though the fish in the streams and the animals in the woods were more real to me than all the grand families of the capital, I knew that merely shooting at the deer with my child's bow would not advance me in the greater world.

Having learned to use a sword, a rusty old blade, its edge long dulled, I already longed to be a soldier and was happiest dueling with the farm children, with their equally cast-off weapons. We would go into the fields and announce ourselves to our opponent, giving name, family, and rank. I, Kumagai Jirō Naozane of the Taira . . . I can still hear my adolescent voice. Then the farmer's boy would invent some name for himself and after such formality we would begin hacking away at each other.

That was the way men fought back in the old days. It was formal. One knew whom one was fighting. Not like now—masses of men milling anonymously about. To be certain, this formality was exercised only by the leaders, grand warriors all. Nowadays, when there are so many grand warriors, they no longer have the time for such lengthy preambles.

Back then no soldier—not even an officer—was considered grand. Rather, these new soldiers were all despised. They were thought to be useful only for settling land disputes and keeping order in the provinces. The imperial house was perhaps grateful for their protection, but the Fujiwara regents held the new soldiery in disdain.

Nobles and Fujiwara leaders alike used this new military then as we use servants now, with the difference that we order our good domestics carefully while back then the aristocracy exerised no care at all. They simply sent their soldiery into small and local battles where they were eventually butchered, and the roads made safe for the tax collectors. These warriors were, after all, only simple boys who merely hoped for spoil and, like myself, an escape from the farm.

How different now—a mere lifetime away. The warriors' estate is high indeed. There are ranks, and ranks within those ranks. There is protocol and something of an imitation-of-court ceremony. The peasant's son is now a high-ranking officer and has learned to use the new recruits as he himself was once used. And there is a rise in prestige as well. The warrior is now truly grand and even the rich merchants are in awe. Different indeed from the scruffy lot that first shuffled into the capital.

All this occurred during my time, one that destroyed a world and created another. Two strong military clans—the Taira and the Minamoto—each holding some claim to authority, finally turned against each other, and it was during these years that I played my part and attempted to rise in this world—I who as a boy had once stood in the paddy and called out: I, Kumagai Naozane of the Taira. . . .

* * *

Perhaps I should here say some words about myself and my character. I was born with good health and was blessed with a strong constitution which has not, until recently, failed me. I am of middling height and middling appearance and am unexceptional in most things.

In one, however, I am not. I have a temper, which I frequently lose, and doing so has lost me a number of advantages that ought to have been mine. It has consistently worked against my best interests.

My best interests are devoted to making a career for myself in climbing to the top of my chosen profession. That I have now had several—farmer, soldier, lay priest—would indicate perhaps that my success has been partial. Indeed, I so regard it. However, as my deposition indicates, I still attempt to reach the top. My aim right now is to get to the highest paradise.

This life of striving has, I must admit, been questioned. Hōnen, my mentor in matters religious, himself wondered why the opinion of the world should mean so much to me. He thought, you see, that my aiming at eminence was to ensure regard. It is not, however, the opinion of the world that matters to me. Rather, it is my opinion of myself. And it is with this that my famous temper interferes.

It—and another weakness. I am all too often able to look behind or beyond the proffered motive, able to see the other side. This makes me needlessly question. It may also lead to a kind of fellow feeling—a sentiment continually curbing my advantages. Try as I have to reform my character I have not been able to do so. It is the stubborn beast, a mind of its own, upon which I am forced to ride.

And finally, to end this list of afflictions, there is a regard for truth which will not be subdued, no matter how I try. An example of this is the dilemma I experience when I find myself credited with the head of Atsumori. Truly, I took it, and the fact is noted in the military lists. My argument is that I do not wish to see myself regarded as a villain—although one who, according to rumor, attempted a kind of restitution. I am not a bad man—in fact, I am a worthwhile one, and I desire to be known as such. At the same time, however, rumor gets the matter wrong and it is this which upsets me, even though getting the manner right would perhaps go against my best interests.

This is what I am like, always working against my true aims in this life. Having ruined my chances for the military life, I am sitting here plotting the ruin of an ecclesiastical career as well. For in these times, to be discovered writing so plainly of the past, as I intend to, would result in serious censure.

Yet here I sit, scribbling away, and for the most paltry and impractical of reasons. I want to make some sense of this past, and of myself; and I want to tell the truth. Is this not ridiculous? But, then, I am like that.

And now I have dwelt enough upon the sage person I have become. Let me return to the unformed youth that I was.

* * *

After a number of such military visits—bands of warriors on the road—we in the provinces understood that both the Taira and the Minamoto were gathering troops and that something important was about to occur.

Something did—a war. It began in the first year of the Hōgen era [1156] in the autumn. To it went my fencing instructor, an excellent man named Kurō. He was accepted by the Minamoto to train recruits. Having long looked with envy at the passing soldiery, fine youngsters off to make their fortunes in the world, I took advantage of Kurō's going to join him.

My adoptive uncle, Naomitsu, had no objection; indeed, he was pleased to see his expensive little charge go off. And so, one ripe day in early autumn I set out with a sword but no mount, walking the curving country road between the orchards of glowing persimmons, on to where I had never before been.

The road led to the Minamoto encampment, the only one in our part of the country. There I joined Kurō and made myself useful. It might now be thought strange that a Taira boy should attach himself to a Minamoto camp, but back then we did not yet know that the two clans would finally seek to destroy each other. Rather, we saw our families as united in seeking to protect the imperial house from the rapacity of the Fujiwara regents. It was thus not unusual for brothers to attach themselves to these different houses, or for father and son to join their respective troops only shortly to find themselves on opposite sides.

Clan loyalty was, unlike now, unimportant. Opportunity was what counted. If, as one strode into the capital to defend his

imperial majesty, one could attach oneself to a rising officer—
no matter his clan—then one's fortune was made. Thus, I saw
that becoming a soldier under a Minamoto officer was of practical value. At the same time, however, this customary lack of
family loyalty led to complications.

My own commander, Minamoto Yoshitomo, was the only
member of his family who had close relations with the Taira.
These he was later to demonstrate when, during the Hōgen
War, he was the only Minamoto to side with Taira no Kiyomori.
Consequently, in order to protect the emperor, Yoshitomo (as
we will see) besieged the imperial palace at the very time that his
own father and brother were defending it.

Though I too, through Kurō's influence, found a place in
Yoshitomo's ranks, I was too young and too low ever to move
close to our leader. He was then in his early thirties and going
about his business with that air of earnest preoccupation, which
I now recognize as a family trait. Nonetheless, I thought him a
great man (since my own fortunes were now so attached to his)
and longed to prove myself of worth. I followed him about with
shining eyes.

Finally word came. Our troops were to move to the capital to
protect his imperial majesty. It was, I remember, one of the last
days of autumn, and I yet retain the musty smell of grain, the
sudden scent of apples. We marched through forests, over
mountains; we forded rivers and strode through villages much
the same as those we had left.

When possible, we camped in these hamlets and treated the
inhabitants not much differently from the way those traveling
troops had treated us. Food, drink, even girls, we took. We were
already soldiers: we ate what we had and fucked what we could.

I use the word precisely—that was the way we talked. Now that
the late Yoritomo has so cleaned up the army—even instituted
baths—such plain terms are no longer heard. But back then we
farted at will, pissed where we were, shat where we slept, and
smelled to high heaven. We were an unpretentious lot.

After days of marching, one cold, late afternoon, rounding a high crest, we saw lying in the valley the great capital, Heiankyō. It is now much changed, but I well remember my first sight of the city, lying there below us in the low sun of early winter.

The city was square, which surprised us, and it had long, straight avenues, quite different from the straggling roads of even our larger towns. And these cut through each other, creating great rectangles. The city was so large, so planned, that we stopped to gape.

It lay there before us and we could see, tiny in the distance, the gates and the larger roofs of temples, the squares of green lawns that held the palace enclosures, and block upon block of dwellings. The smoke from the cooking fires rose into the air and the late sun turned it to gold.

This was a view with which I was shortly to become very familiar and eventually much irritated by. This was because it was there, in that pass, that we stayed. The ostensible reason was that we were to stand guard lest armies of mountain warrior-monks, suborned by the Fujiwara, should attempt to storm this pass into the capital. The real reason was that this Hōgen Incident (as it is now called, having been downgraded from being called a war) was essentially a local fracas. Calling in the troops from as far away as Musashi had not been warranted. Therefore we were kept out.

My reader will understand our chagrin as we observed the battle laid out before us yet remained stuck up on the hill, unable to descend into the capital to make our fortunes. All we could see were the fires as they blazed, though occasionally we made out the lines of soldiery and the scattered ranks of the fleeing populace.

Later we learned what had happened. Our war had been occasioned by disagreements within the imperial house. Emperor Toba had retired—as was the custom. This common process of retirement was variously seen as a Fujiwara ploy intended to weaken the imperial house and strengthen this family line, and

as a reasonable imperial decision. Reasonable because the ceremonial duties of an emperor were such that the only possibility
of actually having the leisure to rule was to abdicate and then, in
time-honored fashion, wield power as retired authority.

The now-retired Toba announced the ascension of another
son, Go-Shirakawa, who duly took the throne at the age of
twenty-eight in the second year of Kyūju [1155]. No sooner was
this decision made than ex-Emperor Toba died and his son,
Lord Sutoku, at once challenged Go-Shirakawa. This rivalry
between the two was soon known to all. Nothing like this had
ever before occurred, though the court librarians at once
embarked on fruitless search for precedents. Each of the two
claimants had his own faction. The Fujiwara believed that
strength lay with Sutoku, as did the Minamoto, already agreeing
with these regents whom they were eventually to supplant. The
Taira, on the other hand, lent their support to Go-Shirakawa.
Thus, though troops were there to defend the emperor, the
problem was which emperor. All parties were thus to a degree
rebels, and which side had been all along truly loyal would be
determined only by victory.

It was this process that I impatiently watched from my hilltop
perch, looking with longing at the billowing flames and straining my ears to hear the distant neighs and cries. Then it was
over. One morning I awoke and saw only smoke and the tiny
lines of the military, like ants at parley. These were the victorious supporters of the Emperor Go-Shirakawa. This meant that
the Taira had won: the Taira, Kiyomori, Yoshitomo, and
myself—for at once I saw the advantages of being by birth a
Taira, despite my presently wearing Minamoto colors.

Down below there seemed to be much activity. I could not
decipher it from my distance, but it turned out to be the executions. There was such a blood-letting in the capital that back on
the farm that year even the tax collectors failed to appear.
Everyone was busy at the execution grounds.

Among those being dispatched was Tameyoshi, the father of

my commander, who had been on the losing side. Yoshitomo pleaded for his father's life; but Taira no Kiyomori sensibly asked him how otherwise the victors were to deal with that pretender, Sutoku, and strongly suggested that he do something about his troublesome parent. I was told that the son was forced to call the palanquin into which his father was placed and carried off. To safety it was assumed, but the soldiers stopped the palanquin on a mountain path and made the old man get out and kneel. Following orders, they then cut off his head. Tameyoshi was said to have behaved in a composed manner and occasioned no difficulty, and the head was then brought back to the capital but not displayed.

Other heads certainly were. Soon most of Tameyoshi's sons— Yoshitomo's brothers—all had their faces on view. One who had escaped, the eighth and last son, Tametomo, famous as the greatest archer of his day, was soon captured, the tendons of both arms were severed and he was banished to the distant island of Ōshima, never again to bend the bow.

This living death excited favorable comment, since it was not bloody. Both the imperial house and the Fujiwara regents had been taken aback by all this post-battle carnage. For centuries, punishment had been by custom restricted to flogging and banishment. Now, however, the law having been changed, something as permanent as beheading was becoming so common that people no longer even turned to look at the staring eyes of former acquaintances.

Thus, while we were perched up on our hill over a hundred had their heads chopped off. It was said that the executions halted only because no more necks were available. As for my commander, Yoshitomo, he became infamous as the man who had executed his own father. The Fujiwara minister Michinori, due to marry, had refused the proffered hand of Yoshitomo's daughter and accepted that of Kiyomori's.

Our forgotten band on the hill was also disappointed, because we had attached ourselves to a now disgraced leader.

When Lord Yoshitomo finally remembered us and came to review our resisting ranks, we were a sullen lot. I no longer gazed at him with shining eyes. He had lost all attraction since he could no longer assist me—could not even get me into Heiankyō. I was ready to seek my fortune elsewhere. This resolve proved fortunate, for it was not four years before the man lost his own head as well.

* * *

Here, now, as I write in these newly spartan times, the Minamoto—the reigning family I later had the good fortune to join for a second time, otherwise I would not now be sitting here—have simplified history by smoothing the complications of what actually occurred.

Earlier political machinations are not now mentioned, since it was, you see, the will of Hachiman, great god of war, that occasioned the Minamoto rise. With the imperial family now so tractable here in ruined Heiankyō, where foxes walk the boulevards and badgers roam the palaces, the rise of the Minamoto is seen as something preordained, the defeat of the Taira certain from the beginning.

The Minamoto may have saved the country as they claim, but they also ruined it. Much that was natural, innocent, and simple, vanished when the Taira were finally run to ground. A new suspicion, complicated by political considerations, by distrust, entered when the Minamoto acquired more power than had even the once powerful Fujiwara.

This I know I should not ponder, much less write. It is careless of me. After all, it was the Minamoto clan that won this war. For me to feel this fondness for another time, an era beyond recall, can obtain me no gain. But then I am sometimes like that: practical, looking properly to my own interests and then, in a moment of weakness, feeling for the lost, the gone—the vanished world of the Taira, even the head of little Atsumori bobbing in the surf. It is doubtless a grave defect.

* * *

The Hōgen Incident over, our Emperor Go-Shirakawa properly enthroned, we were dispersed and I spent a despondent time in the wandering entourage of the humiliated Yoshitomo.

I languished—it was as though my life had not yet begun; I was a farmer who could not return to his land, a soldier who had never fought. Though I did not despair, such emotion being thankfully foreign to my character, I was certainly not pleased with what I had so far been allotted in this existence.

It was then that I heard a rumor which interested me. The Taira, victorious, were in need of further troops in the capital in order that the person of his imperial majesty, Emperor Go-Shirakawa, should be safe from harm. Such numbers were necessary, since the Minamoto were again moving their soldiery into Heiankyō on the pretext of guarding the same emperor.

This being so, Taira warriors were being called to service and one of them was my uncle Naomitsu back in Musashi. Being no warrior and, further, as will transpire, no man of honor, he much preferred to sit by the manor hearth. It was a simple matter to have me made his substitute. It was also easy for me to mention my grandfather, innocently dead because of the discredited Fujiwara and the now diminished Minamoto.

Thus, eighteen years old, I was finally descending into Heiankyō—even, thanks to the influence of my martyred grandfather, in charge of a small group of men. Impersonating a seasoned soldier, I fittingly disciplined my marching troops, convincingly lost my temper when necessary, and at the same time attempted to hide the wonder I felt when I finally entered the gates of the capital.

Yet, truly, I was astonished. The people—never had I seen so many in one place at one time. Everywhere I gazed were men, women, children. Wherever I looked were warriors on horseback, foot soldiers with halberds, merchants with servants carrying bundles, women strolling, ladies riding in oxcarts or palanquins, little boys running errands, girls playing games with each other, and beggars of all descriptions. I remember the first simple question I asked myself upon viewing this unexampled spectacle: What could all of these people find to do?

We stared at them more than they at us. Already they were becoming used to the sight of daily arriving raw recruits led by gangling boy sergeants. Even the beggars, having learned that nothing was to be gained, did not approach. We, however, gaped at everything and found a stout merchant's wife as much of a marvel as a fully mounted officer.

We were dazzled by the new colors—vermilion armor, indigo cloaks, jet-black lacquered bonnets—sights never seen on our dun farms. And we were intoxicated by the odors—the tang of cut cedar, the scent of fine incenses, and spices we had never before smelled: cinnamon, nutmeg, aloe.

And so, on that first day we wandered the long, wide avenues of the capital and it was already late afternoon before I found where it was we were supposed to go. This was in the eastern part of the city, across from the new Gojō Bridge, and out into what had until recently been open country.

Here our commander, Taira no Kiyomori, had built his residence—at Rokuhara. More a separate city than a house, building after building, courtyard after courtyard, it covered what had been groves and meadows and now extended up the hills leading to the Kiyomizu Temple. Everything was still quite new and the smell of raw lumber hung in the afternoon air.

Approaching the main gate of this vast Rokuhara residence, we met a group of smartly marching troops and then glimpsed through the dust several men on horseback. I ordered my men off the road—we had no idea whose soldiers these were and our heads were still full of stories of Hōgen happenings. And at that moment the man on the lead horse passed us.

Thus, on our very first day, we saw Commander Kiyomori. I remember that moment well for this sight was the main marvel in a day filled with wonders. He was in black armor and rode a black horse, while his black helmet was carried by a page who paced beside the man and his mount. Of his person I remember mainly the nose. It was large and strong. And his ears. They also were large and stood out in a manner which might have been comical had his appearance been otherwise less impressive. He must have been around forty at the time and he was a fine figure of a warrior.

There he was, the mighty leader of whom we had so much heard, the head of our clan, the man responsible for the new ascendancy of the Taira. I gazed and my eyes shone.

* * *

In those early days in Heiankyō, during that year before the Heiji War, I recall that soldiers were everywhere: Minamoto troops—all traitorously working for the disliked Fujiwara, we said; or our own—staunchly protecting his majesty. Every grand building in the capital seemed to have a guard post; troops were forever trotting from one section of the city to another, officers on horseback cantered by and members of the high court military were jogged to and fro in palanquins. Everything was surprisingly disciplined.

Where we had come from, soldiers had the reputation of being unruly. Back in Musashi, farmers hid when troops went through. Shutters were put up and so remained until they had passed—usually carrying off with them whatever they could lay their hands on: barley, yams, the occasional peasant girl.

The only value of a soldier seemed to lie in his ferocity. The Minamoto were openly the teeth and claws of the Fujiwara and we Taira were likened to the fabled dogs of Chang-an in distant China. Like these animals, our soldiers were encouraged to bark and to bite. Yet now, in Heiankyō, we were suddenly civil, and able to take our proper place in a proper society.

This had been ordered by Kiyomori—we were to behave as befitted our new station. Previously, having no wealth, few military men had been allowed financial dignity. The fiefs given deserving army officers were notoriously in barren mountains or on desolate moors, where the unhappy recipients existed on what the court threw their way. Now all of this was changed. Kiyomori, to suit his own dignity, took to rewarding and disciplining his troops. Never had I seen soldiers so clean, nor so ready to obey commands.

It was thus a heady season. For the first time we soldiers had a future. Kiyomori had been one of us—and now look at him. His opportunity was ours. And in this possibility dwelt hope. We thought well of our prospects and became, for the first time, well behaved. We were on the right side, the one on the ascendancy.

There were various accountings of our leader's rise to power. One of our favorites was that he was in actuality the son of the Emperor Shirakawa, now dead these twenty-five years. This meant that royal blood flowed in the veins of our leader and that in protecting the present emperor he was also performing a filial duty. Another accounting—this one popular among our enemies—was that he was the unfortunate issue of a deranged priest who had gotten to his mother. We called this a typical Minamoto story. Back then anything contrary to the Taira cause was called Minamoto.

Lord Kiyomori was himself careful to appear the best-bred warrior the capital had ever seen. He showed great concern never to infringe upon any of the imperial prerogatives and was always punctiliously laying this or that idea before his highness. In this he was conspicuously different from the Fujiwara regents, who were often overbearing to all, including the emperor, and from their Minamoto lackeys, who were always surly.

The good manners of our leader were not, I think, actually due to any especial reverence felt for the imperial person. Back in those days an emperor was just another man, an important one, one to whom duty was owed, but quite mortal. Thus it was not at all like these Kamakura days when the emperor—though of little political significance—is treated as though he were a deity.

No, Lord Kiyomori behaved respectfully because it was politic to do so. I think any man in his position might have so behaved. I certainly would have.

* * *

All this chronicling. For whom, I wonder, am I writing? Certainly not for the ballad boys whose racket I daily endure, though they might gain by my sober example; they are getting everything wrong as they turn history into entertainment.

For whom, I wonder—not, certainly, for the young louts now in charge up in Kamakura. They know nothing of history. For them the world began with Yoritomo. Even Kiyomori, his great enemy, means nothing. But one can understand this. When the infant Antoku went into the depths, he carried with him an age. A civilization was swallowed and nothing is as it was. For the soldiers now in Kamakura everything earlier is useless.

Not for me, however. I experienced those days and, though I do not want to be one of those doddering ancients forever bewailing necessary change, I cannot believe that my years have meant nothing. That is why I now wish to put them—my life— into some kind of order.

Also to create a permanence where none unfortunately exists. I well realize that impermanence is our natural state, one that we would—as the Lord Buddha suggests—be wise to accept. Nonetheless, I am human enough to resent such eternal evanescence. So I scribble to explain myself to myself, though none but perhaps a few of my descendents will read this after I am gone. Yet, like everyone else who has ever lived this sorry life, I want to be remembered. And I want myself and my times to be remembered accurately, which is among the reasons I resent those sensationalizing scribes down the hall.

Things as they then were . . . as I write, I remember how Kiyomori appeared that first day, sitting there, black upon his black horse. He seemed so much himself. That is how I thought of him: this man is entirely who he is. And behind this thought was my own idea of myself—so unformed. Kiyomori could experience no doubts, and I was myself at the time composed of little else.

To become a consistent, understandable person; all of a single piece, standing firm against the tides of time; one who logically looks after his own interests—steadfast and memorable, a worthwhile person. That is what I am still wicked enough to want, priest though I am.

* * *

Time passed swiftly. It was now two years after the Hōgen War and its grand head-display, and there had been many changes. The imperial palace, fired during the disturbances, had been rebuilt, and there were new departments, new ministers. Traditional court ceremonials not practiced for a hundred years were revived; the music academy and the training school of court dancers were again opened; wrestling contests were once more seen in pavilions in the palace park; the pleasure houses were filled with ever younger girls; and Commander Kiyomori policed the capital so well that there was the promise of lasting peace.

A part of this welcome change was ascribed to the ascension of the new emperor. His Imperial Majesty Go-Shirakawa retired and in his place was installed the young Nijō. The welcoming of a sixteen-year-old was in part due to dissatisfaction with his predecessor. It was not so much Go-Shirakawa's taste for low-life, though he did tend to fill the palace with popular singers and stay up till all hours. Rather, it was felt that with such popular tastes went a certain inclination toward intrigue and machination. In addition, it was well known that Go-Shirakawa had his own wealth—he was a major landlord. The new emperor, on the other hand, was said to be properly poor, possessed of a probity much beyond his years and of a conservative turn of mind, which much resembled that of earlier rulers.

Under his reign, then, people hoped that things would be like the good old times, when the emperor smiled upon his subjects and all went well: a time of eternal peace. The people, however, did not have the opportunity to discover if this would actually have come about. Late in the last year of Hōgen, the first year of Heiji [1159], this lasting peace ended.

It ended on the fourth day of the twelfth month on a cold and windy night. We were all in the guardhouse. It was too chilly to wander the streets or to go to the pleasure quarters, so most of us were asleep. To be sure, we should not have been, we were on guard duty, but the Commander had left the week before on a pilgrimage to Kumano Shrine and had taken a large number of officers with him, so our discipline was relaxed.

Though a full complement of guards was on watch, none of us expected anything but more days and nights of nothing happening, and so we were unprepared. At midnight I was sound asleep, and it was just at this time that the Minamoto attempted their coup.

Later we discovered how. Vice-Councilor Nobuyori, a Fujiwara courtier, formerly favored by Emperor Go-Shirakawa, had earlier in the year applied for a higher position. The retired emperor, no longer favoring the man, had refused. In this he had been counseled by yet another Fujiwara, Councilor Michinori, a man who had the imperial ear—and who had, incidentally, also had the death penalty reinstated and was consequently responsible for the executions at the end of the war.

Michinori was also, in addition, something of a joke. His wife, a large, stout woman, had been the nurse of Go-Shirakawa and thus enjoyed special privileges at the cloistered palace. A great gossip, she was always running in and out with this story or that. This amused the low tastes of the retired emperor and so she was eventually able to forward her husband's career. The joke consisted in how she so obviously managed her spouse—the bossy wife and the henpecked husband are usually figures of fun. What made it more amusing was that he had earlier chosen the tonsure and had become very holy. It was said he had taken holy orders in order to escape from her, but if so the ruse had not succeeded and now we were daily diverted by the sight of this man of the cloth being led about by the nose.

The aspiring Nobuyori was incensed that advice from this upstart priest had kept him from what he believed to be a deserved appointment. Not that he deserved much. Already Captain of the Outer Palace Guards, he could not even ride properly. There was a now famous incident (a part of those disturbances for which he was himself largely responsible) where he could not successfully hoist his considerable bulk to mount his horse, while a group of his own guards stood about and hid their smiles.

Still, though indolent and overweight, Nobuyori was not without a political sense. He decided upon a coup that would chasten Go-Shirakawa and ruin Michinori. Taking his case to the aggrieved Minamoto, he received discreet sympathy. Indeed, he and his chief sympathizer, my former commander, Lord Yoshitomo, kept their plot so successfully secret that few in the court, and no one among the Taira, knew what they were about.

In this peaceful interlude no one was thinking of dissent. There were, to be sure, many Minamoto officers and soldiers in the capital, but there had been no recent incidents between them and us. Everyone knew that the Retired Emperor Go-Shirakawa favored the Taira—one had but to look at the grand state allowed Lord Kiyomori—but the opinion was that our two families had gotten their various allegiances so confused in the Hōgen War of two years before that there was little likelihood of our again fighting each other. In current Kamakura terminology, the necessary polarity had not yet been achieved.

But such opinion was mistaken. Yoshitomo continued to be angry at the slights suffered at the conclusion of the Hōgen War, and hence had entered into this plot with Vice-Councilor Nobuyori. Thus, on that cold night, the vice-councilor took his troops and went and hammered at the gates of the palace. His majesty was still awake, late as it was. Always fond of night life, he and two of Michinori's sons were watching the court dancers practicing for a performance scheduled for the New Year's celebration. When they first heard the racket outside they thought it was a fire.

Everyone was thinking about fire that evening. It had not rained, the air was dry, and the wind was strong. Also, less than a month before there had been a conflagration in one of the riverfront palaces and a young princess scheduled to dance at New Year's had burned to death. Now, hearing the noise, Retired Emperor Go-Shirakawa became perturbed and it was then he learned that an armed Nobuyori was author of the commotion, that he had—having perhaps been hoisted onto his animal—ridden over with all of his soldiers, and that he was now demanding audience.

There are various versions of his reception, but the most likely one finds Vice-Councilor Nobuyori complaining that Councilor Michinori had brought false charges against him and that this same person was going to have palace troops come to arrest him. It was upon Nobuyori's having learned this that, escaping, he had come to bid farewell to his imperial patron.

As was intended, the retired emperor was confused by this explanation. He said there was no truth in such allegations and that he would himself go and see the reigning emperor—the sixteen-year-old Nijō—and make certain that such rumors were silenced.

Nobuyori well knew Go-Shirakawa's habit of pretending powerlessness and referring all decisions to the inexperienced Nijō, so he could now say that this seemed an excellent thought and if his majesty would but get himself ready then he—Nobuyori—would loyally accompany him.

The retired emperor, angry at this, asked what he meant, to thus order about an imperial person. Several of the attending officers indicated what was meant by seizing him, shoving him into a palanquin, and rushing him out of the gate. Michinori's two sons were then dispatched, and the palace set on fire.

In the meantime, the Emperor Nijō had been awakened by Yoshitomo and his men entering the palace they were supposed to have been guarding. He was taken to an outlying building and locked up just as the retired emperor arrived and was secured in the palace archives. All of this was completed by two in the morning.

The Minamoto were now in command. They had both reigning and retired emperors, they controlled the guards' office, the heads of the councilor's two sons were already on view at the east gate, and now all the rebels had to do was deal with Michinori himself, with the absent Kiyomori, and with us.

By the following morning, Vice-Councilor Nobuyori was installed in the offices of the Police Commission, issuing proclamations in the name of the reigning emperor. Soldiers had already surrounded Michinori's mansion and burned it down with everyone in it, including the bossy wet-nurse wife. Her husband managed to escape but was several days later discovered in Uji and decapitated.

The tonsured trophy was brought back and displayed on the banks of the river. After that, any household members remaining—some nineteen, we later heard—were one by one beheaded under the sightless eyes of the man who had himself revived the death penalty.

The morning after the insurrection the wind had dropped, but it was still cold and the capital remained shuttered. We too at Rokuhara did not venture out far. Our leader was away and Minamoto soldiers stalked the streets. We were safe—Rokuhara had been designed as a fortress, there were several wells and enough food—but we were confused.

And so we remained. Though messengers had been at once dispatched to Kiyomori, our commander was still far distant and he had so made himself sole leader that without him none of us knew what to do.

While we remained inactive in our fort, there was over at the Fujiwara residences a scramble among the usurpers for the various offices of state. Nobuyori finally obtained his wished-for title of General of the Imperial Guards and a ministerial post as well; Yoshitomo was given the province of Harima, and at the following banquet a triumph for the Minamoto was officially announced.

Why at this point an attack was not launched against us at Rokuhara I do not know. It was later said that Yoshitomo had so counseled but that the indolent Nobuyori overruled him, saying that it was an unlucky day for such an enterprise and that, in any event, he—still the cautious Fujiwara courtier in all things—thought they had best wait to see what the forces of Kiyomori would do.

We did nothing—stayed inside and so remained for ten whole days. It was a strange period—now sharply cold and us holed up in our fortress like wasps in winter. Except for the cooking fires one would have thought the place deserted. Then on the nineteenth day of the month, Kiyomori returned.

How happy we were to see him. All of us cheered and his wife ran to greet him just as she was, barefoot, right out into the snow of the courtyard. He had with him many more men—soldiers from Ise—and though this meant that room had to be found for them in our already crowded encampment we were pleased to welcome them.

At first we thought it was their vast number that had intimidated the Minamoto into letting them through to Rokuhara. Later we learned that this was rather the doing of Nobuyori himself. He reasoned that, since he held both emperors, Kiyomori could do nothing. And so this newly appointed General of the Imperial Guards allowed his enemy safely to return.

Others did not reason that the leader of the Taira could do nothing. By the morning of the twentieth day of the month, Nobuyori was all alone in his palace, except for Lord Yoshitomo and his men. All the others, terrified of the anger of Commander Kiyomori, had deserted. The peace had ended.

* * *

This war between the Taira and the Minamoto officially began in the early morning of the twenty-seventh day. At three, a group of masked soldiers entered the palace archives and roused the retired emperor. They took him—again protesting, it is said—from the northwest gate, eventually depositing him at the Ninnaji, a temple well outside the city gates. Just how easily this was accomplished I myself learned, since I had been ordered to serve on a like mission: the liberation of the Emperor Nijō.

Accompanying us were two Fujiwara officers—Tsunemune and Korekata, head of the police. That they had come over to our side was a surprise, yet there they were, right in our compound, their horses shaking the snow from their manes. They then rode out again, our men following, to lead us to the enemy, now unlawfully occupying the imperial palace.

Entering the grounds was simple. We were unchallenged. Either Nobuyori was asleep or, more likely, the guards had already defected. Once inside, Korekata led us directly to a small building on the north side. There he battered at the doors until they were opened by the terrified retainers, and in we marched.

When his imperial majesty the Emperor Nijō appeared, I did not recognize him. To be sure, I had never seen him before—still, I was not prepared for this pale and beautiful sixteen-year-old with eyebrows plucked, lips painted, lacquered teeth shining in the candlelight. Only when this wonderful figure moved did I see that it was a boy. With him was a real girl—his sister.

They made no complaint but entered their palanquins and we traversed the entire length of the city unchallenged until we came to Gojō. Here a group of Minamoto soldiers guarding the avenue to Rokuhara halted us, and the wisdom of Korekata's disguising the emperor became apparent.

The soldiery was told that two palace entertainers were being escorted to their homes by express orders of Nobuyori.

Suspicious, they demanded to be shown. And so the young emperor and his sister were ordered out. Here, while the guards were looking at them, I also had the opportunity of gazing at his majesty.

He made a boyish girl when one knew he was a boy. While his sister cowered, his confusion was masculine, resolute. I felt a strong emotion—I was only three years older than he—which I set down to reverence. It began again to snow and there he stood, flakes in his locks. I gazed at the sight and my eyes shone.

Satisfied, the guards let us pass and we proceeded up the road and eventually reached Rokuhara at four in the morning. And about an hour later there came another knocking at the gate. After the lookouts signaled that there was no danger, we unbarred it to a most miserable and bedraggled lot. It was the emperor's household, whole dozens who, having no place else to go, had followed us out, wandering after their emperor in all their finery through the slush and sleet.

We had no room for them. With us, the Ise army, the imperial suite, and now these; there might be food and drink enough, but where would everyone lie down? Quite a number had no beds, but I was permitted my pallet because I had had the duty that night. And with me under the coverlet I took a young page who would otherwise have had no place to sleep. He was about fourteen, knew nothing but life in the palace, but was anxious for his own safety and hence willing to please.

His name was Tamamaru and though he came from common folk he had been chosen for imperial service because of his beauty, which was great—cold, wet, and crying though he was. I thought he looked just like my young emperor, though his teeth were white and his eyebrows his own. At any rate he was frightened enough to do whatever I made him, and we then fell into an exhausted sleep. Which was just as well, as I got no more sleep for some time.

By dawn the torpid Nobuyori awoke to what had occurred and in the snow and the dark called for a review of his troops.

Two thousand lined up, icicles doubtless on their visors. With the awakened general were Yoshitomo and his three sons— including the thirteen-year-old Yoritomo, whom I would come to know so well. Nobuyori gave his orders and Yoshitomo left with a mere battalion of soldiers to declare war.

They reached our bridge shortly after dawn and stood there in the white light on the other side of the river, a smallish group of men. Then Lord Yoshitomo rode forward and delivered his challenge.

It was a stirring one. A Minamoto, he shouted, was true always to the throne. And now that his majesty was in mortal danger due to the ambitions of the Taira, he—Minamoto no Yoshitomo—was ready to engage in righteous battle on behalf of his imperial majesty.

After this, he was, we later learned, to have been suddenly joined by Nobuyori and his two thousand men. The resulting sight—masses of armed men in the cold light of dawn—would have thrown Rokuhara into confusion and the attack upon this stronghold would have at once begun.

In the event, however, Nobuyori dawdled. He was still in the palace with his two thousand soldiers. And so the day dawned, the snow stopped, and it was a bright and sparkling morning— not at all appropriate for a sudden, nocturnal attack.

Kiyomori took advantage of this indecision. In fact, he had already dispatched his eldest son, Shigemori, with five hundred horsemen to take the palace, Nobuyori, and Yoshitomo's three sons.

When Shigemori galloped into that courtyard, Nobuyori turned and ran. Only Yoshihira, one of Yoshitomo's sons, held his ground and challenged Shigemori. This resulted in their famous duel, right outside the great hall, just in front of the sacred cherry tree.

Then, when Shigemori was getting the worst of it, some of the Minamoto horsemen who had run off with Nobuyori returned and attacked the Taira warriors. At that point, the chronicles tell us, the snow turned the color of cherry blossoms—a phrase which doubtless occurred to no one during the actual battle.

As more Minamoto returned to fight, more Taira were sent up from Rokuhara and the war raged. Four times the Taira were repelled and even the lazy Nobuyori, encouraged, returned to take the field. When Shigemori received an arrow there was a general rout and our men were forced back all the way to the Gojō bridge.

At this point I was wakened, and both Tamamaru and I were sent up to the wall to repell the invaders and, when none came, were sent outside to begin tearing down our side of the bridge.

It was a stirring sight that met our eyes. The far side was alive with men, all fighting in the slush. Horses were milling and slipping, and sometimes one of the horsemen would give a great cry as he fell with his mount into the black and icy river.

There was no telling which army was which, all the uniforms were wet and muddy and the flags had become indistinguishable, but we knew that the Minamoto must at all costs be kept out and so we all—soldiers, valets, pages, housemaids—worked to destroy the bridge.

Hard work it was too. That bridge had been made to last, and here we were trying to tear it apart with our hands. Since we were frantic, however, we managed to do so, throwing the loosened planks, the uprooted posts, one by one into the ice-filled stream below.

The housemaids' fingers were soon bleeding and Tamamaru dropped a railing on his foot. We worked hard and well but it seemed all for nothing because the enemy circled about and a group of men, led by Yoshihira, crossed downstream and was attacking us from the south.

Then Commander Kiyomori himself took full control. He seemed everywhere, his large nose and big ears all around us. He even found time to gather together the children onto the parapets and have them throw rocks down upon the invaders.

Tamamaru, limping about in his torn silks, hit a climbing Minamoto squarely in the face with a paving stone.

Though this invader fell back, joining his fellows at the base of our walls, still the soldiers came, slipping in the mud and blood, wading through the slush and slime, climbing on the bodies of their comrades. Soon we were tearing the very tiles from the roofs because both our arrows and our stones were gone.

This desperate battle lasted all day. I saw a child slip and fall on the soldiers beneath, where it was at once butchered; a young serving girl was disemboweled; our commander took an arrow in the sleeve. And all accompanied by a noise so great— shouts, cries, yells, screams—that eventually one no longer heard it, as one no longer hears the rush of a nearby waterfall.

The battle was going much against us, but we were saved by the foresight of Shigemori's lieutenants who now returned to the palace and took it, killing those who had remained on guard. When news of this reached Yoshitomo, he realized that he had no place upon which to fall back and so, with Rokuhara all but assured, he began a retreat.

He did not, to be sure, know how desperate our position was. Plans had already been made that it would be we who retreat-ed—back up the hills toward the Kiyomizu Temple. But we well knew of this desperation, and so when the unwise Minamoto showed us their backs we swarmed out of our gates like angry hornets in full pursuit.

So close had we been to defeat and death that our sudden reprise was like wine. We became instantly drunk and, leaping the small gap we had made in our bridge, we raced over the dead and the dying and set out in pursuit. From all of Yoshitomo's company only fourteen, it is said, reached the far hills alive.

I remember running after a wounded foot soldier, dragging himself along as swiftly as he could, and slicing through his neck—then being surprised that killing was so simple.

Even Tamamaru, who stayed near me all day, frightened but

elated, became carried away. He had found a sword and with it went limping about attacking the fleeing soldiers. He pinned to the ground a boy not much older than himself, then cut his throat. It was strange to see this fourteen-year-old page, blood-covered, his silk garments in shreds, grimace ferociously as he sliced through the living flesh and then look up to me for approbation.

Eventually there were no more to kill. The dead lay deep in the streets, in the river, and they were piled like earth-filled sacks around the snowy ramparts of Rokuhara. We went back to the fortress, my captured head bumping against my thigh—secured by its hair to my scabbard belt. Tamamaru's was held fast in his bloody fist, since his silken belt was lost. Already, the servants were making cooking fires, soldiers were pulling arrows from the gates, and valets were rolling bodies into the river where the winter current carried them away. It was sunset.

We soldiers were assembled in the big courtyard and Kiyomori himself addressed us, praising our fidelity to the emperor. This imperial personage was then brought out. No longer dressed as a girl, he now carried a ceremonial sword, and we all knelt and bowed.

Then we turned in our trophies. Mine was marked beside my name and added to the growing pile. Tamamaru's was not, since he was but a page. I thought I might get credit for his as well but it was instead added to a separate pile, later allocated to the credit of our leader. We were then given something to eat and sent to our barracks and to bed.

Mine was again my own. Tamamaru was herded back to the apartments of the young emperor and when I next saw him he was in a new silk outfit, purple on a cream background, and he looked straight through me. Again he was an imperial page and I was a common subaltern. The delightful disorder of battle was over.

* * *

The Minamoto were now in full rout. Yoshitomo and his sons

attempted to flee to the farther side of Lake Biwa; Nobuyori tried to reach Ninnaji to ask the retired emperor for pardon— neither succeeded.

Kiyomori's soldiers were everywhere and found nearly everyone. Officers, nobles, soldiers alike, all were decapitated the following day. The headless corpses were stacked like firewood and the heads were neatly laid out, as in a pumpkin field, scribes busily attaching labels and marking which was accredited to whom.

The following day Kiyomori ordered an inspection of the imperial palace and a ceremonial reinstatement of the Emperor Nijō, so we all bathed, put on clean uniforms, and made ourselves a splendid sight as our grand procession left Rokuhara, proceeding up from Gojō to the palace, the emperor and his sister in a ceremonial oxcart flanked by an honor guard. Along the way, homes and stores were unshuttered and the people of the city appeared, also all dressed up. The winter sun shone. It was like a holiday—as indeed it was, since that day no work was done.

At the palace there was an amusing occurrence. After the fighting, the place had been deserted and into it poured the destitute, all the orphans, beggars, and criminals of the city. Here they made themselves at home, dressed themselves up in silks and brocades, and built bonfires in the chambers. Not finding food, they butchered and barbecued some horses and left the remains. A corner of the council chamber was their lavatory, but in general they relieved themselves wherever they happened to be and cleaned themselves with whatever came to hand.

When our procession arrived, they were still deep in their revels, having located the imperial wine. Once it was discovered that we were there, however, they all emerged, looking like mice when the pantry door is opened. There they stood, still clutching their stolen finery, teeth chattering. However, much as they may have deserved it for so desecrating the imperial chambers, they were not executed. Rather, they were made to clean and repair their damage as best they could. This took the rest of the day.

I know—since I was there—that the guards considerably savaged the beggars while they were attempting to remove the mess they had made. And I know—because I saw it—that one pretty outcast girl, kicking and screaming, was raped by five soldiers in the back of the state chamber itself. Nonetheless, the townsfolk thought this all a marvelous leniency on the part of the stern Lord Kiyomori, and mercy was welcome after all the killing.

Perhaps further seeking to ingratiate himself with his subjects, at the end of the day our lord actually ordered that each of the laboring beggars should be given a measure of cooked millet. This sat well with the citizens of Heiankyō, who reasoned that if our new lord was this understanding and generous with the lowest, then they—somewhat higher—would have little to fear from him.

Then, finally, the Emperor Nijō—who had spent the day waiting in an undespoiled pavilion—was reinstated. It was not really a ceremony, since there was no precedent for it, but Kiyomori saw to it that it at least appeared ceremonial.

There were torches that made the palace rooms even brighter than day, and musicians were ferreted out, and the dancers who had been practicing their New Year's numbers when the disturbance began were brought forward and made to perform—and so with great pomp and splendor the sixteen-year-old emperor again ascended his throne and the Heiji War was over.

* * *

The day after that we were assembled by the Kamo River and the conclusion of hostilities was signaled by the tallying of the heads. These, somewhat preserved by the weather, were laid out in long lines and the scribes read out their names, if they had any, and those to whom they were credited.

It occurs to me as I write that my reader may well no longer be familiar with this particular military custom. Routine behead-ing after battle is no longer practiced because in this era of peace we have no more battles. Back then, however, the taking and cataloging of heads was an important part of military life.

The reason was that promotions and other rewards were allot-ed to those of greatest valor, but the determination of just what that consisted was difficult. Hence this quota system. He who had the most heads was most valorous.

In theory, the system gave greater credit for better heads. If you killed an enemy officer you got more points. In practice, however, since there were so many fewer officers than soldiers, numbers as well began to count.

As a consequence, though collecting heads was important, whose heads these were became less so. Indeed, the innocent passerby was sometimes slain so that he could contribute his head to a soldier's account. As in this war where, I was told, there were five heads all labeled: Traitorous Monk Enshin Akamatsu.

Heads being this important, there was no question of taking prisoners of war. Surrender in battle ceased to be a soldierly option. The head was taken and the corpse was sometimes used for weapon practice. It was then thrown away, but the head was kept.

While still a common soldier, I had sometimes been assigned to the washing of a head or two. These round objects soon ceased to be human. One caught them by the ears or by the nose to turn them around and scrub away the gore. Occasion-ally, a dead eye would blink at the indignity and this always brought a laugh.

Naturally, each of us foresaw the possibility that our own heads would be handled in this disrespectful fashion. And when the thought occurred we would be rougher than ever, slapping that pale cheek or scrubbing away at those young lips.

There is nowadays none of this. Indeed the entire quota sys-tem that supported all of these decapitations has disappeared.

One is judged not by the number of staring heads collected but by more abstract trophies: diligence, perseverance, loyalty.

Perhaps I am again being old fashioned, but there was something reassuring about those melonlike objects bumping about the knees, held by their long hair from the belt or the saddle pommel. At least it was something to see and to smell. It was not, like loyalty, invisible. And there was something satisfying about the scrubbed face staring at one—for all the world like a small son—as the scribe called out, To Officer Kumagai Naozane—one head: name unknown.

* * *

Here in this time of peace I should perhaps say something further about war, specifically about killing. It is not something we often go about these days, and if we do, it is in an impersonal and executive manner. One side in a skirmish is sent against another and in the muddle a number, indeed, are killed. This is the result of administrative considerations. At the same time, however, it divests the slain of a kind of dignity that is his due, and it deprives the slayer of distinction. Let me enlarge.

Back in the time of which I am speaking, he who was killed had been chosen and he had had the opportunity of defending himself. Thus, due to misfortune or ineptitude, he could himself observe the transition from life to death and this conferred upon his position a sort of dignity—one which we demonstrated by the removal of his head.

He who killed was acknowledged as being better at his job, always a welcome compliment, and he was proved so at considerable risk of discomfort, always the sign of a competent craftsman. Hence the satisfaction at a job well done, as signified by all the smiles of those gathered around the piles of heads.

I was to be found there, grinning away with all the rest, for I had just returned from the excitement of battle. I had chosen my man (or been chosen—that sometimes happened as well) and we had chased each other about the field. With my sword held high, two hands gripping its handle as my two thighs gripped the heaving side of my mount, I experienced the full glory of battle.

How can I best describe it to you who have perhaps never felt it? First, perhaps by suggesting that the glory of battle is no empty phrase. What I felt was a kind of resplendence, a kind of bliss or, if you will, perhaps happiness. Racing away, sword in air, I knew I had never been more myself.

I might compare this feeling, in myself, to the loss of temper to which I am prone. When I allow this to occur I am as though filled with a liquor which fleshes me out, defines me. I am gratefully engorged and become a single entity. No longer do I reason and consider, doubt or worry. Rather, I am solid all the way through, as my sword is. I am utterly and only myself.

This feeling is defining, but now imagine it amplified until it eclipses even any consideration of the matter. Solid, now more a part of the mount than the mere rider, more the sword than the simple wielder, I am so entirely consistent that thought is stilled.

That blessed state—when thought is stilled. There are only a few occasions when the miracle can occur. When deep in prayer, when engaged in love, when lost in anger, and when committed to battle. To be filled with faith, with lust, with ire—it is all the same: one is filled.

Without a thought I urge my mount, I must be first in battle, first to burst upon the enemy, first to kill. Racing, my steed leaping over the barricade, I am inside the camp, my sword swirling as I grip my mount and see my adversary as he, as mindless as myself, comes racing to meet me.

We are so much more similar than we are different, but we have designated each other, and we must now fight. I grab at his bridle, he makes a fast pass at my sword arm; I wheel, aim for his neck, that exposed sliver of flesh just under the back rim of his helmet; he whirls and aims at my neck, that small V-shaped wedge of flesh between my cuirass and my collar.

If we miss, we wheel and try again. If one of us does not miss, the other falls slowly from his mount and lies in the dust, still or writhing—awaiting the coming sword and the final separation of spirit from body.

I have known only victory, never defeat (on the battlefield, that is) and so cannot share with you the emotions of the loser, but I wonder if these are so different from mine. I am filled still with my purpose. So is he with his. I have not returned to that dappled person I was. Nor has he gone back to any previous self. We are there, still alike—heroes, if you will, in that we have sur-mounted our petty persons to become these armored beings still filled with pure purpose.

You may wonder that I, a priest, would continue to so express myself. Yet it is something akin to this feeling I have been describing that I expect to discover in myself as I enter the blessed land—this sense of being whole, this miracle of the sun-dered parts together assembled.

I remember the forty-eight vows of Amida Buddha and dwell upon the eighteenth, the *Namu Amida Butsu*, Amida's "Original Vow." It is this I invoke to allow me passage. And it is I who opened this very road to those whom I bested in battle. My ambition to stay behind and guide the dead is perhaps best understood when one remembers that I have already led so many.

* * *

There followed a long era of peace—a full decade. It was, to be sure, an uneasy one, but I wonder if there is any other kind. These years of Taira peace were so filled with dissent and intrigue that I was not surprised the other day to hear one of our ballad-making novices singing away about the bad old times of which I am now writing.

Back then, sang this young voice, men both high and low lived with no peace of mind, lived as though walking always upon the thinnest ice or treading the narrow ledge above a precipice. The world had waxed corrupt and lax, and vice had outstripped virtue.

And so it had. To begin at the very top, there was an unusual discord between the retired emperor and the Emperor Nijō. The younger would not defer to the older, and Go-Shirakawa in turn could not countenance such disrespect in the younger.

The retired emperor would deprive the reigning emperor of several of his most trusted officers. Nijō would retaliate by decimating the attendants of Go-Shirakawa. This intercine and largely bureaucratic warfare made life difficult for those in the imperial service. A lord one day, banished the next, men's fortunes so fluctuated that great houses came tumbling down, whole families were sent weeping into the wilds, and suicides grew common.

With imperial bickering in plain view, political machinations, usually decently hid, slid into sight. The customary intrigues and maneuverings of the court cast off their shrouding layers of ceremony and flaunted themselves. One result was that the imperial house lost an amount of respect. Another was that the court of Kiyomori, himself so carefully circumspect, gained a like amount.

At the same time, though the Taira had supported the now-retired emperor against his elder brother during the Hōgen War of five years before, Lord Kiyomori presently desired that Go-Shirakawa should be deprived of some of that new power. Consequently, the imperial sniping pleased him.

Not that his pleasure was obvious. No one was more solicitous of both emperors than was Kiyomori, no one more punctilious in regard to visits and presents, no one more patient during long, closeted sessions than he.

I was often a member of the retinue that accompanied our lord on these imperial visits. We used to believe that our accompanying throng was so large because we had little else to do and so had somehow to be given employment, but I now think the real reason was that our numbers were meant to intimidate the court and to impose upon their majesties.

We would stand around in the grounds of the new palace while Lord Kiyomori was being entertained by the retired emperor. The sun hot on our helmeted heads, we waited, our noses filled with the smell of freshly cut lumber, which this modest little palace still exuded. Nor were we allowed to amuse ourselves. No talking, neither with each other, nor with the sometimes pretty palace servants who came to gawk. We stood or squatted or knelt, holding our flags and halberds and making a fine show while the higher officers were offered refreshment in one of the outer rooms where the future was being decided.

All to the Taira advantage. In recognition of our great service against the insurgents, Kiyomori was elevated to the senior grade of the third court rank. And over the years further promotions came fast; he was made member of the court council, then captain of the police commissioner's division, then vice-councilor, councilor, and finally state minister. Further, upon entering palaces he was no longer required to dismount from his carriage—a grand if cumbersome affair drawn on these occasions by a large ox, on others by us.

His privileges were those of premier, though that title was still withheld him. It was one he wanted because it promised ultimate power. In practice, however, the position was vacant. It was waiting for the proper person to be found. Since this person— someone capable of instructing the young emperor, someone who could govern in his stead, someone who was a model to the people—was scarcely ever found, the title usually went empty.

I well understood our Kiyomori's ambitions and his irritation at having the title withheld. After all, it was the ultimate indication that he had made something of himself. This was also my intention. And I too had my share of irritations.

My small platoon, originally boys from Musashi, now included city youths as well, and all had in this lazy peace grown insubordinate. They could not accustom themselves to being supervised by someone as rustic as myself. Their leader—me— they said, was such a country boy that he could not read even the simplest Chinese character. Jocular remarks about radishes were made, horse manure as well. And cow patties. Even my father's bear was joshed over.

I caught one of the men at such pleasantries and had him publicly flogged. The gathered men stared at the red muscle as a buttock split and there was a respectful hush—disturbed to be sure by the culprit's screams. Though this display muffled the ridicule, it did not increase my popularity.

Since I was determined to make something of myself, however, a good reputation was called for and so I continued to enforce discipline. I detained the entire group for the remark of a single man and had numbers of them locked up, beatings were common. During such sessions I became terrible in my wrath, and thus, in a modest way, emulted our respected Lord Kiyomori.

* * *

Our Taira policies were successful. In less than two years, by the second year of Ninnan [1167], Lord Kiyomori had assumed the highest position in the civil government and had finally received the coveted premiership. And in the years to come he would marry his daughter, Tokuko, to the new emperor, Takakura, and their son, the child-emperor Antoku, would be our lord's own grandchild.

In this our leader proved that he had learned well from our former foe, the now much diminished Fujiwara, for it had long been their policy to so intermarry their women with the imperial house that relations of fealty became those of family.

The resemblance of the new Taira clan to the old Fujiwara was openly commented upon. It was said Premier Kiyomori and his family controlled almost half the country. At that time the land was divided into sixty-six provinces and those governed by the Taira certainly numbered more than thirty. Too, Kiyomori's sons were all ministers, all of his daughters were married to royalty, sixteen of his close relatives were nobles, and thirty more were courtiers, while others—his was a large family—were made provincial governors or the heads of imperial guards.

He became as grand as he was powerful. Our Rokuhara fortress was transformed into a palace, at night as bright as day, lanterns everywhere. The most brilliant was the chamber housing our master's gem collection. It was so stuffed that there was no room for further offerings, though such appeared daily. People said the place shone even in the dark.

In the corridors the attendents were so brilliantly costumed that the popular song of the day called the palace a garden and these servants butterflies. The splendor spilled into the courtyards, which swarmed with horses and carriages, visitors and petitioners. And in the apartments were rare woods, incenses, spices, brocades, embroideries, jewels, gold, silver. By comparison the imperial palaces, homes of the emperors Go-Shirakawa and Nijō, were shabby. It was in regard to this successful splendor that Lord Kiyomori's brother-in-law, Tokitada, famously said: If one is not a Taira, one is not a man.

This was a sentiment to which the general populace enthusiastically subscribed. A rage for things Taira swept the capital. Our winning color (red—the Minamoto color was white) was everywhere: red flags, red bunting, even a few red robes on the more patriotic wives of merchants. There were also a number of fads—a way of wrapping the kimono sash, of doing the hair, of twisting the brim of the headdress: these were found to be in the Taira manner and became the fashion.

So overweening was this new regard that when Kiyomori took up with a young dancer named Gio, other young dancers began calling themselves by such names as Gini and Gifuku and Gitoku and Gichi. Equally, there was a gradual move of the capital to the east of the city, where stood the Rokuhara, now a palace in itself with a splendid new bridge leading to it. Property around the Kiyomori estate, in particular the Gojō gate, became extremely expensive as the gentry bought to build.

In consequence the western part of the capital, never much,

became even more unfashionable. It was here that the beggars found their homes. They swarmed everywhere but were mainly about the temples. Guards had to be posted to protect the faithful in their prayers, since those in need of alms became more and more demanding.

Yet, for those already prosperous, these years of peace were indeed rich times. Money (newly minted, ordered by the new premier) was to be made from almost every enterprise, and the newly rich set about aping their ruler. Here the house of Kiyomori set very high standards. Take, for example, the sudden fad for learning it engendered.

As I remember, it began around the first year of Eiryaku [1160]. Younger officers were encouraged to visit the Imperial Academy and there read the Confucian classics, long moldering in their old Chinese bindings. Few, of course, could, but such is the power of fashion that there shortly appeared an entire race of military scholars whose sole purpose was to make simplified adaptations into the native tongue and to indulge in learned disputation on this arcane point or that.

The officers passed the fad onto their men who shortly memorized a few tag-lines with which they now decorated their observations. From here the craze descended to members of the merchant class. Having soon become learned as well, they in turn passed it on, and eventually even the cooks and postillions could supply a sage quote if so required.

I remember that ladies' letters—I was paying some attention to a daughter of the minor gentry at the time—became almost impossible to read. Due to the cost of paper, they were always crammed with afterthoughts, but they now became even more illegible, since the new learning had to be given a place. Confucian precepts, historical quotations, Chinese poems—the letter would arrive so scribbled over that it would appear entirely black.

Attempting to read one of these indecipherable missives was doubly difficult for me in that I knew no more Chinese characters than did my correspondent. I could read *kana* script but my rural upbringing and her sex had kept us both from learning the cumbersome *kanji*. When I answered her, I had to go to a common scribe, and perhaps my correspondent was forced to a similar extreme.

I, however, unlike her, could otherwise better my estate. With the rage for learning burning so brightly, it was simple to receive permission for further schooling and easy to find a teacher. I again chose a priest and he was happy to get the money. In return, this elegant personage, much given to aphorism, weekly drilled me in the intricacies of our written language.

Consequently, I could at last finally get through one of those letters of hers in which she elegantly remembered on the back of page two to remind me to honor my parents and observe the laws of society, all in Chinese characters. And I thought how wise of Kiyomori to have insinuated these conservative observations of the venerable Confucius, since, if followed, they made ruling an easier task than it might otherwise have been. Such a thought was mine alone, however. One does not question the naturalness of a new fashion—its very attraction lies in its apparent spontaneity.

There was, however, nothing spontaneous about Kiyomori and the men with whom he now surrounded himself. Everything was nicely calculated. And he who commanded two emperors had small difficulty in ruling a willing and bemused populace.

For so doing he fashioned many tools. One of the most effective was his young cadet corps. This consisted of three hundred boys, all from fourteen to sixteen years old. They had their hair cut in a distinctive bobbed fashioned and they wore a special costume—a quite dazzling shade of purplish-blue elegantly called azure. These lads were the rage of the city, feted, dined, welcomed everywhere, since it was they who in large part created the various diverting fashions that kept everyone agog.

It was well known, of course, that they were also spies and that it was through them that Kiyomori and his court learned of covert happenings in the capital. But it made small difference to the populace that the boys were little tattletales, puffed up with their own importance. And the small spies could also be used for benefit as well. If Kiyomori heard a lot that the merchants would prefer he had not, he also heard much that they wanted him to. Since the Rokuhara lists of preferment were based large-ly on the reports of the boy-spies, it was merely proper manage-ment for merchants and the middle classes to court them and then send them home with messages of exemplary faithfulness and undying fidelity.

We in the army did not take so well to this effective little corps. They were always running about self-importantly in their azure outfits, combining within themselves the sullenness of adolescence and the stupidity of childhood. They were all un-commonly good looking, it is true, but none were to be trusted.

Nor did they much take to us. Hence I was surprised when one of their mentors—all of whom had been pages or red-robed spies themselves—came to the barracks to call upon me. Several years younger than myself—I was then in my later twenties—he looked to be plumply dissipated and seemed to be full of him-self.

Though his ostensible purpose was to speak of a minor mat-ter concerning a certain platoon, his questions were so pointless and his methods so circuitous that I soon realized that it was I who was being investigated.

Such had become routine and, as I afterward learned, I was up for a promotion and this always required routine investiga-tion. In the platoon in question was a soldier who was friendly with two of the young men in the retired emperor's imperial guard. Official suspicion of myself was, however, unwarranted. I knew none of the people involved and was, perhaps conse-quently, promoted.

During our talk, my interlocutor sat there staring at me and fanning his bulk with his fashionable red-lacquer fan. Did I not remember a certain night, the night the Heiji War began? Think now, didn't I remember?

It was little Tamamaru whom I had befriended some dozen years before, now quite unrecognizable. I should never have known him had not some impulse made him tell me. He lowered his eyes, then looked up through his lashes.

If this casual and by me almost forgotten episode was known to Rokuhara, then what, indeed, was not known? Tamamaru had been sent to me because of our casual meeting when we were boys. Though disturbed by the implications of the investigation, I was nonetheless moved by admiration for Premier Kiyomori and his administrative system. He had become truly successful.

* * *

Since I had been in the service of Kiyomori for nearly a decade now, my fortunes had risen with his. From a provincial foot soldier turned troop leader, I became a subaltern and, eventually —my fidelity tested by Tamamaru—I was made lieutenant.

Among the reasons for the appointment was that it was discovered, with some help from myself, that my family had long been firmly Taira. Also, that my imperial-guard grandfather had indeed been forced into suicide by the scheming Fujiwara. Making me officer to the near-imperial Premier Kiyomori was a way of righting ancient wrongs and, at the same time, affirming the benevolence of the current reign.

Further, I had learned to put myself before my superiors, to be always there, always seemingly occupied with my duties. Lord Kiyomori liked his men to be busy, to serve long hours, to prefer to remain on post even when nominally free. Having little otherwise to do, I often stayed behind the others and this after a time attracted admiring notice. I kept my men on an uncomfortably short leash and was obviously dedicated.

The promotion to lieutenant meant more money, a new uniform, increased prestige, and not much more responsibility. It did not, however, increase my popularity with my men. Rather than congratulate me upon my success in my chosen profession, they made yet more jokes about bumpkins in uniform. For this they received welts upon their naked backs and were thus encouraged to slander more quietly. But I never became a popular officer.

We officers were, however, popular with the populace. For one thing we kept our men in order and prevented rapine and pillage. For another, we belonged to the most powerful man in the empire and there was no telling when any of us might be further elevated. In addition, we were decorative and entertaining and gave the townspeople the pretexts they needed for parties and excursions.

I was consequently often invited out, and often accepted, having now accomplished my purpose in having stayed inside working overtime. At one such tea party I had the pleasure of again meeting my old fencing teacher, Kurō. Now he sat cross-legged on a round cushion expertly balancing a teacup on his knee and expressing surprise at how big I had gotten. And I—though I did not say so—was equally surprised at how this provincial sword teacher had become such a polished fencing master, now fit for the best Fujiwara society.

Perhaps, however, it was just our lingering rustic airs that so capitivated those folk in the capital. One proper matron, I remember, asked my name and, when I courteously replied, she was not able to repress a small shiver. It must have sounded barbaric to her—that bear reference—and this both alarmed and attracted the lady.

Popular, we were commanded to the homes of the minor aristocracy to attend lengthy dance recitals followed by delicate fare served with becoming modesty by well-born daughters, or were invited to the richly ostentatious homes of merchants, offered Chinese wines and other delicacies from distant climes, and had commoner daughters thrust upon us.

The desired ends were identical. Both aristocracy and merchants wished to connect their houses with that of Kiyomori in any way that they could. Marriage with one of his lieutenants was a tenuous connection but was thought better than none. And there was not that much choice. All of Kiyomori's proper offspring were reserved for the imperial line.

Then too, we young officers were also occasionally invited to the imperial palace—not Emperor Go-Shirakawa's but Emperor Nijō's. While we did not view the young emperor himself—I was never to see him again after those early glimpses—we saw a lot of his court.

It was not all that much fun. There were moral readings and the slower of the court dances. Flirting was not encouraged. The Emperor Nijō had grown up serious. Far different, we heard, were the evenings at the retired emperor's palace. Here the rooms were brightly lit far into the night and the air rang with those popular tunes of the day, the *imayō*, which Go-Shirakawa so loved. There were contests where singers vied with each other, and dances to go with all the music. I imagine that dalliance was encouraged as well. To these, however, we were not invited—only the higher-ups from Kiyomori's court were.

At one of the imperial parties at Emperor Nijō's palace there was a pretty girl, daughter of a minor official, who had apparently been told to interest me. Though her parents were forward in their attentions, I grew to like her because she neither fawned nor complimented, but went about pouring my cup full just as she had been ordered.

After the graces of the others, her undemanding and straightforward manner was strangely attractive. Indeed, her very lack of interest interested me. Ten years as a rising and likely officer candidate in what had become an increasingly dissolute capital had accustomed me to easier conquests.

Most of our evenings out were given over to dissipations of various sorts. We young officers gambled, drank, quarreled, and ended up under the coverlet with someone we did not know and often enough did not even desire. Under such circumstances, making love becomes as ordinary as eating and when food is plentiful one does not think of hunger.

As a consequence of my disordered life, I was thinking of some alliance that would bring domestic comfort and at the same time would strengthen my chances of rising further in my career. So I looked into the background of this girl who, unlike the others, paid so little attention to me.

Her name was Ōto and she was of good Taira stock, of blood fine enough for her to serve as lady-in-waiting to Fuji no Kata, the wife of Tsunemori, a younger brother of Kiyomori.

He was, as I have indicated, encouraging courtly ways, so we now had our own nobility, and both Ōto and I were on the edges of it. Her parents thought that marriage to one of Kiyomori's lieutenants would forward their daughter in the world, and I believed that an alliance with a close associate to the wife of Tsunemori would elevate me. Consequently, it was a union made in heaven, as they say, and we were shortly wed.

It was winter, cold and dry, the air smelling of charcoal fires. She was in her red-brocade ceremonial garb and this brought out the color in her cheeks. On my side were a fellow officer and my old instructor, Kurō. On hers were her parents and her patron, the pregnant Fuji no Kata—though the lady's distinguished husband, brother to the Nation's Protector, as we were now styling the Lord Kiyomori, did not appear.

This wife of mine turned out to be as truly indifferent to me as she had originally appeared. She had married me because she had to marry someone and I seemed the best of the lot. I had a parcel of land in Musashi, I did not drink too much, and though I had a temper, I rarely quarreled. She had probably heard I slept about, but that was no problem. She now had her husband, her own small house, and the promise of a child. And she was, I must say, an excellent wife. They called us an ideal couple—and I suppose we were.

* * *

There they go again—always the same time, and every morning. Initially I thought their chantings were acts of devotion to allay the spirits of the dead. After all, these youngsters have the reputation of being able to appease the beyond. But now I am not so certain. Perhaps there is some popular demand for their efforts, since these are all war tales. But if so, the future audience is going to receive some peculiar historical information.

Right now they are still going on about times under Kiyomori. All obeyed his commands. As the grass bends before the wind, they received his favor as the earth welcomes the rain—pretty figures of speech. The singers down the hall are fond of the poetic; they are not, however, very accurate. No one welcomed anything—they were made to put up with it, but the methods used were much more subtle than those the scribes are busy ascribing.

The pageboy spies, for example. As they have it, if one word was heard against the Taira, the pretty horde would burst into the offending house, confiscate the belongings, and march the owner off under arrest. Not at all. Their methods were much more sure, and much more successful. I wonder why our young balladeers do not take the trouble to ascertain their facts.

Having just returned from down the hall, I now know why. As I was rounding the corner one of these musical youths ran into me. Blind as a bat. Turns out the majority of them are. Consequently, they can't ascertain anything.

Ah, there they go again. Singing away about a time they have never seen, and never could have.

* * *

When I remember those last days of the Taira at the capital, they have something about them of a golden autumn, of the fullness of an orchard just past its prime, where the late sun is reflected in the fat cheek of the apple and winter is still only a thought. It was the end, but none of us saw it, though it was plain, standing there before us.

It is said that when a man reaches his mid-term he falls prey to doubt. This afflicted Kiyomori in his later years. To find the answers to the questions plaguing him he was filling his chambers with shamans and rural magicians of various sorts; he even moved his palace (and hence the capital itself) for a time to far Fukuhara on the sea, certainly to attend to trade relations with China but perhaps also to escape from such doubts and demons as had possessed him. I remember the very stink of magic in the place, all that smoke and incense, the stench of burned hair and the smell of blood from the little animals he had slaughtered to placate those demons.

They possessed us all because this was a time of great doubt. The reason was that while we were lolling in the capital, the end of the world was approaching. Though we saw this shadow we did not yet guess its cause. We did, however, recognize our forebodings.

There were, I remember, signs of this event even when I was still a child. An oak, older than the oldest family, withered; a spring failed; a horse had a two-headed colt. In the second year of Kyūan [1146] there was a comet. It was viewed as a dire portent, coming at it did from the unfortunate northeast. I, being six or so at the time, remember it well as it sailed over us during the hot, late summer nights.

There were, in addition, other reminders: an intractable younger generation, a lowering of morals, an absence of bravery, things not as they had once been, and so on. These are all common enough events but we saw them as portents.

Nor were we wrong to, for we had divine proof. According to the Buddhist faith, we would pass through three ages—we had, in fact, already done so. First had been the era when there was divine law and enlightenment; then came the period when the laws existed but there was no more enlightenment; and, finally, this time, when the law itself dissolves and there is no enlightenment because we have fallen away in the far reaches of time from the Lord Buddha's example. Radiating from so long ago, his divine light can no longer reach us.

As to just when these latter days of the law were supposed to have begun there was disagreement. Chinese priests from long ago are said to have calculated that they were beginning even back then, but our own clergy seem to have early moved this unhappy era as far forward as possible. Even so, more recent clerics were eventually forced to conclude that the latter days could not be held off much longer. That, indeed, they were now upon us. Should anyone keep to Buddha's precepts, they lamented, he would be as rare as a tiger in the marketplace.

Our church in making this pronouncement proved it. A belief in the three stages of the law is itself doctrine. We of this degenerate third age—*mappō*—can no longer experience enlightenment, for the law says that we cannot. And now, as I write, with the dissolving of even this law within the law, the world indeed turns dark.

To live at the end of things is to prefer the sunset to the sunshine, to view each birth with pity and each death with satisfaction: we grow more expectant of failure than success; we prefer our petty known to the great unexpected; and we hover near our hearth now that it is about to flicker and die.

How singular I now find our fears. We had expected devastation and ruin, but these in our minds took the forms of conflagration and earthquake. Yet it was not these that destroyed our world, but something quite different from what we could have imagined.

As I look now from my retreat, I see that a whole new world has taken the place of ours: new ways of thinking, of acting; few of our cherished beliefs observed; gone our superstitions and our fears, gone too our solaces.

* * *

In order to explain the onset of *mappō*, the downfall of the Taira, and the consequent vanishing of our world, I must now return to that story which I have neglected in following the anecdotes of my own fortunes.

Only a year after the Heiji War, the Minamoto lost their

leader. Lord Yoshitomo in exile was slaughtered naked in his bath by one of his own men, one presumably in the pay of the capital—the Taira, the Fujiwara, or some imperial agency.

His head was exhibited in the capital. And there I viewed for the last time my former commander. Here was the man who had fought against his brother and killed his father, led a great coup and almost succeeded. I stared at that empty face—the hair loosened for the fatal bath, the fine ash used for washing still whitening one ear, the features holding that oddly expectant expression that decapitated heads often carry—and wondered if, had he lived, the Minamoto might have sooner won. We used to joke about this. When something displeased us Taira we would say: Oh, if Yoshitomo had never taken that bath.

Lord Kiyomori would not have appreciated our joke. He understood the danger that still-living Minamoto members represented. This was the reason for his policy of extermination. It began directly after the final battle, as I have recounted, with the decapitation of the eldest son. They say that he wept—the youth, not Kiyomori—because he was to be beheaded rather than allowed to kill himself in proper military fashion. These tears were cherished by the vanquished for a quarter of a century.

Kiyomori would not have wept. He was a great leader with great ambitions who looked after his own people and must, for that reason, exterminate the enemy. Though he is now, in this Kamakura world of the Minamoto, regarded as a great villain, Kiyomori was but doing his duty. He thought the killings a necessity.

Ah, but history is now merely the Minamoto version or, rather, the Hōjō version of the Minamoto version, now that that family rules us. The ballad makers here have Yoshihira not only refusing to weep but also seeking to confront his executioner. Ah-hah, he cries, it is you who will behead me. Well, get on with it, for if you do not do it right my head will fly up and bite your face. What? asks the warrior whose duty it is to behead him: How could a severed head bite my face? And Yoshihira says: Just do it right or in a hundred days I will kick you to death. And so the head was sloppily decapitated and just one hundred days later the decapitator was kicked to death by his horse—who was really, you see, Yoshihira's divine incarnation. And so on.

So, Kiyomori knew that killings were a necessity. This is what he had Retired Emperor Go-Shirakawa told, that this continued chopping off of heads was part of national security. After a time, however, the decapitations ceased. It was becoming impolitic for Kiyomori to continue, since the sight of blood—at least in such quantities—was becoming repellent now that peace was at hand. Also, head chopping was time-consuming. Our lord was required to be present at each execution and he could no longer spare the time, what with the press of those other administrative duties upon which the prosperity of the Taira now rested.

Twenty-five years later it was said that he stopped too soon. If he had but persevered, then the Taira might have ruled forever. Executions are indeed necessary, but when he halted, two of the enemy's sons were left alive. The elder, Yoritomo, thirteen when his father was killed, was sent to—of all places—the eastern provinces where his own father had ruled. Though the officers there were now all newly appointed by Kiyomori and hence Taira, the people themselves—soldier and peasant alike—were all Minamoto, and it was upon these that, when old enough, Yoritomo worked. The youngest son—Yoshitsune—was kept in the capital. Again this was not wise, but he was only one year old at the time and infants are not thought dangerous.

Lord Kiyomori's reasons for such uncharacteristic restraint remain obscure. Now it is said that he fell in love with the boys' mother, a beautiful lady, who became his concubine upon the understanding that her sons' lives be spared. Perhaps, but that would have been unlike Kiyomori, for it is impossible to imagine the man ever falling in love. His only stipulation was that the boys become priests—as though that would ensure their pliability. He need only have looked to the priests of Mount Hiei to have seen that war and devotion are scarely incompatible. And, even if Kiyomori had his reasons for sparing the infant, what could possibly have been those for leaving the elder boy, Yoritomo, alive?

The question is one still heard. People are fond of inconsistency and yet they wonder it about. Kiyomori seems all of a piece, eminently understandable, and yet this is something not like him at all. It is a mystery. We sagely wag our heads. This inconsistency is seen as a sign of humanity. He felt sorry for the child, hard soldier though he was—ah, he was but a man for all that, not one of us is perfect, and so on.

Mercy—that is what is being hinted at. But Kiyomori was not merciful. He was a man singularly devoted to his clan and its ambitions. For these he worked unsparingly and devoted himself entirely. Far from being willful, he was selfless. And far from being merciful, he was ruthless. Thus his leaving alive his enemy's two captive sons can be seen only as dereliction of duty—unless he had some further plans of his own of which we now know nothing.

So, the boys lived and thrived. And as the years went by, Yoritomo—the elder—became a strategist, an able administrator, a skilled politician, a man who lived only for duty and the prospering of his defeated clan. He sounds like his great Taira enemy, does he not? And indeed after the death of the lord of the Taira, the lord of the Minamoto became much like him. The same executions, the same regard for duty—except that Yoritomo, unlike Kiyomori, left no enemy alive.

I myself saw the young Yoritomo shortly after his capture and just before his pardon. He had become separated from his father and was found wandering in the snowy mountains of Mino. Consequently, when I viewed him he was dirty and hungry. Nevertheless, this thirteen-year-old boy behaved with great dignity. He stood there, slightly apart from his captors, and regarded us. We could, in his eyes, have been grooms or scullions rather than the Premier Kiyomori's honorable guard.

I remember that look of his. It was appraising. The gaze alone convinced me that this was no ordinary boy. Though I was myself then only eighteen or so, I remember thinking that this child—already calculating—would bear watching.

Later, when I was once again a Minamoto and in the company of Lord Yoritomo, I remembered this early gaze and compared it with that occasionally now directed upon myself. And in that self-possessed look—considering, planning—I saw before me the face of the long dead Kiyomori of the vanished Taira.

* * *

Since I have become a priest, I incline to see the similarities in things rather than their differences. Perhaps, indeed, in the end all things are identical. Which is to say, meaningless, since meanings are merely those attributes we choose to bestow.

Nowadays the Taira are thought to have been wicked, though they were once held good; and the Minamoto are held virtuous, though they were once thought bad. But in time the wicked Taira will in people's minds become again elevated and the victorious Minamoto—now succumbing to that very bureaucracy which so wearied the Taira—will become once more wicked. I see this occurring. Now that Minamoto no Yoritomo is dead—and Yoshitsune as well—there is a small but definite inclination to feel sorry for the once powerful Taira.

All things being equal in this sad world, both the Taira and the Minamoto claims to virtue will perhaps always be debated. They could certainly not be denied. The sensible Fujiwara Teika famously said: This strife between the white and the red is no concern of mine. Yet it so became. His Taira patrons lost their power to the Minamoto, and he remained permanently poor, himself powerless in his minor post.

At the same time, despite such recent claims of the Taira's having been admirably pitiful, there is one member of the Minamoto who has always been spoken of with concern and affection: Yoshitsune, the youngest son of Yoshitomo. He is now seen as a compassionate and sympathetic person who was hounded to his death by a disagreeable half-brother, Yoritomo; he is pictured as a virtuous and manly warrior who, like the cherry blossom, bloomed but to fall.

People now believe that at the age of six he was refusing to have his head shaved by the priests of Kurama Temple (as though they would have tolerated that), preferring to learn the martial arts from virtuous if renegade monks, and then, at ten, finding a genealogy of the Minamoto and thus for the first time discovering his true identity and his future role. I have seen a painting of him at this moment, a pretty child, his face illuminated with this new knowledge, one small hand firmly clamped about the scroll as though it were the pommel of a sword.

I knew him—at least I saw him often enough. I remember him as excitable, impulsive, impatient, bug-eyed General Yoshitsune. Now, however, in a mere two decades, gone forever is my skinny ex-commander. In his place stands a beautiful youth, aristocratically languid but, naturally, terrible in his anger. Poor Yoshitsune, doomed, hounded, decoratively dragging himself from place to place.

Poor Yoshitsune, indeed, since he has now been buried under this pathetic popular image as well. He, terrible enemy of the Taira, has been given all the Taira attributes—he is aristocratic, bewildered, pursued from place to place. Even his crooked teeth are hidden under the layers of courtly lacquer gratuitously lent him. And Yoshitsune was nothing like that, though this is now the only Yoshitsune left to history.

* * *

It was upon a hot day in late July during the first year of Eiman [1165] that the Emperor Nijō, having for some time been ill, died at the age of twenty-three. Retired Emperor Go-Shirakawa concealed whatever satisfaction he felt, and Kiyomori was punctilious in his obsequies.

When I heard the news, I well remembered that brave boy standing there on a distant snowy night and so, having no duties that sad day, resolved to accompany the imperial procession bearing him away for burial. And a sorrowful train it was, the body carried through this heat by a double-brace of oxen, trampling the summer dust, accompanied by members of the court sweating under the sun, mourning dirtied, brocades wilting.

When the mausoleum was reached, myriads of monks were waiting, intoning, and clouds of incense boiled up to darken the brazen sky. Then came the famous occurrence that was to have such repercussions for all of us.

It began as a simple bureaucratic incident, one perhaps typical of those times. Customarily the monks of Heijōkyō [Nara] and of Heiankyō, the north and south, new and old capitals, gathered at imperial funerals and hung the tablets of their respective temples in invariable order on the gates at the four sides of the tomb. Today, however, one of the holy delegations—that from Enryakuji—for what reason I do not know, defied tradition and put up its tablet out of turn.

The monks of the insulted temples at once instituted a fearful clamor, one which could be heard well over the chanting of the others. Then two young priests from Kōfukuji, the institution feeling itself the most injured, rushed forward wearing monkish armor and carrying sickle-bladed halberds. With no hesitation at all they raced into the imperial mausoleum and cut down the offending tablet. This fell to the stones beneath and broke.

The incident was one in a series of ecclesiastical rudenesses. Indeed, for some time, these mountain monks had been more of a menace than a solace. In disregard of all Buddhist injunctions against violence, armed bands would roam about attacking one another's monasteries. They descended into the capital as well, where they made their various demands and would block the homes of even imperial ministers until these were gratified.

They were also, I now understand, just as much a part of our age as we ourselves were. Kiyomori had arranged that most of the Taira native lands now no longer paid imperial taxes. The priests were thus also seeking exemptions for their various temples. Like the Taira they wanted power, and they were obtaining it through offering protection or threatening disruption, just as we were.

It was regarding these renegade priests from the nearby mountain that the Retired Emperor Go-Shirakawa made his celebrated and oft-quoted remark to the effect that there were three things in the world over which he had no control: the fall of the dice, the flooding of the Kamo River, and the misbehavior of the monks of Mount Hiei.

This was proved correct, but two days after the funeral runners brought to Rokuhara at dawn the news that a great number from Enryakuji, nursing their grievances and the shards of their broken tablets, were making for the capital. At once the city, having before tasted holy violence, shut its doors. Those who could, ran to Rokuhara for protection. Among these was Retired Emperor Go-Shirakawa, the imperial litter brought in on the run.

Thus began a terrible day, the twenty-ninth of the seventh month. I was on patrol with my men outside the walls of Rokuhara and so I saw what happened. We were near Kiyomizu Temple, by now an ecclesiastical city with its five-storey towers and great verandas, home to more than a thousand monks and servants, majestic in the light of the noon summer sun.

And it was here, near the main entrance of the temple complex, that the huge monkish mob racing down from Mount Hiei suddenly erupted like some wild river. Running they came— screaming monks with halberds and scythes, flowed swiftly into the temple precincts, striking as they went. I saw a group of young Kiyomizu acolytes, caught up in this flood, cut to pieces as they stood. Others rushed out and, monk against monk, these men struggled. The floor of the great hall was soon slippery with blood, and over it all, golden in its great pavilion, sat the image of the merciful Kannon.

The shouts of the furious mountain monks and the screams of the dying mingled, and beyond their struggling masses I saw the first flames, licking around the pillars, then billowing into the great hall itself. I remember one old monk, appallingly burned, rolling down the stairs, his robes all aflame. And a young one, his leg cut off, trying to kneel, to pray, as he bled to death and the fire covered him. And a youngster, perhaps an acolyte, perhaps a serving boy, impossible to tell, naked, his head so battered it seemed no longer human but rather something from the kitchen, and his back all aflame.

All of this and more I saw from my place on a little island of green, surrounded by these running monks as though by a raging stream. I was standing there half hidden by a large memorial stone, attesting to the mercy of Kannon who did indeed mercifully protect me. There I was, standing in my Taira uniform, unnoticed by everyone. My men were not so fortunate. They had scattered at the attack and eventually some straggled back. As for myself, after the river of armed and irate monks had streamed past, I made my prudent way home.

Back, inside Rokuhara, I found a singular state of affairs. Though the retired emperor had come to Kiyomori for protection, some of the higher officers were openly saying that this raid, like the scandal at the funeral two days before, was part of a plot—that someone most powerful was attempting to overthrow the Taira. This, indeed, they had heard the noble Kiyomori himself saying.

Others, however, questioned: if this was a plot, why then was not Rokuhara itself attacked, and why was it that this most powerful someone had come to take refuge within our very gates?

They were answered that this was because the mob had allowed itself to become diverted. Kiyomizu was, after all, a branch of the offending Kōfukuji, and the crazed monks, forgetting their true purpose, had turned to rend the affiliated temple. And as to the retired imperial presence—was it not obvious that in this way he hoped to cloak his treacherous designs?

Here I ceased to lend my ears. There is never an end to speculations of this sort and, in any event, we already knew that Lord Kiyomori and Emperor Go-Shirakawa held each other in suspicion.

His imperial highness appeared affable, allowing our lord regularly to ride his litter—carried by us—directly into the palace itself, permitting him even to go into and out of the palace wearing but informal dress. And our lord seemed punctilious in his regard for these privileges, but we knew that the true state of affairs was different.

Kiyomori now chose to make public this difference. When, danger past, the retired emperor desired to return home, it was only Shigemori, Kiyomori's first son, who did the honors and not our lord himself. This was a scandalous slight. Though the return was accomplished with full military retinue, nothing could disguise this intended insult.

Thus came about the first public break between the retired emperor and his chief lord, indeed, his premier, and it is from this that one may date the open enmity of the imperial house— one of the factors in the Taira decline. From this day too, I believe, may be seen another reason for the ruin of the proud clan. It was after the return of Shigemori that the first rift within our own family became visible.

Back from his seeing home the imperial guest, the son is said to have asked his father why he himself had not accompanied the returning emperor. Kiyomori is then reported to have stated his suspicions: that the retired emperor was plotting against the Taira, that his taking refuge was but a ruse, that Go-Shirakawa had had the mad monks goaded on, and that he was secretly plotting with that other family, the Minamoto.

The loyal son is then reported to have advised his father that such suspicions were ignoble. He then turned and left. After the virtuous son had departed, the censured father is said to have shaken his head and remarked upon what a bloodless lord Lord Shigemori was.

In whatever form, words had been had, and it is just here, in this schism between father and son, that one may place the beginnings—by the retired emperor's design or not—of the fall of the Taira.

Certainly such an interpretation was suggested that very night in the palace, where, according to an account later told, the Emperor Go-Shirakawa said that it was passing strange that an idle idea was circulating that he wished harm to the Taira when, as all knew, he had no such desires at all.

Here, a favorite chamberlain, Saiko, himself a priest and one from Enryakuji at that, said something to the effect that rumors were never idle; that, indeed, one ought perhaps to remember the old saying that heaven has no mouth but speaks through the lips of men. He then added that since the prosperity of the Taira had gone beyond measure, perhaps such a rumor as this was heaven-inspired.

While the rest of the court looked on, incredulous, the emperor—as though in corroboration—turned to the chamberlain, pulled a long face, and nodded as though there were indeed, unfortunately, something to the old saying.

Yet nothing further at once occurred. The irate monks, mollified, went back home, and in due time the retired emperor succeeded in placing a new emperor—the nine-year-old Takakura—on the throne. And two years later, it was Go-Shirakawa himself who, in the name of his son, asked that the hand of the seventeen-year-old Tokuko, Kiyomori's daughter, be joined with that of the then eleven-year-old emperor.

During this time, despite presages and prophecies, life in Heiankyō continued as I have already described it—ten years of prosperous peace under the Taira. It was now the first year of Shōan [1171] and our lands, so seemingly secure, were being called Akitsushima—the Islands of Autumnal Abundance.

This was a recent reading. My elegant *kanji* instructor has told me that the term earlier meant merely island of dragonflies but that a more felicitous homonym had replaced the insect with the season so that the familiar description would refer directly to the prosperity that the great Kiyomori had brought us.

Abundance indeed. All Heiankyō was by now a vast marketplace. It swarmed with horses and carriages and townsfolk, strolling about in their finery. There were silver and jasper from Yangchou, jewels from Chinchou, the twill of Wuchin, and the brocade of Shuchiang—all imported from far China and now contributing to our local magnificence.

Islands of autumnal abundance—now there was such a fullness, a ripeness about the capital, that in these lean and wintery days of the Kamakura shogunate the Taira Heiankyō seems to me to have had an age of gold, more imagined than remembered.

Nonetheless the autumn was upon us and the decline of the Taira had begun. In the months that followed the burning of the Kiyomizu Temple, the words between Kiyomori and his son, and the retired emperor's open resentment, further incidents presaged the fate of my family.

* * *

One such marked a yet more open breach between Taira and Minamoto. It involved Lord Yorimasa. He was a Minamoto who had remained loyal to the Emperor Go-Shirakawa during the Hōgen War but had never affiliated himself with the Taira. Nonetheless he remained a powerful person and his anger was to be reckoned with.

His eldest son, Nakatsuna, owned a very fine horse and this much piqued the curiosity of Lord Kiyomori's second son, the ill-natured Munemori. Envious, he had the animal abducted and brought back to Rokuhara. There it was branded Nakatsuna, the name of its owner, and locked up in the Taira stables. Thereafter, whenever a celebrated visitor came, Munemori's pleasantry was to call: Bring out Nakatsuna. Saddle Nakatsuna. Oh, what a wicked beast! Beat him! Whip him!

The unfortunate animal soon enough passed away, but not the humiliated anger of Nakatsuna and that of his powerful father. It is said that from this ludicrous incident sprang the resolve that led the latter to seek the downfall of the Taira and to pursue the renewal of his own family, the Minamoto.

Another incident, one which marked the further deterioration between the imperial house and the Taira, was the scandalous affair of the topknots. Lord Shigemori's second son, Sukemori, a spoiled and impetuous thirteen-year-old, out hunting with a group of his equally pampered young friends, bumped into the procession of Prince Motofusa, at that time serving as regent to the young Emperor Takakura.

The prince's attendants, outraged, demanded that the boys dismount and apologize. The lads, excited by the quail and skylark they had been slaughtering, refused. They were therefore pulled from their mounts and given a shameful beating.

Young Sukemori, already a full lieutenant general in those frivolous times, ran home to Rokuhara and his grandfather, Kiyomori. Irate, the premier said that the proud prince-regent must be punished. Shigemori, a prudent man, said that, no, his son was himself plainly at fault and should have apologized.

Relations between Kiyomori and Shigemori were already such that without a word our lord ordered a number of raw recruits, as crude and violent as any in our forces, to lie in wait and cut off the topknots of the attendants of Prince Motofusa in the next procession of the prince-regent.

This they did, knocking the courtiers down and holding them by their necks against the dirt while the topknot was sliced off. Even the secretary of the palace archives was not spared, even the captain of the imperial guard. They were then released, their hair all flowing like that of so many violated virgins.

The rude soldiers next cut the harnesses of one of the oxen, battered the prince-regent's carriage and ripped away its screen, then departed for Rokuhara and an audience with Kiyomori. He received the louts all dressed up in his ecclesiastical robes—for he was now priest-premier—and told them how well they had done.

The prudent Shigemori was alarmed. Behind his father's back he dismissed all the soldiers involved, sending them penniless back to their barbarian provinces. His own son he

banished to the farther reaches of Ise. It is said that the Retired
Emperor Go-Shirakawa much admired these gentlemanly acts.
Lord Kiyomori did not, however, and the incident widened yet
further the rift between father and son.

Likewise widening was the conflict between the imperial faction and the Taira. In fact, a real plot was being hatched to overthrow the impossible family of which I was then a member. The
plotters were meeting at a mountain villa in Shishigatani,
beyond the capital. They included various provincial governors,
the chief of the board of ceremonies, men of the police comis-
sioner's division, and more, including Yorimasa himself—all
united by a distrust and dislike of the Taira. Among the more
vocal was—again—the priest Saiko.

This group was, one evening shortly after the topknot affair,
joined by the retired emperor himself. He spoke most openly,
and Lord Narichika, a favorite who had high hopes, was so excited that he knocked over his wine bottle. All turned to look at it,
as it gurgled away on its side, and then Narichika said, Oh, look,
the *heiji* has fallen.

The object was the rustic bottle; the reference was to the
Heike, that is (different reading of the *kanji*), the Taira—us.
This sally his imperial majesty found amusing and said that
there were so many *heiji* still standing that he wondered if Lord
Narichika were not already drunk.

General laughter—then, from a temple secretary, who indicated the bottles: But, what shall we do with them? Silence—
until Priest Saiko stood up, drew his sword, and said: The best is
to behead them.

This he did, chopping off the top of a nearby bottle while the
others stood about, smiles fading. False pleasantry had turned to
true violence and the plot was acknowledged.

* * *

I, a mere lieutenant, knew nothing about our coming tragedy.
My marriage had brought me a raise in both position and pay,

and my wife made no more demands on me than I did on her. Her only complaint was that she gave birth to a boy rather than to a girl.

Nowadays, of course, it is baby boys who are welcomed and baby girls who are not. This is because ours has become a military society and more soldiers are always needed. Not back then, though. My wife wanted a girl, because in that peaceful capital a girl could always make a marriage above her station and with her rise elevate the entire family.

So she apologized to me for this birth, and it was here that I perhaps first detected that her ambition was as great as mine. Just as my first concern was to look after my advancement, bettering myself in this life, so Ōto's was to ensure a social progress that included our family only because it was hers.

So we were better matched than I had thought. We went our separate ways together. While she busied herself with social calls, with the family budget, with the baby, I went about my daily rounds.

I will record such a typical day because it was so different from the typical days of soldiers now. And the days were filled with a variety that seems rich indeed as I sit here solitary in my threadbare old age.

Though troops might still be awakened early, their officers were not. Often I was late abed, occasionally nursing a throbbing head occasioned by drink the night before. Rising from my solitary pallet, I would clap for the servant girl, some cheap country relative of my wife's, who brought in water for me to rinse my mouth and wash my hands. I would get back into my uniform, having slept in my undergarments, unlike now when the warrior sleeps in everything but full armor.

Then, after a kind of barley mush, which was all the girl could contrive, and the news that her mistress had gone early to one of the Fujiwara houses with a present of fresh mountain fern, I would stroll over to Rokuhara—we lived not far away in a narrow and unfashionable ravine near Kiyomizu—and report in.

There I would have a bite of whatever was on the fire, a bit of deer haunch or part of one of the boars our men were always bringing down from Mount Hiei. After that I would look to my platoon, a group of men almost as indolent as myself. They would already have been out on parade, morning exercise supervised by a subaltern, so all I had to do was observe their general effect.

Then I would sit around and crack jokes with the other officers and endure comments on my rustic origins and un-remedied bumpkin ways. Then, eventually, there would be a midday meal of some kind. Before, on the march, we Taira had had but two meals a day. Now, in the capital, most of us ate three. We also, despite Buddhist prohibitions, ate meat. At least the army did; the court ate mainly fish, and the monks snacked all the time.

After this, stomachs full, we would parade our troops or attend administrative meetings, where we listened with respect to whomever happened to be talking to us and also occasional-ly fell asleep.

Then, awake again after such ceremonial duties, it was time for a bit of pleasure. This varied but it always included drinking. Usually it was spent with a petty official or a worldly priest, or with some minor Fujiwara anxious to ingratiate and willing to begin at the bottom. Sometimes it also included the opportuni-ty to go to bed with someone—particularly in the grander tem-ples. Then back to the pallet and a sound and healthy sleep.

So the days went on, with such a calm inevitability that it seemed they would last forever. I was by then past thirty, a respectable man with a dutiful wife and a little boy whom I bare-ly knew. And I had begun to put on weight. Life was comfort-able, and though we felt what breezes of change were already blowing, we paid small attention.

Yet into this peace, slowly at first, then more and more, intruded the plottings of the retired emperor, and the differ-ences between our lord and his son.

* * *

As for myself, I was not particularly loyal to Lord Kiyomori . . .
Having begun this sentence, I now gaze at it. What a singular
sentiment for me to have written. As though such loyalty was
ever one of our concerns back then.

It but indicates that, though now sequestered in this temple,
I nonetheless remain a part of this new age where loyalty is
everything. Down in Kamakura, Lord Yoritomo's example continues to exact the most unexampled personal devotion. If one
is suspected of lacking this quality—as was poor Yoshitsune, for
example—then one's head is removed. This, said our leader, is
the way in which our stern new state is forged.

But back in the old and innocent days of which I am now writing, fidelity was but an expedient. Some of theirs came over to
our side, some of ours went over to theirs. Our lives were like
those of the merchants—healthily moved only by thoughts of
self and its advancement. Surely, I think, such is the more natural—natural to the state of man, certainly to men back then.

So, as I say, I was not particularly loyal to our Kiyomori, that
commander whom I had first glimpsed on his black horse nearly fifteen years before. And my having attached myself to him in
hopes of gain did not prevent my seeing him now as despotic,
besotted with his own power and hence less likely to be of advantage to anyone under his control.

It was with this in mind that I, in those lax old days, enrolled
myself under Lord Tomomori, Kiyomori's youngest son, who
though only twenty at the time was already known for his good
sense, his skill in keeping free of entanglements, and his cool-
ness toward his impossible father.

He was, in short, rather like myself—if I may be allowed the
vanity of the comparison—and in this move I made the first,
which eventually led me away from the Taira family entirely. I
was, however, in consequence no longer the junior officer I had
been. My transfer meant a loss of status—bitterly regretted by

my wife—but I thought that under the son opportunities for advancement were greater than they would have been under the father.

The fact that such a move as mine, so open, so noticed, so transparent, was possible indicates how things were at Rokuhara. Nowadays in the military capital of Kamakura where personal loyalty is regarded as a virtue, such a move as mine would have been refused and, if the suit was persisted in, would have met with dismissal from the forces.

My foresight, however, did have some unwelcome consequences. By removing myself from my original obligation I was also removed from the jurisdiction of my uncle, Hisashita Naomitsu, back in Musashi. His retaliation for having his authority so publicly flouted—I was still nominally standing in for him in the capital— was to take over my native lands, giving as reason a claim that the boundary had been mistakenly drawn.

I was so informed by my old teacher, Kurō, who kept up with the country folk. He said I ought to complain to the military court at Rokuhara, but this I did not do. I did not want to call Kiyomori's attention to myself just then and I did not want to begin my service under Lord Tomomori on such a doubtful note.

Instead I lost my famous temper, was rude to my equals and awful to my inferiors, scowled, refused to drink or else got drunk, made a great racket stomping down corridors. I am like that. Though I am solicitous of my future to a degree, given the opportunity, I usually work against my own interests.

Still the loss of land was serious. Nowadays, of course, it would have been calamitous. In Kamakura you are always judged by your potential—how many men you can bring with you, how much land you own. And even back then in Heiankyō a man alone had less chance, though progress remained possible.

Naturally, Kiyomori said never a word. His little purple-robed spies would have informed him of my defection, but what was I to him? Some dissatisfied minor officer down the line meant nothing to Kiyomori, Premier, High Priest, Commanding General, and Great Leader of the Taira, he whose power was absolute.

* * *

Kiyomori, nevertheless, cannot have seen what was going on about him. Otherwise he would not have acted in the manner in which he did during the next complication. This occurred when an important imperial post was coming vacant and Councilor Narichika, newly appointed, was thought especially favored by the retired emperor. The man apparently truly desired the position because he brought together more than a hundred priests from the Yahata Shrine and for seven days put them to work chanting holy texts appropriate for his success.

This pious and expensive act accomplished nothing, however, for it was no longer the retired emperor who conferred rank and title but Priest-Premier Kiyomori. Consequently, despite Narichika's prayers, our lord elevated his own son, Shigemori, into the coveted position. It was then that the furious Narichika made his famous statement: The whims of the Taira are the only law of the land—them I will therefore overthrow.

Kiyomori heard of this boast but did nothing. His power was seemingly so absolute that he could ignore even open dissent. Narichika's complaint, however, gave others the means to voice theirs. With the Taira in such complete command who would protect those not of that clan? Retired Emperor Go-Shirakawa himself was asked at court what he would do if, for example, the monks, angry, unwilling to be appeased, were again to come down with some impossible petition. And this seemingly powerless imperial majesty sadly replied that, indeed, he should be forced to grant that appeal.

As though on cue, the monks again appeared. It was, as I well remember, the thirteenth day of the fourth month of the third year of Angen [1177]. Early in the morning they came, heralded by the sound of their massed drums, their holy symbols swinging at their shoulders or held aloft over their heads. They made a fine sight. The open areas northeast of the capital were covered with their multitudes—thousands of monks, followers, servants. Their holy palanquins glittered in the early morning sunlight, and the people of Heiankyō crowded into the fields to gaze upon this wondrous if dangerous apparition, while the retired emperor, prudent, called out the imperial guards. Both Taira and Minamoto troops fortified the approaches to the palace and prepared to repulse the monkish horde.

The Minamoto were led by Yorimasa, long the right arm of the retired emperor, with only three hundred men. Our side was led by Shigemori, now state minister and general, with some three thousand men. Not, however, me. After my transfer I was back at Rokuhara doing quartermaster work.

The other family won the day. Yorimasa was diplomatic and persuaded to retire the very monks besieging the gates he was guarding. The would-be attackers discovered that the Minamoto were fine people and that Yorimasa was a perfect gentleman. They then ran around to the gates the Taira were guarding, where Shigemori—no gentleman—charged into their ranks.

Some of the priests were wounded, and arrows struck a few of the holy symbols. Retiring in angry confusion, the monks shouted imprecations against the Taira, the holy symbols were taken to the nearby Gion Shrine, where the sacrilegious arrows were pulled out, prayers were said, and dark vows taken. The local gods were angry; disaster threatened the capital.

So it did—the very next evening, around midnight. Once again a mighty mob from Mount Hiei invaded Heiankyō. Once again the Taira forces deployed. Once again the retired emperor nimbly hopped into his palanquin to be carried to safety. Though that evening repulsed, the holy horde eventually had its way.

On the twenty-eighth of the month at around ten in the evening, a sudden fire broke out. Since a strong spring wind was blowing, the flames swept diagonally across the city, gathering force and ferocity as they came.

It was a dreadful sight and I saw it from the battlements of Rokuhara. One after another, whole city blocks were engulfed by the flames and then, nearer, the minor palaces, some thirty in all as well as sixteen of the new mansions at the foot of our hill, and the homes of courtiers and high officials beyond number.

This wall of flame fed upon the city in its path. I remember not only the sunlight brightness of this conflagration but also the sound it made, carried high on the spring wind: the crackling, the cries of those trapped.

The fire spared Rokuhara. It passed so close that we could feel its terrible warmth, but then the wind turned and carried the tide of flame directly north. We stood there transfixed as the wall of fire swept past, sparks falling on our armor, our eyes bright, mirroring this sea of flame. It marched past us with its great munching noise, punctuated by screams and bellows, burning everything in its path, finally to attack the imperial palace itself. The great gates, the hall of music, the assembly chamber, over eight of the major administrative bureaux and the office of records itself, all were shortly burning fiercely, and amid the flames curled the documents of centuries.

There was never, I believe, an estimate of the damage. Several hundred people were believed consumed and certainly many more animals were broiled in their paddocks and pens. The material damage was beyond calculation: everything was swept away in that mighty conflagration.

By morning a third of the city, including its entire center, was lying in smoldering ash. So much of the past, so much antiquity, so much beauty had vanished during that night. And with it had gone the spirit of that wonderous capital of Heiankyō. The conflagration dramatized for all of us the truth of our times—we were living in the latter days of the law, and for us there was to be but one sorrow followed by another: not sentiments for a strong society nor for an efficient soldiery.

As to who started the fire . . . this was never discovered. Someone had a dream in which two or three hundred large

torch-bearing monkeys were seen coming down from Mount
Hiei and firing the capital. So it was left at that. Something
incomprehensible, a malign miracle, allowed by the Buddha
himself, now that he no longer cared.

* * *

Whoever was truly responsible for the conflagration, a suitable
object for Taira wrath, was shortly apprehended. This was the
priest Saiko, the one who had chopped the head off the bottle.
It began when a colleague of Councilor Narichika, Yukitsuna by
name, paid a call on Kiyomori.

Since our lord Kiyomori knew that Narichika was gathering
imperial troops, apparently to chastize the unruly monks, and
since the visitor called at the unusual hour of midnight, he was
curious as to its occasion. Once Yukitsuna was in the presence of
the great man, he was asked why he had called so late, and he
answered that by day there were too many people about the person of the priest-premier for him to say what he had to.

What he had to say was that the true reason for soldiery being
raised at this moment was that forces were preparing to overthrow Kiyomori and his house. Keenly interested, our lord
asked if the retired emperor knew of this, and Yukitsuna is said
to have answered with: Must I, my lord, spell out to you the
details? It is by express imperial authority that Councilor
Narichika is gathering these soldiers about him.

The great man exploded with a sudden access of rage, posi-
tively blazed with anger, I am told. Always volatile, the temper of
Kiyomori was like a flame. The poor, singed Yukitsuna, who had
perhaps thought this revelation would win a bright advancement, gathered his robes about him and was fortunate to flee
the place.

Word of what had occurred soon reached the retired emper-
or, but not at once the betrayed Narichika. Rather, he received
a Taira messenger who respectfully informed him that Kiyomori
apologized for the lateness but prayed he would honor him with
a meeting as to what do to about the importunate monks. The

councilor had himself been getting soldiers together on the pretext of doing just that so that he now, thinking his true intentions unknown, went trustingly off to Rokuhara in his fine carriage, dressed in an elegant hunting suit, accompanied by a full complement of servants and ox-tenders.

He did not get very far. A troop of Taira soldiers shortly surrounded his vehicle, dragged him from it, and pulled him into the chambers of our lord. There he found that his crony, the priest Saiko, had already been apprehended and was sitting bound hand and foot.

The furious Kiyomori appeared, strode over and kicked Saiko in the face. He had heard about the beheaded bottle. Also, apparently, the talk of the mouth of the people telling the truth, for the unhappy priest was then held down while his own mouth was split from jaw to jaw, the cheeks cut through, gashed to the very ears, back teeth glinting white in the blood. He was then taken to common ground by the river and summarily executed.

This torture had been witnessed by Narichika, also now trussed and bound. The priest-premier then turned to the guards, who happened to be those belonging to his elder son, and ordered them to beat the man. When they hesitated to raise their hands against so important a member of the imperial court, our lord, still in his rage, shouted: So—you respect the orders of Lord Shigemori more than you do mine. I no longer, it seems, have any authority.

And off he stomped into his inner chambers, leaving Narichika lying bound in the courtyard to sweat away in his fine hunting suit as the hot sun of the sixth month rose. He was not, however, executed, only exiled. This was Lord Shigemori's clement doing—an act which had the further result that relations between father and son were yet more weakened.

Kiyomori himself, believing the retired emperor to be behind the plot, was now resolved to exile that imperial presence—an expedient unheard of and indicative both of the power of the priest-premier and of his abuse of it.

Our lord therefore had quite a few people arrested, including the entire family of Councilor Narichika and any courtier whom he thought might have been implicated in the plot. Then he gathered together his military forces and made a speech, reminding us of how he had supported His Majesty the ex-Emperor Go-Shirakawa, and how often we had compromised our own safety for that of this august person. Now, however, the imperial ears had been poisoned against us. Our emperor might even be prevailed upon by our enemies to issue an edict deposing us.

It was a not unsuccessful, if transparently self-serving, speech. And Kiyomori made it all the more effective by choosing to appear before us in full battle dress: red-and-gold brocade skirt, light, leather-body armor laced with black silk cords holding his tightly fitting silver breastplate. He even carried his silver-handled halberd, the one he claimed was given him by some god or other.

In a rousing climax he concluded: Therefore His Imperial Majesty must be escorted to a place where he cannot harm His Imperial Self, in the commission of which we will yet once more be affirming our allegiance to the august throne.

He then dramatically called for his sword and his steed. These were not forthcoming because, while we were standing open-mouthed at the very idea of turning against the retired emperor, Shigemori had appeared. He now stood before us and burst into tears, saying that we had long been loyal subjects of our emperor and that such a transferal, even for the sake of imperial safety, was not to be countenanced. In our land the gods did not permit any irreverence, even one merely seeming so.

Lord Shigemori was standing there in court dress, wearing his high black-lacquered headgear, facing his father in his grand battle clothes. It was like a drama: civil diplomacy facing military might. To make it even more metaphorical, Kiyomori at one point went into the next apartment and put a raw-silk priest's robe over his armor. Whatever his motives—appearing first as premier then as priest—it seemed of some symbolic significance: Lord Kiyomori's silver breastplace shone through the holy robe—force hiding behind belief.

After a time the conversation turned practical. We Taira, reminded Lord Shigemori, still held Councilor Narichika, and one might doubt a successful conclusion to their plot, now that its principal agent was in our hands. But the son went bravely on to demonstrate to the father his own convictions.

He had had his say, he said. Well may he be condemned, he added, looking at his father who was standing there clutching his robe over his breastplate. And when my head falls, you will do as you wish. Now I return to my palace. And, turning to us: Follow me, those of you who will.

It was an extraordinary speech for it marked a now public rupture between father and son; it was the earthquake that struck the house of Taira and caused now this great fissure to appear.

Into it we leapt. After such an impassioned speech, such drama, such spectacle, even I was carried away. As our lord galloped out of the courtyard, all of us ran after him. Yet, as I panted down the dusty road leading to Shigemori's villa, my eyes shining, I wondered just what I was doing. But then I realized that his younger brother, my new commander, Lord Tomomori, would undoubtedly side with his sibling, and I understood what I was doing.

It is said that the priest-premier stood there for a time looking at the empty courtyard, then went in and took off his armor. It is also said that the imperial presence, Retired Emperor Go-Shirakawa, having faced exile in his own palace and now perhaps wiping a relieved brow, said of Shigemori: What indeed a princely lord this is! He has repaid a foul plot against his family with understanding and with kindness. Then the retired emperor invoked a proverb: If a son dares to advise his father, then his house will hold to the way most just.

Strange prophecy, given the outcome.

* * *

Nowadays it is said that had Lord Shigemori lived, the fall of the Taira might not have occurred. My ballad-mongers are of that opinion. I am treated to their plaint: Truly this person was most missed, for he had been to the depths of his spirit loyal to the emperor, his speech as eloquent as his deeds were virtuous.

And so they may well have been. Shigemori had his ambitions like everyone else, but he was also, unlike his inflammable father, reserved. I saw him everyday because I was in the retinue of his younger brother. Reserved he was, but affable, and, in the Fujiwara fashion, artistic. He loved poetry, wrote a fine hand, and if there was an excursion to view the blossoms or a party to gaze upon the moon, he was often the only Taira to attend.

This love of beauty seemed in him not ostentatious, as it did in so many, but natural. It went with a certain simplicity in tastes: the rich plainness of his clothing, the sober splendor of his house. He was not the man to collect gaudy gems, as did his father.

All of which makes me take as true his plea for a conservative cooperation with a possibly treacherous emperor. He felt that only through harmonious understanding could peace and hence culture continue—a belief which was, of course, correct. But what strange thoughts to have held in that corrupt age of ours, and what a pathetic ambition to cling to when all was crumbling about him. Still—and the ballad boys have it right there—while he was alive there was still some hope.

But he died. It was in the third year of Jishō [1179], in the heat of the first day of the eighth month, a year or so after the arrest and exile of the rebel Narichika. Lord Shigemori was forty-two years old and the physicians could not make out the cause of his death.

Perhaps it was a disease sent by the gods. Lord Shigemori himself said so. The gods of Kumano—a number of which Lord Kiyomori had appropriated as his own—had sent him a sign, he said. What did the sign portend? This he did not say. Perhaps never again to cross his father, Kiyomori, to whom these deities belonged.

After the dramatic rift of father and son things had gone on as before—there was no other recourse. The only difference was that the world now knew that the difference had occurred. When Lord Shigemori was struck with his wasting disease, there were those who, as expected, said this striking down of an unfilial son was the judgment of heaven.

Surprisingly, Shigemori himself was among their number. How could I now be so foolish as to ignore the will of heaven and to crave health, is what he is supposed to have said. And when a famous Chinese physician came all that distance to see him, he was refused. And the patient, apparently believing in the judgment of heaven, certainly became religious. During his long illness he had built his own temple. It was very grand—had forty-eight lanterns set up, each standing for one of the forty-eight vows of Amida Buddha.

Having despaired of this life, Shigemori was ensuring himself of a good position in the next one. To this end he also had himself ordained in his own temple. His head was shaved and the robes were placed about his shoulders. Those around him mourned as though he were already dead, but his counsel was still heeded. There are some who maintain that the world remained at peace as long as it did entirely through the advice of this military man turned priest.

* * *

I, as soldier turned priest, may without undue familiarity compare myself to Lord Shigemori in that both of us, denied our opportunities for advancement and command in the military sphere, opted for advancement in the spiritual plane.

He desired the highest place available to him within paradise, and I would seek no less. The difference, of course, is that as a soldier I could not afford my own regiment and my own mounts, and, in preparing for the next life, I do not have funds for temples and sutra readings. Nonetheless, within our separate categories, the deceased lord and myself are similar.

Certainly we were both aware of the deepening presence of this decadent age—*mappō*—these last days of the Law. I have already indicated something of the gathering gloom, but now, between the deaths of Lord Shigemori and Kiyomori, the sky turned yet darker.

With mountain monks a continued menace, the populace came to believe that there was no virtue in giving further funds. With the temples becoming poor, more marauding monks appeared. These men of Buddha's teaching, with the Buddha now so far away, turned mercenary and robber. Truly pious men became excessively rare. As rare as tigers in the marketplace, it was said, and Lord Shigemori was our last.

There now seemed equally no path for us to attain that bright paradise we had so confidently perceived, and conversely no way to avoid that dark hell the vivid descriptions of which were now to be heard at any corner of the capital or seen hanging pictured in gaudy horror outside the discredited temples.

Hell was a dramatic affair: ogres with clubs and saws, beating and then dismembering the living dead; boiling cauldrons, screaming beings within, unable to die because no longer alive; mountains of swords these poor creatures were forced to scale, slicing to ribbons their immortal flesh; and great grills where the recently dead were cooked and then made to partake of each other while greedy demons hovered beneath to catch the drippings. One naturally wished to avoid such an unpleasant place.

This one could now do. In these latter days of the Law, the merciful Buddha had vouchsafed a path that led past this sideshow to the meadows of salvation and from them onward to the radiant heights of the further shore. This path was provided by the relatively recent sect we now call Jōdo, in reference to that Pure Land paradise toward which we elect are bound.

Its qualifications are uncomplicated. All one does is to pray. We of this latter age are so decadent that we can no longer attain our reward through righteous conduct, nor would the reciting of scriptures and the saying of holy texts now assist us in achieving our aims.

However, the Lord Buddha has opened for us this single way —we but intone, again and again, our simple request—I call upon you, Amida Buddha. If we but do this a sufficient number of times then our rebirth in paradise is assured.

It is an excellent belief in that it is so suited to our times. Though in more primitive form it has been around now for many years, in our age it has come to excite the hopes of thousands of new believers. Though these were originally lowly people, farmers and servants, the faithful now number not only the merchants and the military but even the aristocracy itself. Originally one heard the formula mumbled by tradesmen and serving people; now it was heard in military barracks and palace corridors. The holy words were on all lips.

Including mine. I am now a lay priest of the Jōdo sect and occupy many a stray hour invoking the blessed name. Indeed, my mentor, the priest Hōnen, remembered or invented a proverb to fit such as myself: Even fools who hold strong faith have a better chance at the future life than thinkers who doubt.

Like many proverbs it is unarguable. If, indeed, one is to be saved through rebirth into the Pure Land, then faith in this occurrence demonstrates the belief. And Hōnen believed what he said. The here and now was so hopeless that one could not hope for salvation during this life. It was only by being reborn that one could hope. And so during these decadent latter days it was only simple belief in this rebirth that could provide salvation. The endless reciting of the formula kept one from all doubt. It also kept one from all thought.

Hōnen once wrote me a letter in which he answered some theological questions I had. In it he said that the vow of Amida had nothing to do with sutras, meditation, and the like. If you wish to concern yourself with these that is all right, he wrote, so long as the repetition of the Name is steadfastly observed.

Tamemori Saburō, another disciple, had said that both he

and myself had been told merely to practice this *nembutsu* because we were ignorant, that if we had been men of learning, it would have been different. Here Hōnen was adamant—this was quite absurd, he said. There is no distinction at all among believers, he averred. All are equal.

This I find difficult to believe, since nothing else on this earth is equal. And if it were, where would fit my own distinction? I believe it to be a man's duty to strive to put himself forward, to occupy eventually the highest place, to become a worthwhile person. What sort of earth—and what sort of heaven?—would be one without one place higher then the other. When I remember this I feel uncomfortable and then I am gratefully filled with ire, like one of our bath buckets being filled with hot water.

I remember that in this same letter the good Hōnen gave me grave counsel about this temper of mine. I really ought to curb it, he said, even though the Original Vow of Amida does not forbid this. He is hinting that it would work against both my good death and my successful afterlife.

Nonsense. If the Buddha should refuse me welcome because of this temper of mine he would be breaking his own Vow in that the refusal would be a defect in his professed perfect compassion, and all this talk about certain fulfillment would not be true. Really, I sometimes quite lose my temper. But, enough.

During those days when the Reverend Hōnen was most active, there were a number who even tried to force the gates of the Pure Land by throwing themselves into the Katsura River. Theirs was death by analogy. Since it was thought that the Pure Land existed beyond the sea, it mattered little into just what water you threw yourself.

Others were more orthodox in their attempts. Believing that the benevolent Kannon had created a staging post between our mainland and the farther shore of the Pure Land, a number decided to sail for this miraculous island. It was called Fudaraku and contained a high and sacred mountain that could be seen from a distance and hence guide the pilgrims to the happy shores.

They even knew the location of the place, so deep was their faith. It was just off the coast of the Kii Peninsula, far to the east of Naniwa. There they journeyed in their numbers and there they disembarked in their boats. Since they would not be returning, they also took a number of tools with which to stove in their craft once the island was reached—or before. One enterprising shipwright even created a boat with a detachable bottom— instant submersion guaranteed. It sold well, I am told. And, while the enthusiasm lasted, people spoke with enthusiasm of *jūsui ōjō*—rebirth in paradise through drowning.

But, like all fashions, it ran its course. It appealed only to the faddish. Once these were gone, no one requiring so instant a rebirth was left. Most of us were content to plod along, following the daily routine and awaiting rebirth on its own terms. We still do. And as I listen to my few fellow believers here at the temple intoning that familiar phrase—*Namu Amida Butsu*—I wonder what now will happen to our simple faith, now that Hōnen himself is in exile, now that our temples have been turned over to passing folk such as these ballad makers, now that our masters in Kamakura have turned to other sects.

Yet, I congratulate myself that I declared myself early, in the days of the true popularity of our belief. In this way I acquired a place for myself, a position in the hierarchy of our church, and— if I may so phrase it—in the regard of the Buddha. In the afterlife I compliment myself that I have at least some right to a place of privilege. An officer during my earthly career, it would seem that no less is awaiting me in my posthumous existence. It would be satisfaction indeed to sit in a high place amid this throng.

Well do I remember when I was first animated by the spirit of this sect. Still a common soldier I had been sent for some reason, with a number of my comrades, to the old Toba residence, some distance from the capital—and for that reason the place where the retired emperor Go-Shirakawa was later incarcerated.

It was a small, provincial palace, old-fashioned and dirty and containing a number of shabby decorations, among them a large hanging scroll.

It was a mandala of the type that the young Jōdo sect was specializing in: easy to understand, attractive. There was the Buddha, sitting on his lotus in the center and looking down at his poor suppliants so far below that they were all but falling out of the picture.

What struck me in this otherwise conventional rendering was his wonderful confidence. Never had I seen a delineation of the Buddha in which gratification was writ so large. Often the features are neutral, withdrawn, aware but uninvolved. In this old scroll, however, his satisfaction was palpable. And I thought how wonderful to be in such a position: ambition satisfied, success assured. Bad painting on the part of the artisan? Unseemly imagination on the part of the viewer? I do not know. I do know, however, that for the first time an image of our deity had a meaning for me. In his own way the Buddha had spoken to me. My eyes shone and I can count my priestly vocation from that day.

* * *

No sooner was Shigemori dead than his father turned openly against Retired Emperor Go-Shirakawa. It was in the third year of Jishō [1179] that this occurred. The event began with a strong earth tremor at eight in the morning of the seventh day of the eleventh month, and was followed by the head of the board of divination in the palace running to the retired emperor, falling on his face, and blurting out that his texts had announced within the year, or within the month, or within the day some great disaster.

Since this is the forecast for every day of our lives, one wonders that anyone found it exceptional, earthquake or not, but his majesty did. Perhaps because he knew of what the disaster would consist: the head of the house of Taira coming to force him into exile.

To this end, the retired emperor sent messengers to Premier

Kiyomori. This was not a wise move because it smelled of guilt, and also gave his enemy a way to state his case, to make rebellion against the imperial house seem a necessity.

Consequently, standing in front of these imperial messengers, Kiyomori made yet another speech. He dwelt upon the death of Shigemori, admitted that he thought it an evil portent, wondered what the Taira might have done to have so forfeited the regard of their beloved emperor, then went into a citation of services rendered endangered emperors, all decorated with the precedents from Chinese history that his librarians had dug out of old books.

Then he mentioned an incident at Shishigatani—the wine-bottle affair. The emperor must be protected from such drinking companions. Though Kiyomori was but an old man now much enfeebled by the death of his eldest son—thus like unto an aged tree that loses one by one its last leaves—still, never would he be derelict in his imperial duty. His last strength would be consumed in delivering his imperial majesty.

To this end, on the twenty-eighth day of the eleventh month, Premier Kiyomori had Retired Emperor Go-Shirakawa's palace surrounded by troops. There was no escaping, and courtiers, lords, and ladies alike milled in the corridors, white with fear. The rumor spread that just as Nobuyori had burned the palace in the Heiji War, so now Lord Kiyomori was about to burn this one—with everyone in it.

This, however, he did not do. Rather, he sent Munemori, his second son, with troops to see that our emperor was properly guarded. When told he must go hence to the distant and rustic Toba palace, Emperor Go-Shirakawa said that he would but that Munemori must accompany him.

Fearing his father's anger, this feckless second son hesitated and the emperor said: Ah, how inferior you are to your late brother. It was he who saved me from such treatment before, but now that there is no one whom the Lord Kiyomori respects, there is no one to restrain him, and I am afraid.

He really said this. I heard him because I was there, standing in Taira battledress in the second row. Munemori had caused Tomomori, his younger brother and my commander, to come along and bring his troops.

Having spoken, the retired emperor began to weep. It was not a skillful performance, but it moved us soldiers because the tableau was so pathetic—imperial presence with sleeves to his flowing eyes. I remember my own eyes growing moist at the spectacle of such greatness so humbled. Our hopes for preferment and advancement within the ranks should have seen us cheerfully carting off the imperial party, but instead we were in tears as true as those of our emperor were feigned.

He kept this up for some time, until we were sniffling and wiping our noses on our sleeves. Since I was standing close to the imperial presence, I could see him peeping over the edge of his own brocaded sleeve to judge the effect. His intentions were apparent, yet we were all taken in. I suppose we wanted to be.

He was wily, our retired emperor, yet there was something childlike about him. Though he was well over fifty at the time he had—like so many of the palace people—retained an air of youth. Or perhaps it was an air of inexperience.

Along with his beloved popular music, his troupes of singers, and his bands of scribes who wrote down these tunes of the day, he entertained a readiness to be surprised at the most common fact of ordinary life. When he first learned that palanquin bearers sometimes wore deerskin gloves to protect their hands, he shook his head with childish wonder. This naiveté was, I think, quite genuine, as was his intense interest concerning that of which he knew little.

Sometimes I think that Retired Emperor Go-Shirakawa was moved solely by these infantile interests of his. What will happen if I do this, he asked himself, and then did it. Perhaps the fall of the Taira was merely the result of the same kind of curiosity with which he once confined a large unfed monkey to a lacquered cage in order to discover how many days it would live.

Such detached curiosity, uncommon then, now even more so,

would have been a virtue in a leisured noble or even in a wealthy merchant with few responsibilities. In an emperor, however, it was fatal. He had such power that this curiosity naturally turned itself to political ends—such as the plot against the Taira.

In any event, his experiment with weeping failed to attain its object and he was carried away to distant Toba, there to rusticate in the endless snowfalls of that year, to look out into his whitened garden and wonder why the mallard on the pond had green cheeks.

The reigning emperor, Takakura, son-in-law to our Lord Kiyomori, escaped blame and censure alike by shutting his palace and sequestering himself, giving out that he was not well. He had recently returned from a pilgrimage to Itsukushima, one which everyone knew he made only because his father-in-law had ordered him to. Kiyomori had made him go to this Hachiman shrine of the Taira so that he would be seen ordering an emperor about.

This accomplished, Emperor Takakura surprised Kiyomori by shutting himself up. He is said to have wept a good deal of the time and to have spent the rest in composing aphorisms. One is well known: The emperor is like unto a ship, and his subjects are as unto water. The water enables the ship to float well, but angry waters can capsize a noble vessel.

Not much of an aphorism, but then Takakura—his wife so under the hand of Kiyomori—was not much of an emperor. That he had the strength to lock himself up and refuse to hold court showed a character which at the time surprised us.

But it did him little good. In the following year, the fourth of Jishō [1180], the priest-premier simply had him abdicate. That Kiyomori could successfully do so indicates the strength that he had now gathered about him. If there had been a precedent for his becoming emperor, no one would have been surprised had he availed himself of it.

As it was, he did the next best thing and, as I have recounted, became the grandfather of an emperor. His daughter had been delivered of an infant, and it was this child who was placed on the throne only two months after the father had been deposed. Not that it was put this way. Rather, because of these troubled times, it was thought advisable. His Imperial Highness the Emperor Takakura was not well, confined as he was to his rooms. He could thus no longer execute imperial tasks. Better then for the noble child to take up the reins of duty. That the child was but three years of age occasioned no problem. The busy librarians had found precedent: was it not true that some distant emperor in China had attained the throne at the even more remarkable age of two?

This argument accepted, Kiyomori could enjoy the benefits of his new position. So could we all. I ingratiated myself with my superiors and Ōto with their wives. My son was found to be a likely little fellow in the eyes of my peers and the joys of peace were ours.

* * *

While our Taira family was enjoying its reign, the Minamoto had not been idle. Yorimasa, representing that house in the capital, had come truly to hate the Taira. And now, with the news of this recent enormity of Lord Kiyomori on all lips, he went secretly to the palace of the second son of the retired emperor, Prince Mochihito, and, pleading the impotence of the throne and the general unhappiness of the people, confided that if the prince were to raise a rebellion against the Taira, the Minamoto would rise in their numbers to send the hated Kiyomori to his death, to depose the infant Antoku, and to put upon the throne the rightful emperor: Mochihito himself.

These were dangerous words, but the prince saw wisdom in them. He had already been twice by-passed for succession—the second time only two months earlier when the infant Antoku had been propped up on the throne. He was thus ready to sign the documents necessary for Kiyomori's removal.

Though Prince Mochihito was a brave young man and, as an

eligible imperial bachelor, a popular one, he was ill-advised to have so compromised himself. In no time, Taira commissioners were on their way to his residence. That he was not then apprehended was due to the vigilance of one of his admirers. She also arranged his escape.

Just before the Taira party appeared, a small procession might have been seen leaving the backgate of the palace: servants, a young page holding a high umbrella and under it a palace lady wearing a lacquered reed hat. This peaceful group hurried along the back street and when it came to a ditch, the lady leaped across it in such a manner that passersby wondered at her breeding.

The young lady was, of course, Prince Mochihito. For this saving disguise he had ample precedent. Not only was there the young Nijō but it was said that the Emperor Temmu himself, when still a crown prince, escaped attacking rebels by disguising himself as a female.

The transformation was, of course, easier back then than it would be now. The nobles still wore their hair long and though palace robes had many a class and station difference, there was not much to differentiate men from women. Now, in Kamakura, with full armor for the men most of the time, and hair cut short in any event, there would be less opportunity for such time-honored impersonation.

So the prince escaped. On his way to Miidera, a temple on the reaches of Lake Biwa, he and his little company tramped over the hills, since the roads were dangerous. When the goal was reached, the prince, his female robes all stained and torn, was a bedraggled sight. There is a poem about it: His poor torn feet left tracks behind, staining the earth like scarlet maple leaves.

Thus apparently ended one rebellion against the Taira. The next, however, began almost at once. Though perhaps instigated by the Minamoto, it came from the troublesome monks of Mount Hiei. These issued a proclamation to their fellow temples. Since His Imperial Highness Prince Mochihito had been hounded to Miidera, it would follow that the tyrant would now turn his arms against this temple. Had not these soldier-monks best take up arms to face this danger?

While it is true that the two temples, Miidera and Enryakuji (where this document was written), were of differing opinions on most things, still—continued the missive—as fellow sects under the Tendai-shū were they not like unto the two wheels of the wagon of enlightenment, and should they not join to suppress the tyrant Taira?

That nothing initially came of this alliance was due to these two allied sects bickering in their usual manner. Thus, though there were great plans for a march on Rokuhara, the arguments went on for so long that the nocturnal attack had to be called off by the approach of day.

We waited for an enemy that never appeared. All night long we stood inside Rokuhara, in full armor, listening to the occasional owl and becoming weary indeed. Dawn found us red-eyed and foul-mouthed. Had an attack been then launched we might have been an easy prey, but the monks were still squabbling.

Nonetheless, a battle was in preparation. Prince Mochihito, this time dressed as a member of his own sex, was on his way from Miidera to join the monks. He rode all night and at dawn stopped at Uji.

We heard about it, of course. Back then spies were already almost as common as they are now. And so we left on the run, sleepless but determined, gathering more troops as we raced along, eventually reaching Uji and its fast-flowing river. We were invigorated in that we knew we would win—rabble priests and renegade courtiers were no proper enemy.

We did not know, however, that the entire Minamoto army had gathered itself behind Mochihito. Nor did we know that they had destroyed the great bridge at Uji in a much more thorough manner than we had torn up our little Gojō bridge.

Consequently, as our men came racing up the rise of the road, they suddenly found themselves on the brink of the rushing river. The impetus of those in front and the push of those behind was so great that over two hundred of our vanguard horsemen pitched into the water, where most of them drowned.

I, farther back, heard the terrified neighings of the horses as they were swept downstream and the cries of the poor men as they, weighed down by their armor, sank beneath the stream.

Then the two enemies, Taira and Minamoto, occupied the ends of the broken span and shot arrows at each other for a very long time. I had a good view of these proceedings. There, just opposite, on the ruined causeway, stood Yorimasa, leader of the Minamoto, wearing a grand set of armor, blue and white leather, and over it a brocaded robe—white, the Minamoto color. He wore no helmet, either from bravado or because he had lost it, and his bald head shone in the sun.

The arrows—big-tipped battle arrows—flew back and forth. I remember seeing a horse getting one in the eye, and a young soldier receiving another in his open mouth as he shouted his battle cry. Perhaps we were getting the worst of it in this battle of arrows because shortly there came an order from our commander, Tomomori, who had been put in charge of the entire operation, to move across the river and fight on solid land.

Our battalion leader, the young Ōba Kageyoshi—brother to the more famous Kagechika—made a speech. We are warriors of the east, he said, and though this stream looks swift it is no more so than our beloved Tone River back home. Let us ford it!

This homely appeal carried the day. Three hundred of us, all mounted, galloped directly into the flood, where—ordered to turn the heads of the stronger mounts upstream and the weaker ones downstream—we let them have their rein. Gentle with our mounts, we were firm with the stream. As a result, all the beasts kept their footing and all of us kept our saddles.

We came, as was later said, like a tidal wave, and behind us, seeing this success, Tomomori ordered forward the rest of our army, thousands of us. Though some were drowned—three were later found in fishtraps—most clung to their saddles and barely got their heads wet, surviving for the grand battle on the other side.

This I shall not describe. I must later relate battles more important both to the Taira and to myself. Suffice it then to inform you that we soldiers retired in triumph to Rokuhara, carrying bobbing from the pommels of our saddles some five hundred heads of the fallen foe.

Among these were the heads of all of Yorimasa's sons, though not that of the father. He had been wounded, escaped from the field of battle and later, seeing all was lost, killed himself at the nearby Byōdōin, piercing himself with his blade and calling— since he was a recent convert—upon Amida Buddha.

The head of the unfortunate Prince Mochihito, however, was there, staring at us with those handsome, dead eyes. His lady was called to Rokuhara and after a single glance she buried her face in her sleeves. Thus the identity of the severed head was proved by the discomfiture of the woman, and to the satisfaction of the archivists.

Later the children of the unfortunate prince were rounded up. The eldest was made a monk. I don't know what happened to the rest. All held high court rank but this was now annulled by our priest-premier who, not content with having killed a son of the retired emperor, now degraded his unfortunate offspring. After that we celebrated by going and burning down Miidera.

* * *

Back in Heiankyō, Taira popularity had by now considerably lessened. The good people of the capital were afraid of us. Doors were closed in our faces and folk fled when asked a civil question. There were also a number of portents. The sound of tall trees falling was heard in the night, though there were no longer any tall trees around Rokuhara. And rats made nests in the tails of Kiyomori's horses, a singular activity that was seen as indication of further anomalies to come.

One such was the news that Yoritomo, exiled son of Yoshitomo, spared by our Kiyomori, had gotten an army together in Izu, his place of exile, had killed the Taira governor, and had then had the further effrontery to set up a small fortified camp at a place called Kamakura.

Some said not to worry, that the Hōjō family, loyal Taira, would certainly not support the upstart, since he was now a declared enemy of the imperial house. Others said that Kiyomori had now so distanced himself from this house that to side with Yoritomo could be interpreted as siding with the emperor. Still others said that since Kiyomori had so disposed of emperors, such imperial power no longer existed.

Lord Kiyomori also said a few things. That he should have put that damnable Yoritomo to death. The whelp had gone and forgotten all of his obligations to him who had spared his life. Now he kills the governor. He makes himself a fort. I should have cut off his head.

He ranted because he was alarmed. Yoritomo had been exiled when he was thirteen and he was now in his vigorous thirties. And, unbeknownst to us all that time, he was not without resources. In the fifth month, Prince Michihito had Yoritomo sent an imperial order, addressed to the members of the Minamoto clan in the provinces of the three regions of Tōkai, Tōsan, and Hokuriku, as well as their soldiers, in which it was ordered that the Lay Priest Kiyomori and the rebellious cohorts who followed him be pursued and destroyed at the earliest possible time.

Even as our leader stamped and shouted, an emissary from the Izu Minamoto branch had in answer placed a petitition before the retired emperor. His humble servant, Yoritomo of the Minamoto, was fearful lest any of his actions be misinterpreted as against the imperial house. He desired to reassure his majesty that such was not the case. Retired Emperor Go-Shirakawa graciously signed the petition—read and understood—and it was spirited back to Yoritomo's rural retreat.

Though he now held what amounted to imperial instructions, Lord Yoritomo was still militarily weak. And yet, as we dithered in the capital, he was slowly gathering an army about himself. Since I myself was to benefit from his methods, I will describe them.

Yoritomo was willing, even eager, to embrace former enemies. He sought out the disaffected, the defeated, and won them over. This he was forced to do, since, originally, the prudent local Minamoto families did not respond to his call to arms. He did, however, have recourse to a number of the disaffiliated, the rancorous, the disappointed.

It was a simple ceremony. All you had to do was roll up your banner and take off your helmet. This latter was known as yielding the neck and was taken as symbolic of defeat. You were then enrolled among the Minamoto.

At the same time, however, Yoritomo—already the able administrator—was making a private distinction between such newcomers and those other true Minamoto who had earlier entered his service. He had a book in which he kept it all written down—name, signal services, how many generations a true and loyal Minamoto, and so on. When I myself became again a Minamoto, you may be assured that my name did not figure well in that little book.

* * *

But back then I was still with Priest-Premier Kiyomori. And so it was that on a cool but sunny summer morning, we Taira marched out from the capital to go and chastise the Minamoto rebels. Glorious sight that we were, the citizens of Heiankyō gave us no rousing send-off. Those few who gathered merely stared and the majority did not come out to look at all. They would have been happy had we never returned—so much was Kiyomori now feared and hated.

And many of us, myself included, wondered if we would ever again see the capital. We knew what our lord had done—he had exiled an emperor, he had slain an imperial son. We wondered that he could have done this without punishment. Perhaps punishment was merely awaiting him, awaiting us all. These thoughts are not those of a soldier who goes to victory.

And so we marched on, banners floating red above us, the sun glinting off our polished helmets. Bright and colorful, like brilliant and cumbersome beetles we made our slow way out of the valley and up the mountain, taking the road down which I myself had traveled twenty years before.

At the first pass, I—a grown man, a soldier, a husband, a father—turned to look where my young eyes had first gazed. There lay Heiankyō, shining in the bright summer sun, seemingly unchanged, and I found myself thinking: It is as though we had never been there.

Yet, the years had left their marks on us. Back then we were all young, raw, determined. Now we were middle-aged professionals, all of us too dressed up, some of us a bit paunchy. We looked like a bunch of Fujiwara on the march.

And we were, after all, courtiers. That is what we had become under Kiyomori. A number of the officers had even taken to using makeup and adopted the courtly custom of lacquering the teeth black. The paint was mere vanity but the lacquer proved practical. In the coming carnage it offered a way to tell the Taira from the Minamoto heads. Ours were the ones with the blackened teeth—dead courtiers of Kiyomori.

And here we were going off to battle against the young, raw, determined army of Yoritomo—going off to fight against ourselves as we had been twenty years before. But we were no longer confident. There was little conversation when we camped and we did not sing as we marched.

We showed our plight in other ways as well. If the capital had come to dislike us after twenty years, the countryside grew to hate us in a mere two weeks. We stole, we raped, we murdered. Poor Ōba Kageyoshi tried to keep the men in some order but it was impossible. Poor Ōba, soon to become one of the ablest of generals and one who . . .

* * *

How soon, how easily is one reconciled to the historical mode. My only purpose in occupying my days in writing is to recount what happened and perhaps find some meaning in the patterns of those distant days. This being so I really ought to limit myself to what I know.

And back then I certainly did not know that Ōba was to become a famous general. Nor did he. And now, as though my ink has splattered the page, I have cast the future and revealed his destiny. In so doing it is as though I have killed him. Worse, I do to him what rumor attempts to do to me—makes me the sniveling soldier turned priest, makes him into a famous general and only that.

But I do not remember a famous general. I remember a brash young man who beat his horse to make it go faster, who once cut his leg deeply in some fight but raced on nonetheless, who drank the most and sang the best. To be with Ōba when he was young was to be with an unformed promise—to see life and vitality and to wonder if it was to be spared.

I want to remember and want to write of his freshness and his laughter and the day he got drunk and did a monkey dance of his own devising. And yet, as I write, I see the jowls of the general and the unhappy way he had of shifting in his saddle after he hurt his back. Knowledge is fatal. We know what happened after that, and this in turn colors our memories.

As I pause, brush in hand, I am more mindful of the difficulties of the blind balladeers down the hall as they struggle with their own historical accountings. Just the other day these adolescents were improvising away and began to sing of the death of the Emperor Nijō. He was a blossom fallen in the bud they decided. But this was not enough for the needs of the posthumous picture they were painting. So they made him a great gallant and have him asking a private in the guards to go outside the palace to procure women for him.

The reason for this singular account is that some Chinese emperor was said to have done just this and ended up with the beautiful Yang Kwei-fei. But our musical historians are not disturbed by the unlikeliness of it. Actually, had an imperial majesty felt this need he would have ordered a staff officer out— certainly no rank lower than that.

* * *

Poor Ōba—still young, given to jokes and laughter—but right now concerned that his men behave themselves. This was his first large command, a reward for exploits at Uji Bridge, and his desire to have a good time was warring with the need for discipline. So it was stocks for our thieves, public floggings for our rapists, and no monkey dances.

This discipline had some result: we became an effective army. When we reached the eastern provinces we swarmed into that post-town of Kamakura that the enemy had there created— hemmed in by the mountains, facing the sea—and in no time drove them out. A signal Taira victory—three thousand of us against three hundred of them.

I myself fought well—even wildly. About that time I began to learn that there were benefits to losing my temper. You can still read about me in the old military lists. There I am. My name is one of those under Ōba Kageyoshi, along with some thirteen others.

There I am slashing about, my temper lost. First into the camp, my sword irresistable. I remember yet the sound it made cutting through armor and into flesh, a kind of bang, like a hand drum loudly hit, followed by a liquid sound, like silk being ripped. And the way it felt—at first my sword was as though it had struck a tree, and then the blade slid on as though into water. As I rampaged around, my military reputation had begun.

And shortly suffered what might have been a permanent setback. For, having routed our understaffed foe, we settled back in Kamakura—then as disagreeble a post-town village as it is now a disagreeably fortified city—and went back to our courtier-like ways. We lounged about, complained of the food, admired ourselves on parade, and neglected our defenses.

This was taken advantage of when Yoritomo with a whole new army, gathered from the families of the farther eastern provinces, descended upon us—all as unmindful as dormant squirrels—and grabbed back his little capital.

With us in it. We were taken quite by surprise. Our scouts had not even noticed the approaching enemy. Ōba was sound asleep, having drunk too much the night before. I was myself still abed with one of the young sword bearers.

I suppose we put up some sort of resistance—I do not much recall, though I remember well enough running around trying to find my clothing while the alarms were being sounded. At any rate, the gates were breached, the enemy army poured in, and there we were, all three thousand of us, on our knees in the courtyard. And there, standing in front of us was the sole restorer of the Minamoto, Lord Yoritomo.

Here was the man who would destroy our world, and yet I recall being disappointed at the sight. Remembering the res-olute thirteen-year-old I had once glimpsed, I had expected someone more dashing, someone who might rival the young Kiyomori in baleful presence.

Not at all. Lord Yoritomo was already what he remained until fairly recently—an able administrator. Though he happened to deal in warfare, he could, with an equal amount of skill, have dealt in rice. He had the eyes of a bureaucrat.

These were now regarding us. He looked as though he were trying to decide how much we were worth. Perhaps he was. I later learned that he had originally thought to hold us in ran-som and make a profit. Then he stood over the kneeling Ōba and asked if this was all our forces. The poor man said it was. At this Lord Yoritomo went into visible thought, hand on chin, a gesture I later discovered to be habitual.

We all expected to die. Kiyomori would have had our heads

off at once. But the Taira leader was a man with many a personal passion. Lord Yoritomo was, on the other hand, an administrator who must see to the best interests of his house, no matter what he himself might feel.

Did he feel anything—ever—this cold man who created that cold capital wherein now lies all power? Remembering that day I find even the false and flaming anger of Kiyomori preferable to those pursed lips, that precise gesture—Yoritomo, hand on chin. Nonetheless, it was to this calculating intelligence that I owe my life, because—as my reader will have understood— Yoritomo did not have me killed. He spared us all. I remember Ōba kneeling there with his mouth open—surprised, perhaps even shocked that propriety had been thus flouted. Then Lord Yoritomo made a speech in those reedy tones, which were to become very familiar to us.

He said that he knew we were good soldiers and that he respected this. It was this knowledge that gave rise to his desire to be generous. He would spare any or all of us who would pledge loyalty to himself and to the Minamoto cause.

Knees pressed into the courtyard gravel, we were all amazed at this. I remember wondering how he could so trust us—the man must be simple. But Lord Yoritomo was never that. He knew all about us. He already had his bands of spies, larger, better, and much less visible than Kiyomori's mauve-robed band of little rascals. He knew that most of us were at heart dissident, and that even the most loyal understood that he had nothing to gain by remaining a Taira man. He had heard our grumblings; he knew that all he need do was ask.

And so we all gave our oaths. We rolled up the Taira banners and yielded our necks by removing our helmets. Nowadays we are criticized for this. Why did you not kill yourselves? That is a question I have sometimes encountered. And certainly nowadays it would be worth your life to go to the other side, if there were another side. But—as I have perhaps already sufficiently indicated—not back then.

Also, we saw this pardon as a way of getting ahead in the world. At least I did. The tides were moving, the Taira were going out and the Minamoto were coming in. And so I gave my new war cry with much more enthusiasm than I had ever given the old in front of the frowning Kiyomori.

Not that Yoritomo himself responded to our enthusiasm. He stared at us with his measuring eye and then, like a merchant who has struck a good bargain, rubbed his hands and disappeared, leaving us to feel foolish.

Thus it was that I once more changed sides and became again a Minamoto. It was not that I thought the less of my grandfather or my dead parent, both loyal Taira. It was that the times had changed and that the Taira were of such low repute and of so little promise. The Minamoto, young, valiant, were more as the Taira had been than were now the Taira themselves.

Too, and this counted with some of us, the retired emperor had pardoned Lord Yoritomo and this meant that his imperial majesty had already condemned Kiyomori. To one resolved to follow the imperial presence the choice was plain.

So, things being what they were back then, I simply asked for my wife and son to join me and—things being what they were—they were sent on their way.

* * *

And, after a time, off we marched—this new and enormous Minamoto army—off to the west to put down the Taira and to protect His Imperial Highness.

At the same time, after much delay the main Taira army was also setting forth. It was led by Koremori, one of the late Shigemori's sons. He was said to have been fine looking—not perhaps so much the young man himself as his outfit. He wore, it was said, a red brocaded battle-robe and his armor was laced with wide green silk cords; behind him was held aloft his ancestral garment, leather inlaid with tiger skin, and his saddle was studded with gold.

Eventually this splendid sight came to the banks of the Fuji River. Here Koremori himself wished to push on but his elder advisors told him to wait for the allied armies from Izu and Suruga to appear.

This advice was occasioned by their hearing that Lord Yoritomo's forces were large indeed. A Taira messenger, upset and exaggerating, said that there was no clear space left, no land at all, that everything from their river to the distant seas was occupied by the bivouacs of this enormous army; that he himself had been traveling for a week and seen nothing but soldiers—no fields, no forests, no mountains, no plains—just this enormous army covering all the ground.

It is indicative of the state of the Taira that—despite the fact that there were not this many people in the entire land—the tale was believed, a council of war was held, and all of these fat and flaccid Taira officers began to frighten each other with the tales they had heard.

One of our provincial Minamoto warriors, it was said, could easily pull a bow it would take five of them to bend; one of our staff-officers had five hundred men behind him; when we fought we did not retrieve our dead, rather just rode over the corpses and continued into battle. With alarmed reports such as these, it is no wonder that the so-called Battle of Fuji River turned out the way that it did.

It was late on the twenty-third day of the tenth month that we Minamoto darkened the plain with our numbers—as is now said—and lighted the sky with our campfires. Since it was evening, however, we decided to wait for morning. When it was light enough, each side would shoot arrows back and forth, the river would be forded, there would be some initial skirmishes, and then one side would eventually massacre the other.

About midnight it happened that a number of water fowl were disturbed by one of our spies. The whole lot of these birds, nesting in marshes near the Taira camp, then took to the air. Since there were so many, the noise was considerable and it probably did indeed resemble the sound of massed arrows being shot.

This might explain but it did not excuse the Taira dismay. The army panicked. Officers thought they were ambushed and ordered retreat. Soldiers fled, trampling each other. It was said that those who took bows forgot to take arrows, and those who took arrows forgot to take bows. Some leaped on horses that did not belong to them and others, leaping on their own mounts, forgot to untether them and galloped round and round. There was the utmost disorder as the great army of the Taira scattered in the darkness over the plain.

This lamentable and laughable spectacle continued until quiet returned. And when the sun rose and our Minamoto army, gathering properly at the banks of the river, let out its mighty battle cry, there was no answer, no volley, no one in sight.

We sent scouts over to reconnoiter and they returned with the report that the enemy was missing—that tents remained standing, that horses had been left behind, that armor had been tossed away, but that there was no opposing army.

Lord Yoritomo made the most of this. Facing the distant capital, he knelt, bowed and said that it was not he who had won this victory but that it was rather the doing of the great Hachiman, the Minamoto god of war. Then we all knelt, apparently a mighty sight because it is now said that it was as though the plain itself were kneeling.

As for myself, I was grateful that we had had this great victory without having had a battle. None of us were ready to meet in combat friends left behind in the capital—friends for years and now enemies because we were on opposing sides. We were ready to serve the Minamoto but were not yet ready for this consequence of doing so.

So we were grateful for this easy victory. And it was perhaps not due to the intervention of Hachiman but to that of another deity. Later I learned that Lord Yoritomo, always prudent, never went into battle without a small image of the bodhisattva Kannon tied up in his hair-knot, and that he always had his rosary about him. I much admired his foresight and my eyes shone.

* * *

Since I was now a Minamoto, I was able to follow the later fortunes of the Taira only through rumor. But this reached our victorious forces with small difficulty, for it seemed that all the countryside was ridiculing the ridiculous Taira.

Tradespeople were with laughter reciting a newly composed poem, which said that if a man who runs from the sight of the enemy is disgraced, how much greater the disgrace of him who runs from what he does not see.

Itinerant prostitutes were making merry and singing of the young general who threw away his armor at the sound of rushing wings. This personage, though grandson of the great Kiyomori, threw his armor in the river, went to pray to live forever.

When that army, which had set out so bravely, returned bedraggled to the capital, all expected a general punishment, even a few heads to fall. And what happened? Koremori got promoted to the rank of lieutenant-general, everyone under him moved up one place, and Shigehiro—the priest-premier's fourth and last son—was made general of the imperial guard.

Then, to quell criticism, this army marched off to battle against peaceful Heijōkyō, the old southern capital, now an entirely ecclesiastical city. The alleged reason was that the temples there had not opposed the late Prince Mochihito and therefore must have secretly joined him.

Consequently, the newly appointed Shigehiro marched his troops through the avenues of the old city shooting at will, killing anything that moved: priests, peasants, boys, girls. They then began putting the torch to the ancient temples.

At the great Daibutsu-den, largest of the temples, a space so vast that a man was but as an ant, some two thousand of the pursued—old priests, servants, women, children—fled to the second floor and then pulled up the ladders, hoping to be safe.

Observing this, Shigehiro had his men set fire to the venerable edifice. When the flames reached the second floor the screaming began. Those who heard it said that the cries of those burning forever in hell could not have been more horrible.

When the ruins were cool enough the record-keepers went around: two thousand burned at the Daibutsu-den; a thousand more at the fire at Kōfukuji; five hundred in one gutted temple; three hundred in another; a thousand monks died in the fighting itself and some five hundred of their shaved heads were carried back by the Taira to the capital as necessary trophies.

Most awkward ones they proved. Usually severed heads are secured by the hair and swing bravely from the saddle pommel. But these heads were bald as melons and as smooth. The warriors kept dropping them and so an expedient was attempted. Holes were made in the ear lobes and carrying strings were attached.

Originally these heads were to have decorated the walls of Rokuhara and a pretty sight they would have made. But so general was the condemnation of the destruction of Heijōkyō that even the priest-premier realized the inadvisability of this. So, instead of being exhibited, the heads, after having been brought all this distance, were alloted to their victorious takers and then thrown into the river that fronted Rokuhara itelf. There they floated, rotted, sank.

* * *

Another New Year had arrived. It was the fifth year of Jishō [1181] and never had Heiankyō seen a less felicitous year's beginning. There was no music, no dancing. The infant Antoku was kept to his chambers and none of the Fujiwara family made a formal court visit. Even the flautists from Mount Yoshino, whose New Year appearance had been for centuries an annual event, did not appear.

So many temples had been burned, so many of the clergy had been killed, that the priests decreed a time of impurity—the first New Year's ever so designated. An official statement, undertaken by Retired Emperor Go-Shirakawa, took advantage of the general gloom.

How terrible was our age, he said, then pointed to himself as example of this. He, the cloistered emperor, and the present infant emperor as well, and all their line had been deprived of all power during these latter days of the Law; how then to fill the empty passing of the months and years.

He continued for a time in this vein, a well-wrought statement. The courtiers felt strongly against the Taira, authors of this imperial misfortune. They felt even more strongly when the deposed emperor, Takakura, upon hearing of the destruction of the ecclesiastical city, took to his bed and within a very short time actually died. Like the young Emperor Nijō before him, he was carried to Seiganji and, as the blind boys now have it, became as the smoke of evening, rising into the mists of spring. He was twenty-one.

At this, the retired emperor, exiled as he was, found occasion to make a speech again—a most pathetic one. Nothing is more sorrowful for an old man, he said, than to see his son die before him, and nothing more painful for such a young man than to pass on before his father.

When these words were told me I was reminded of those of Kiyomori, uttered only three years before, after Lord Shigemori had died. Both utterances were sincere and yet both speakers were at the same time playing upon the emotions of the audiences, however, there was general sympathy for the pathetic retired emperor and now only hatred for the tyrant Kiyomori.

Can a hate this strong kill? It is now commonly said that it can; that each individual flame of hatred was focused, like a burning glass, upon the person of our priest-premier, and that as a consequence he burst into flame, experiencing a true hell on earth before departing to the proper hell below.

This is what the boys down the hall believe. Yesterday I heard them wailing that when the ailing Kiyomori was laved he turned the water boiling, that the liquid spattered, as though from red-hot iron, that his body was such that people could not bear to be within thirty feet of it, and that smoke from his orifices filled the hall where he lay.

Indeed, he expired amid sufferings, which must have gratified many. Yet, in the midst of these, he did not cease to command. When I die, he is said to have said, do not build a temple, perform no ceremonies. Rather, send an army after Yoritomo. Take him, kill him, cut off his head, and display it before my tomb. I ask only that.

Then, at the age of sixty-four, he died. And I, hearing of this, remembered the big-nosed, large-eared man on his black charger twenty years before. His remains were cremated and a priest took his bones to Settsu, whence he had come. In Heiankyō no funeral rites were performed. Instead, those priests left in Heijōkyō were all pardoned, if that is the word, and their offices were restored. Reconstruction was begun, and Retired Emperor Go-Shirakawa was respectfully requested to return from his retreat and grace the capital.

And, once more, the Taira army moved out to do battle. Through the darkened capital the marching men clanked and rattled. All doors were closed as they passed from the city and the newly reinstalled priests, busy with their divination ceremonies, unanimously prophesied the downfall of this hated family.

So off they marched into the dark, my former comrades in arms and a few friends. And there too I would have gone had I not possessed this talent for looking after myself, both in this world and the next. For had I been among their number it is unlikely that I would now be here listening to the late cicada in my garden, warmed by this late afternoon sun, writing away at my memories.

* * *

The Battle of Yokotagawara, in which this dispirited army next engaged, began on the second day of the month. The Taira forces, gathering on a hill, were relieved and gratified to see approaching several large groups of marching men, some three thousand in all, and floating over them the red banners of their house. As more and more men emerged from the hills and valleys, the Taira commander, delighted, shouted out: See, our allies have come, rallying to us.

But he shouted too soon. At a given signal, the red banners were thrown aside and replaced by white. We Minamoto then raised our war cry and beneath our flapping flags rushed at the incredulous Taira.

Never before had such trickery been employed in battle, such knavery. It was, however, typical of Yoritomo and his rough eastern men. Typical too of the new age that fell upon us all just as we Minamoto fell upon the Taira. For, from now on, such methods of making war became common. No more were there the old comforting rules.

Again the Taira army gave way to panic. Its commander, wounded, dragged himself back to the capital to make his terrible report. This was disregarded and it was decided that, since nothing of the sort was supposed to have occurred, nothing had. Munemori got himself appointed state minister and made a grand procession to court to thank the infant Antoku who, it is said, slept throughout the ceremony.

Not only was this pitiful battle ignored, so was the enemy itself. Though we were swarming like bees, ready to attack the capital, a joint proclamation in the names of both retired and reigning emperors now called for peace on land and on sea. None regarded it. Another New Year had rolled around. There would be no such peace.

*   *   *

But I must return to myself and my own story, writing not of what I was later told, but of what I myself saw.

Formerly an officer with the Taira, I was with the Minamoto given a like appointment—lieutenant, with a platoon to command. This much gratified me for I had feared that I might be made to perform common labor—washing the heads, for example, or worse.

The reason for my prompt promotion was that the Minamoto needed experienced men. There were more than enough raw recruits from the provinces, but they had few who, such as myself, had seen actual battle. We were treated as seasoned veterans and suitably rewarded.

My reward, for example, came after a battle when our troops attacked Satake Shirō at Hanazonoyama in Hitachi. Naozane, reads the rescript, broke into the enemy's camp sooner than anyone else and became known as the warrior who was so strong that he could defeat a thousand warriors all by himself.

The style was common. The hyperbole was to conform to the literary standards of such rescripts. What had perhaps happened was that I had learned to turn my famous temper to practical ends. While I do not remember much about the Hanazonoyama Battle, I must have cut quite a figure, slashing about, shouting all the while.

So, the Minamoto army was shaping up, becoming what Kamakura now calls a prime fighting force. This required some time and, in the midst of hostilities, Lord Yoritomo took two whole years for it. In only eight months he had, as the Kamakura report put it, unified the east. And now, he was, as yet another report had it, consolidating his gains. This took time.

What took so long was the paperwork involved. Since Yoritomo's way was to reward or to bribe, the bureaucrats were kept more busy than the soldiers. After the Fuji River battle more than twenty-four of the more prominent officers received land grants, and all this took months.

It was a calculated investment. Yoritomo would give a deed to the officer that guaranteed the land would remain his. This would bind the person to the court issuing the deed, which was Lord Yoritomo's. It was a new form of loyalty, one quite properly appealing to a person's self-interest.

Other time-consuming duties included the writing of all of

these announcements, letters, proclamations, deeds. The press of paperwork must have been terrible. My own land grant, when it came, was years reaching me.

Also—another reason for this remarkable hiatus—Yoritomo was not originally so certain of himself and of his forces as he later became. After winning these several battles he actually proposed that hostilities cease, provided that the imperial court recognize his forces as protecting the east of the country, while those of the Taira protected the west.

This offer of a negotiated peace would perhaps have been acceptable to the retired emperor, but it was not to the Taira. Kiyomori had died raving that the Minamoto must be exterminated and he had died raving this in public. Consequently, his son and successor, Munemori, was forced to honor the vow he had himself at that time made.

That Yoritomo would have so settled meant either that he was unsure of his forces or that he was playing a deeper game than anyone knew. Nowadays one never hears about this proposal of his. The official history is that after a short period of time the Lord of Kamakura rose and in his wrath crushed the Taira. And so he eventually did, but it is interesting to look at what occurred in between.

Perhaps this will become again generally known. As I write this, Yoritomo is dead and has been so for some time. His successors, the Hōjō regency, will shortly be rewriting a goodly portion of his official account. These gentlemen were, after all, originally Taira. Already they are pushing Yoritomo's hapless son about, and so I should suppose that a vilification of the father will before long begin.

Certainly, the fact that nowadays so much is made of Yoritomo's great rival, the poor, dead Yoshitsune, would indicate that . . .

No, no, enough! I am so fond of wandering about in the corridors of the past that it is easy for me to lose myself in empty speculation as to what actually occurred.

What actually occurs is like a large object that I hold in my hands, turning it this way and that, trying to make out what it could be—a dark, convoluted thing, like an eyeless head; this is what history is.

* * *

Rummaging through my own memories I play the historian. At the same time I must attend to this parallel construction that is being perpetuated by the ballad makers, also historians of a sort.

In so doing I am curiously reminded of an abbot on Mount Hiei who, pursued during one of the many disturbances, recited various sutras to render himself invisible. Interrupted at these prayers by the marauding enemy, he quickly slipped inside a large chest containing sutra rolls and covered himself with the contents.

The enemy searched his chambers but failed to find him. This was because his prayers had been answered. He had been rendered invisible by the sutras, saved by the scrolls. Either way you account for this—a miracle or a stratagem—the facts remain. History must be something like this—a number of observations, most of them true.

I turn and look at the garden. It is evening now and the rocks are fading into the twilight, while here on my veranda the last glow of day yet illuminates my page. Soon someone will come with a candle and after that my gruel will appear with perhaps, as well, a persimmon.

And so another day will have unrolled itself, a day like any other, but one never to be repeated.

* * *

I was now serving directly under a new commander, Lord Minamoto Yoshinaka, and since his rise and fall is important to my story, I must here say something about him.

Son of Yoshitaka, of another branch of the Minamoto clan, he was taken as a child, after the death of his father, to the province of Kiso. There he grew strong and healthy, shortly distinguishing himself with bow and with sword. When old enough he joined the forces of his senior relative, Yoritomo.

Energetic, brave, even dashing, Yoshinaka was irresistible to all but his commander, Lord Yoritomo himself, whose antipathy toward the talented youngster was marked. Perhaps for that reason the young Yoshinaka was not often referred to by his proper name. He was called Lord Kiso, after where he came from, just as I was named after Bear Valley.

Perhaps to prove himself, Kiso willingly followed orders to lead the opening battles in this war. It was he who supervised us in the abortive Battle of Yokotagawara. And he now led some six thousand of us to the stronghold at Kiuchi, in Echizen, midway between the capital and the western sea.

It was a dreary place, filled with bored soldiers and grumbling servants, all on the shores of a stagnant lake. The indoor cooking fires smoked—every night. It was that sort of place.

And there we sat, with no diversions, since Lord Kiso had seen to it that we were not allowed to drink, that no women came to visit, and that the kitchen boys and stable lads were scrawny and pimpled.

So there we sat—with a traitor in our midst as well. He was a priest (such often are) and he sent a message to the Taira, camped on the other side of the lake and, as tormented by the mosquitos as we were. His message, one which later cost him his own shaved and conniving head, was that this was no real lake, that it was an artificial pond, and that all one need do was break down the dam at the far end and gallop across the mud.

One wonders what kind of soldiers these Taira were to have needed this information, what sort of scouts had reconnoitered the area? At any rate, agreeably surprised, the high command sent out a group to hack through the timbers supporting the earthen dam, and in no time we on the other shore were surprised to see the water rapidly receding and a number of fat carp jumping about in the resulting shallows.

It was, I remember, during the fifth month—a hot and unseasonable spring. The frogs had been keeping us awake, since we were not tired enough to sleep, and then quite suddenly an entire lake was pouring away, flooding the deserted farmlands on the farther side and making a roar that brought us wandering to its receding shores.

Though we saddled and girded ourselves, the Taira were already by this time halfway across the mud flats. Encumbered though they were, their horses sinking deep into this new paddy, they still managed to sweep down upon us in style.

I hacked away at several and managed to knock two off their mounts and see them trampled into the liquid mud by their maddened steeds. Then, wading away, up to the knees in muck, I chased a number of others, but we were outnumbered.

It is interesting that, though I was occasionally distinguished by my valor, this time I was perhaps the first to gallop away. But our cause was hopeless. The Battle of Kiuchi, as it was later to be called, was already lost. And it was because of this promptness that I was able to fight in the next encounter.

This occurred shortly afterward, among the hills between Kiuchi and the capital, a place called the Kurikara Valley. It was this battle that both showed Lord Kiso's strengths as a commander and also displayed our new style of warfare—one which much confounded the old-fashioned Taira.

Our commander knew that the Taira forces at this encounter were larger than his own and that he must therefore somehow make the enemy believe that it was rather the Minamoto forces that were the larger. If he displayed us upon the plain, as had Yoritomo in the earlier battles, our weakness would be apparent. He must therefore think of another way.

This he shortly did. By stationing our forces in the hills he was able to parade us in and out of the valleys and thus suggest great numbers. Our white banners shone bravely as we, time and again, wove through the hills and emerged on the edge of the plain where from under the trees watched the waiting Taira. Little did they know that it was the same procession, again and again—continuing until our horses were balking and we, tormented by thirst and flies, were ourselves near revolt.

Having thus displayed our nonexistent numbers, we noted with satisfaction that the Taira were moving forward more slowly and, further, were taking the position that Lord Kiso most desired that they take—opposite us, backed by the valley itself.

It was a large but shallow, green-filled place, like many another, and seemed to lead on into the mountains behind. This is what the Taira presumed that it did. In actuality, however, as our commander had ascertained, it was entirely closed in, ending—just around the valley corner from all that verdant greenery—in barren cliffs.

To the Taira, theirs appeared a safe place because it was open and free from attacks from the rear. At the same time it seemed to offer fair retreat if the battle went against them. There was nothing wrong with such calculations except that, once again, no one had seen to the lay of the land. The Taira were no longer good soldiers, as I—so late of their number—knew but too well.

And so began the famous Battle of Kurikara. It started like a standard battle ought to have—Kiso had seen to that. He thus hoped to reassure the Taira that he might trounce them the better. We started in the most orthodox fashion, except that we began the battle much later in the day than was customary.

Finally, after many a delay, fifteen of our strongest bowmen stood forth and, as was proper, let loose a volley. In reply the Taira, having no idea of our intentions, sent forth fifteen of their own strongest and the volley was returned.

Then we sent thirty horsemen over to prance about and they in turn sent out thirty of theirs. It was a reassuringly normal battle—everything going by the book.

We sent fifty, they sent fifty. Then we sent a hundred and they sent a hundred. And, as was proper, the two armies had now moved closer to each other. Everything, in fact, was going as it ought, except that it was much later than it ought to have been. Given this still preliminary stage of the battle, the sun should have been overhead. Instead, it was already late afternoon and the sun was declining.

We had been instructed to hold ourselves in check. The Taira had, of course, received no such order. They were wild to begin. Blinded, the late sun in their eyes, waves of men raced toward us and then, when we did not respond, raced back again, their shadows long before them. Our enemy had a most touching faith in good manners and were perturbed that we were not following the ritual timetable of battle.

Then the reason for our not so doing became clear. As the sun slowly sank, high on the hills on either side, catching the last of the light stood two new white-bannered armies. Replacements had earlier arrived and been until now hidden by our commander. Already the dazzled Taira believed our forces larger than they were. Now, when these new numbers were dimly seen against the sun, their blinding banners shining, they thought themselves outnumbered.

Once again panic gripped. With a roar, the Taira army was on its feet, men scrambling, horses rearing, as this great body turned and fled. In the twilight, the soldiers behind were unable to see those in front and officers could not find their men. Encumbering helmets were torn off, red banners were dropped, armor was stripped away that the owners might run the better, and they all raced down the darkening valley because they thought that there was a rescuing road at the bottom.

But there was not—only that cruel mortar of stone. And in it was ground the Taira forces. Galloping horses and stampeding men fell one upon the other, neighing and screaming, crushed against the rocks. Son fell on father, brother on brother; servants ended up on top of masters and over these poured yet more fleeing troops.

The valley filled up, the dead and dying lying in heaps, layers deep. When night was full and the stars were out, some seven thousand men, it was said, lay there bleeding, smothering, or already dead. It is said too that these piles of corpses were high as the surrounding hills and that a lake of blood bathed the shores of these new islands.

I was among those who, shouting our battle cry, galloped after those poor soldiers, among whom were certainly former acquaintances and maybe even friends. And in the morning I was a member of the scouting party that went to take stock in the newly risen sun.

Though already accustomed to the sights of war, I had never before seen a spectacle such as this. The mounds of the Taira looked like those piles of sacrificial victims—deer and boar—which after disaster are sometimes found slain at mountain shrines. But these were mountains of men, all of them bruised and torn, one buried under the other, some of them still moving—a hand here, a leg there—in the growing heat of the day.

We went and finished these off with sword or spear. Then, like dogs worrying over some vast carcass, we went after the heads, pulling bodies from the heap, striking, pulling yet another. Burdened by our trophies we staggered away from this mountain of flesh as though from a banquet.

Then we turned and left. There were many more trophies but no way to carry them. And there was no question of honorably burning the remains of the enemy—not when the enemy dead numbered so many. We left them as they were.

They baked and stank and eventually caused a local pestilence. The place is still now filled to the brim, it is said, with crumbling bones. Thus ended the Battle of Kurikara.

* * *

I have diverted myself and, I trust, my reader with this description, but there were so many battles in this endless war that I would end up tiring us both were I in such detail to continue.

I will rather then describe a single incident from the next battle in which I took part. It is one that well indicates the opposition between the Taira and the Minamoto ways of battle, the differences between the ways of old Heiankyō and of the new

Kamakura. In addition it has, as we will see, some relevance to this account of myself.

At the Battle of Shinohara, which occurred later on during that hot and bloody spring, on a day when sweat was pouring off the bodies of the men as though they had come from the bath, the Taira commander, Nagatsuma, was unable to withstand a renewed Minamoto onslaught and had turned to flee the battle—in a manner fast becoming known as "the Taira style" of fighting.

He was a good officer and a brave man but he did not run fast enough. A spruce young Minamoto soon caught up with him. The Taira's armor indicated plainly enough his rank, and the youngster—Yukishige was his name—thought that this capitulation would look well in the battle report.

But he had not counted upon the strength of the older man, and soon he found himself flat on his young back while his would-be captive knelt on his chest and menaced his throat with a dagger.

The youngster was then asked who he was, just as the old manuals said he ought to be asked. And he replied properly with: I am Yukishige, a native of Etchū, eighteen years old.

Here Officer Nagatsuma neglected what the old manuals next advised. He should have at this point removed the youth's head from his body. Instead, he grew pensive and is supposed to have said: Ah, the pity of it all. If my own son were alive he would now be this age. Though I should take his head, I will, in memory of my son, allow him to keep it. Rather, I will take him prisoner.

So they waited until some Taira men came along to assist in the capture. The elder officer sat there confidently because it did not occur to him—long in the capital—that protocol would not be observed and precedent followed. Naturally, when you had bested an enemy, he considered himself a prisoner. Any other behavior would not have suited a gentleman.

But we Minamoto were not gentlemen. Consequently, the

young Yukishige stood up, took out his sword, and began hacking away at his captor's neck. Nagatsuma was so surprised that he sat and stared, this father and grown man, at the impetuous youth who was cutting off his head.

He might have recovered from his incredulity at the manners of the young and gotten in a few jabs himself but that two more Minamoto men came up and joined the youngster. In no time, it was all over for poor Nagatsuma, a gallant man who never believed in treachery.

Now, you, who have perhaps heard of me, may here detect a similarity to an incident in my own career. As you will discover, I too was saddled with another unmannerly youngster, and the encounter ended with the taking of a head. One version of the occasion, which is included in the military lists, sees me besting the boy and smartly appropriating the desired portion. There is another, however, which has me making a show of pity, like the unwise Nagatsuma. Neither of these is correct and I will amend this portion of my history in the following pages.

* * *

Suffice it now to say that of all the many thousands of Taira troops and horsemen said to have set out from the capital at the beginning of the season, not twenty thousand were able to limp back at its end.

It was indeed a bad time for the Taira. But also it was a bad time for my commander, Yoshinaka of Kiso. The reason was the enmity of Lord Yoritomo back in Kamakura, for already he had begun showing that distressing distrust of those who served him.

Yoritomo had earlier conceived and now continued a marked dislike of this dashing cousin. Kiso thus stepped with some care and, perhaps for this reason, this ordinarily violent man attempted a kind of diplomacy in his next encounter with the enemy.

He approached the monks of Mount Hiei, sent messengers with a long list of all the fine things he had done to protect both the Buddha and the emperor against the excesses of the Taira. Someone wrote it all up for him, describing his prowess in fittingly poetic terms: His advances were like the winds of autumn sweeping clean a tree of its leaves, or the fresh snow of winter crevassing the earth—oh truly the gods and Buddha himself had brought these victories to him.

The monks were realistic. They knew that the Taira had now lost most of the battles. So, being priests, they sought divine aid. The word back was prompt: Enemies of the emperor were enemies of the Buddha. So now it was merely the question as to which side was the enemy of the emperor.

At this point the Taira sent their own appeal up the mountain. Would you turn against us when you must know that the Minamoto are at your very door, and when you recall how we have rewarded and supported you? No! May the arms of the emperor's enemies be bound at the gate of our camp and may we bring their heads in triumphal march back to the capital!

The monks again resorted to prayer. Just which side was the enemy of the emperor and consequently that of the Buddha? This was the question they hoped would be answered.

It was—by the Retired Emperor Go-Shirakawa himself. He indicated which was the enemy by fleeing the capital and the Taira. The reason he did so was that the Taira had misunderstood Kiso's intentions at Mount Hiei. They thought it presaged a general attack on the capital—his troops joined by thousands of furious monks, descending yet once more upon the hapless city.

Thus panic again struck this once soldierly but now undisciplined family. Commanders went directly to the palace with orders that the retired emperor retire to some safer place until these Minamoto traitors had been driven back. Retired Emperor Go-Shirakawa, fearing exile once again, was faster than they. He had already hopped into his palanquin and was safely carried outside the city—no one knew where.

This incident occurred on a humid night on the twenty-second day of the seventh month of the second year of Juei

[1183], and news of this unprecedented occurrence at once reached Rokuhara.

* * *

But I see that I am once again ahead of my story, and, further, have left out some important details—important at any rate to myself. Sitting here and looking at my quiet garden, noting an unfamiliar bird sitting by the well or a familiar lizard peering around his rock, I neglect chronology. All seems a warm and pleasant timelessness.

Which would indeed be the ideal of my new profession of lay priest: a constant living in the present with no regret for the past and a firm confidence in the future. I have by no means attained such an attitude, but I have at least managed to lose track of my own chronology in this memoir of mine.

So . . . as I have indicated, it was decided that I had distinguished myself in battle and I received my reward. The citation reads:

> To Kumagai Jiro Naozane of the Osato District, Musashi Province. Regarding holdings assigned him, he is hereby granted the office of land steward of the above-mentioned locality, long his family's holding but lately seized by Hisashita Naomitsu. For having distinguished himself in the campaign against Satake Shiro, this land stewardship of Kumagaya Township is hereby granted. These rights may be transmitted to his descendents. The attention of cultivators is directed to this order and their compliance with its terms is thus decreed. The thirtieth day of the fifth month of Juei 1 [1182].

I have it right here with me still—have just copied it out. Of course it arrived only when I was already a Minamoto veteran. Such was the Kamakura bureaucracy, even back then, that it took years for a simple commendation and land award to find its way from commander down to loyal retainer.

This piece of paper then meant that I was again master of my own land and was hence free from Naomitsu. At the same time the grant gave me a portion of his own land, or so he later maintained. Perhaps it did. He certainly put up a good argument when much later Lord Yoritomo, bored and irritated, had to sit there and listen to the two of us squabble over boundary lines— a result of his own policy of arbitrarily rewarding new recruits.

I often thought of that Musashi tract of mine while I was marching under Lord Kiso through the devastated lands around the capital. It was not, I hoped, like these I now saw. There, in the several years of fighting, no cultivation was done. The fields had gone to weed and then, in that summer's terrible drought, to dust. Great reddish clouds were blown into the sky and fell on our advancing forces, the dust sifting under our armor and into our eyes and mouths—a taste it had: dry, bitter.

It was the taste of hunger because with no cultivation there was no food and a great famine descended on the lands around Heiankyō. We soldiers were kept going through our rations, brought from some distance. But those we passed had no such.

I saw whole farmer families sitting by the roadside, stunned, hands in their laps; too weak to move, with eyes already dark as they watched us pass. And I saw an old couple under a tree, sitting there as though witnessing our grand advance, and then I saw that their eyes were sightless, dead. And a young girl, thin as a spear, who feebly tried to keep up with us, baring her pathetic breasts all the while in hopes of attracting one of us enough to feed her.

And so I thought during that dry and dusty march of my own green and fertile land, which I had not for so long seen. Not since I had been a raw recruit—and now I was a proper officer, cutting, I am told, a fine figure.

* * *

Here I will again digress to describe the grand sight we made, since military fashions are now so different, and since thus will be illustrated one of my themes, the transience of all earthly things, even the hem of armor skirts.

These used to extend all the way down to the knee and much hampered running away, something which the later Taira discovered. The new design, seen nowadays in Kamakura is cut much higher; troops are still expected to run, though now toward the enemy rather than away from it. Indeed, most of the new fashions are designed to accommodate troop movements. The old armor was designed for single combat, an event now all but obsolete.

The helmet for example. It had a much lower back to it. Perhaps this was to discourage any ease during beheading, but it certainly kept the heat in and the breeze out. Now the troops are cooler and not much more vulnerable.

Also back then we had only one sword to contend with, not two, as now. It was much like the present long sword but was much better forged than is nowadays common. It also kept bumping against the back of the shin guards.

These remain as they were, but not our footwear. For some reason back then we all wore fur shoes—bear fur if we could get it. And most uncomfortable they were, kept slipping off at odd intervals and smelled foul all of the time.

We also smelled—not only of wet bear shoes and sweaty jerkins and unwashed bodies, but also the even less attractive stench of scent. Back then we all used it, Minamoto and Taira alike. We used to hold our faces over the smoking incense pots so that our hair grew rank with the stink. The reason given us for this odd activity was that even if the enemy took our heads he could not mock a lack of elegance.

Equally perfumed was our doe skin. This was a piece of hide that we always carried, either folded or rolled up. We used it for sitting on, for marking our places during archery practice; it was also to be our death seat in case we were caught and decapitated. I remember that mine always smelled of aloes, and so consequently did my bottom.

And, oh yes, the fan. It was iron-ribbed and suitably bulky. And in the middle was the big white mark of the Minamoto. I used mine more for hitting my men than for fanning my own sweaty face.

The Kamakura military fashions are now much more sober. The soldiers no longer smell like wayside prostitutes and their raiment is much less bright. In the days of the Taira campaign, however, we were all gold and azure and silver. Yet, even back then, Lord Yoritomo was trying to make us less showy.

Indeed, to the three virtues he required of his warriors— good family, good bowmanship, good horsemanship—he added a fourth: good and modest bearing. He once humiliated one Toshikane, vice-governor of Chikugo, who appeared before him overdressed.

Did he not think it extravagant to wear such clothing? Yoritomo asked the humbled official. Look at these two gentlemen here—indicating two named, I remember, Tsunetane and Senhiro—their domains are more extensive than yours yet they do not wear such rich attire.

The vice-governor was dismissed, chastened, and the new sobriety was upon us. Nowadays the troops wear standard cuts and peasant colors. The men look identical. When they march it is like a centipede, one long creature with many legs. We, on the other hand, used to cut quite a sight, each of us marching smartly down the highway.

An activity we may now continue, I having stopped our procession merely in order to examine our now quaint costumes. We were going to Mount Hiei to further reason with the monks. And shortly, as I have already indicated, the crafty retired emperor would cleverly flee from his palace on that hot summer night.

* * *

In casting about for causes for the Taira downfall the historians have hit upon various reasons, and I have mentioned some of them in this chronicle. But, to my mind, the most important of these was this disappearance of the retired emperor.

Consider—never had anything this untoward occurred. There was no precedent and the Taira, a full generation in the capital, were now so courtier-like that anything without precedent filled them with dread. Also, the retired emperor had been their responsibility. They had claimed him and trotted him out from time to time. His disappearance now made clear that they had not been, in any sense, protecting him. Thus the true imperial enemies must be the Taira themselves, and if this were so then the advancing Minamoto were his protectors.

This the Taira must also have understood. Otherwise it would be difficult to account for their subsequent actions. These occurred so precipitously, one on top of the other, that what ought to have taken months occurred in mere days.

With the retired emperor gone, with the Minamoto almost at the gates, plans were made to evacuate the child emperor Antoku. It was intended that the three imperial treasures were to be carried from the palace in a fine parade, which would then soberly join that of His Imperial Majesty, all padded into his palanquin. Then this mighty procession would proceed with grace and dignity out of the north gate and, accompanied by the army, would march sedately along to an unannounced place of safe repose.

But how different the actuality was from these plans. The confusion was so great that the six-year-old emperor was all but tossed into a waiting wagon; his mother was forced to leap in with him; the straggling lines of men and oxen started at once; and though the three imperial treasures were carted up and taken along, the little emperor's own sword was left behind.

The Taira army was nowhere in sight, and only a few officers accompanied the pitiful procession to the gate. Alone it wandered forth into the famined wilderness, this parade of women and children and courtiers. The reason the protecting army was not in the procession was that both men and officers were packing, preparing to leave, or getting ready to set fire to their own homes, stopping to tear the Taira red badges from their armor.

Nowadays, when all of this is history, you sometimes hear young soldiers asking why the Taira did not stand and fight, why, instead, they turned and fled. After all, reasons youth, it is more glorious to die fighting than to die fleeing.

And so, nowadays, everyone thinks. They have been so taught. Kamakura needs young men who will pursue such glory. Back then, however, loyalty was a lazy thing, as I have indicated, and in any event attack requires a degree of organization and flight needs none.

And so it was that the Taira fled the capital. Lord Koremori himself set the tone in his now famous farewell to his family, a recounting of which I will spare myself. He was not much of a commander—he who ran away at the Battle of Fuji River—but he cuts now a pathetic figure in the accounts as he wets his sleeve yet again. And when he had finished his fine speech he had to scramble because the street was already filled with the smoke of burning mansions.

When the Taira fled the capital they burned down more than twenty palaces, as well as most of the residences of their number. In consequence, fire being the combustible thing that it is, more than forty thousand private homes of the simple residents of Heiankyō went up in flames as well.

Once out of the city these battalions paused. Looking back, they saw the smoke billowing from their burning homes, and one of the vice-councilors, it is said, actually stopped to pen a pathetic poem—such courtiers had become the Taira.

It was this sight that we Minamoto witnessed when we later came through the same pass and saw below us the still-burning city of Heiankyō. The vantage was the same as that I had experienced more than twenty years before when as a youth I had first glimpsed the mighty capital, center of our world.

Then I had seen it beneath me in the golden haze of afternoon, the gentle smoke of cooking fires hanging above it. Now, in the hot glare of that summer, I saw it yet afire, points of flame licking beneath the heavy pall of roiling smoke as the whole city was consumed.

There we again stood gazing and again did not march into the lost capital. We were waiting for the Mount Hiei monks of Enryakuji to give us their allegiance and bring forth Retired Emperor Go-Shirakawa, for it was to their holy arms he had fled.

By the time we arrived in the city the ashes were cold. We marched down blackened avenues along which in peaceful times we had contentedly strolled. Again I stopped my men at the Gojō Bridge, where we had stopped before and where I had seen the mighty Kiyomori—himself now only a few bones stuck in the ground, and a memory like a nightmare.

Then I turned, as I had done before to look at that wonderful palace of his, filled with men and servants, alive with people, over it fluttering the myriad red flags of the Taira.

But now nothing remained of this Rokuhara. All those pavilions, those great apartments, those mighty courtyards—all had been consumed. Gone in but an hour and now we stood in a blackened waste—all that remained were foundation stones and the dead odor of ashes.

*　*　*

Now, sitting in the summer heat, feeling my skin warm in the sun, I listen to a late cicada and idly follow the blunderings of an armored beetle. I feel aged and content—if contentment consists in finally sitting idle and idly remembering.

How simple seems the world when seen from above. I gaze into the short grass as into a forest and there the beetle stumbles on like a lost warrior. Equally, I gaze from the heights of time and see myself, equally blundering, lost in this small area of what I knew.

Nonetheless, unlike almost everyone else, I have survived.

This I credit to my sane policy of looking after myself. Continually throughout my long life I have been surprised at the number of those who fling life away in an attempt to satisfy some demand made by others—whether this be loyalty or simply the urge to do whatever everyone else is doing.

From the first, however, I was gratifyingly free from such feelings of accommodation and of a consequence am still here when most of my contemporaries lie dead. Also, I intend to continue along this road I have so far successfully trod, since I cannot believe that the Buddha, a being so successful in his own right, would have it otherwise.

Now, continuing my saga, I must observe that he seemed to have averted his gaze from the plight of the unsuccessful Taira. This now grew steadily worse: they fled by horseback, by foot, and, once the sea was reached, by boat, but all were sick at heart. As I think of them now I hear yet again their plaint—really hear it, since the blind boys have at this moment decided to elaborate on this very subject.

They compose long lists of those who fled: the former palace minister, the Taira major counselor, the fifth-rank chamberlain, the master of the palace repairs, and on and on. These poets are fond of lists. Fond of poetic detail as well. So unaccustomed were those courtier-feet to walking along rough country lanes that soon the delicate colors of their skirt hems turned the fullest red. Also, one of the fugitives sees a flight of white heron and is terrified, thinking these are Minamoto banners. Perhaps a graceful reference to the Battle of Fuji River.

Anyway, wandering in this wilderness, in place of jade-green draperies in their scarlet-damask bedrooms, they had now had torn reed hangings in rude sheds, and in place of the fragrant smoke of delicate incense, only the black billowings of the burning driftwood of the fisherfolk.

Amidst this the little emperor was carted hither and thither. Since there was now no proper vehicle for His Imperial Highness (the bearers had run off with it), he was carried about on a litter, and was later put into a boat, where he became most ill from the motion, and from which, as is well known, he was later thrown.

Listening to the blind balladeers, I hear of Kiyotsune, a son of Shigemori, and a good man. I used to see him often in the old days in the capital. He loved moon-viewing, I remember, and was always at one of the parties held for such occasions, his sensitive face turned to catch the light, his own eyes alight with the beauty.

Now, down at the water's edge, he looked into the dark. A full moon was rising—his beloved moon. Gazing at it, he drew forth his flute from its brocade pouch and played a final tune. Then he knelt upon the rocks and, after chanting a sutra, threw himself into the waves.

How all of this was known I myself know not. Who could have seen it? Still, even if it did not occur in this fashion, it is a pleasant story. Indeed, the novices down the hall, singing away, seem particularly inspired by this flight to the sea: pushed onward by the passing tides, the Taira boats seem drawn ever higher, into the cloud-filled sky itself. Already, days, weeks, rivers, mountains lay between the fugitives and their lost city. They seem upon the very edge of the earth, a place where all ends, except for endless tears, etc.

* * *

Back in Heiankyō, Retired Emperor Go-Shirakawa had installed himself—his palace having been again burned down—in the Enyūbō, a temple outside the city. Here he greeted his saviors, the Minamoto, and was carried back in glory to the capital, escorted by Yoshinaka, Lord Kiso.

Though usually negligent about his costume, Lord Kiso on this occasion wore a scarlet-brocade battle suit and over it black armor with silk cords. He also carried a sword inlaid with gold and silver, his quiver held black-and-white arrows, and his black lacquered bow was bound with red rattan. This last was a bit criticized. Red was the Taira color. But general opinion was that the savior of his imperial majesty could have anything he wanted. Yoritomo would not, of course, have agreed. Talk about overdressed.

Our Lord Kiso, though handsome in his finery, was uncomfortable. As a decorated officer I was standing quite near and, during the lengthy festivities, could watch the sweat slide down the back of his neck as he fidgeted at his ribbons.

The pronouncements by the retired emperor were particularly long. He most regretted the unfortunate abduction of his imperial majesty, the sacred child, Antoku, and the loss of the three sacred treasures. All must be returned. Something extraordinary must be done, otherwise imperial succession might falter.

Soon, by the eighth month, something was done. The late Emperor Takakura had had several other sons and these, unlike Antoku, had been spared. They were now bid into the presence of Emperor Go-Shirakawa.

The first, a child of five, beckoned into the frightening embrace of the retired emperor, burst into tears, at which his majesty sent him away. Next, his four-year-old brother was brought forth. He, already the little courtier, climbed onto his grandfather's knees, gazed at him with childish charm, and nestled in the imperial arms.

Delighted, Emperor Go-Shirakawa called for the diviners and in a loud voice that all could hear told them to make a very secret divination. Upon noticing the imperial pleasure, they shortly returned with divine word that if this particular four-year-old were made emperor, the line would continue for unto one hundred generations. Thus was little Takanari made emperor-elect. It was he who would later become our well-known Emperor Go-Toba. Of his older, crybaby brother even the name is no longer heard.

This is my quarrel with history—it is forever doing things like this. I would like to know something about the young unfortunate. Did he spend his later life wondering about what would have occurred had he not on that distant day blubbered?

But I am like that, always working against my own interests. Why should I be interested in such failures, from the contemplation of which I can myself gain nothing.

Little Takanari put his small best-foot forward, made a success of himself, if I may so phrase it, and certainly got ahead in this world. And here I am wondering about some small failure lost even to history. I sometimes despair of myself.

* * *

Our Lord Kiso received a number of honors from the retired emperor. He was made general of the Imperial Order, became governor of Echigo and chief of the imperial stables. I was reminded of all that Kiyomori had earlier received after the Hōgen War, and from those same imperial hands.

In the meantime Lord Yoritomo was not forgotten. Many gifts signifying gratitude were sent from the imperial storehouses outside the capital: one-hundred-weight of gold dust, over one thousand rolls of white linen, whole bales of imperial silk—an entire company was required to carry these up to Kamakura.

They were received with some ceremony. Yoritomo was sitting in state in a plain robe, wearing his high lacquered headdress. The court envoy, returned to the capital, dilated upon our lord's gracious good manners and opined that he might well have appeared at court just as he was.

Unlike Yoshinaka, Lord Kiso. This young commander was discovered to be extremely provincial. Evading his dressers, he often arrived in the most awkward apparel, more like a servant's than a gentleman's. And he was always committing social solecism such as entering his oxcart from the back rather than, as long usage demanded, the front. When told of this, he said that it was only a carriage.

Likewise, his rustic manner showed most unfavorably at ceremonies, where he would scratch his head and pick his teeth and openly gaze at the palace ladies. This occasioned an amount of criticism of the sort that I knew well, having myself long been a butt because of my provincial (though presently polished) ways.

Another similarity was that he countered such loose talk much as I had. When he heard that one of his officers was making fun of his dress, he had the elegant fellow stripped in the barracks and flogged until it seemed that the unfortunate was wearing a full suit of red body armor.

This being our lordship's disposition, before long the citizens of Heiankyō had more to put up with than a lack of manners. His officers were sometimes as raw as he was and their men were worse. These thought little of violating the sacred precincts of Kumano, for example, reaping the crops to feed themselves and their horses. Temple storehouses were forcibly opened so that they could take what they wanted. These men, bloated with victory, even took to attacking and robbing citizens on the streets. Of a consequence people were saying that under the Taira one had been afraid only of the priest-premier but that under the Minamoto one was terrified of every single soldier.

The retired emperor knew of this but at first did nothing. He was occupied in installing the new child emperor, for he needed current imperial authority for what he was now going to attempt—ridding the capital of this ignorant Minamoto scoundrel.

His initial plan was ruined by an inept messenger. Kiso, angered, marched upon the new palace of the retired emperor. As so often happened when he was in command, the soldiers got out of control and a real fight began, in the midst of which the palace was fired yet again.

It must have been a scene—I was myself not there to see it, since I was away with my regiment to counter Taira remnants, and so was now only nominally under Lord Kiso. During that palace incident the lord high marshal of Bungo, running away, was caught by a low-ranking soldier and stripped absolutely bare. He was later seen shivering, his behind all goose-fleshed, it is said. He was eventually assisted by a passing priest, who took off and offered his short undergown but kept his own outer robe, with the result that the lord high marshal, pulling this garment over his head to hide his face, again exposed himself, exciting much merriment and many a smiling inquiry as to what new sect this monk could possibly belong to.

Even the small Emperor Go-Toba found himself menaced. At play with the court ladies in a boat on the pond, he was shot at, though not purposely. The Minamoto soldiery involved promptly bowed and escorted the perhaps thrilled imperial youngster and the certainly terrified palace ladies into the safety of a nearby pavilion.

The retired emperor himself was also shot at, though no arrows hit. Again he was fleeing in a palanquin, away from his burning palace, an activity in which he often engaged during troubled times. Now, however, he did not get away. He was caught and locked up in a new mansion near Gojō.

Kiso had carried the day and confounded the imperial enemy. He was, as a result, quite full of himself. During an inspection of the heads—some six hundred and thirty of them—he said that he himself could be ruler if he wished, but in order to become the reigning emperor he would have to adopt the hair style of a child, and to become the retired emperor he would have to shave his head and become a priest, so therefore he had decided to become neither.

This pleasantry sat well with the troops, who, it is said, chuckled about it all morning long. It did not, however, amuse Yoritomo when he heard of it back in Kamakura. His ill humor was further increased when word came that the rash Kiso had dismissed nearly fifty palace nobles and courtiers. Even in the worst days of the Taira, this number had never gone beyond forty-three. So people were saying that Minamoto no Yoshinaka, Lord Kiso, was more tyrannical than even Taira no Kiyomori.

Our lord in Kamakura thus decided upon action and sent forth a large force to chastise the rebellious officer. He—Yoshinaka—hearing of this, had a message sent to the fleeing Taira, inviting them to return to the capital, to join with him and his men, and to attack the east: Kamakura and Yoritomo. At the same time he was demanding from the retired emperor a suppression of the mandate against these Taira. In its place he wanted another that would authorize him to defend Heiankyō and the imperial personage against the other Minamoto.

Eventually he received his mandate. In addition he prevailed upon the retired emperor to raise him to the highest military office, that of shōgun, the very title that Yoritomo himself most coveted. Perhaps it was consequent to this that our Lord decided to march upon the capital. Thus it was that Yoshinaka, Lord Kiso, and now Lord of Heiankyō, as he was styling himself, set out to counter the forces of Lord Yoritomo, of which I was myself one, having returned after my Taira foraging.

And thus I found myself once more at Uji Bridge, four years after my first encounter there. I was under the command of Lord Yoshitsune, one disliked relative sent to subdue another, but now it was the first month of the third year of Juei [1184] and I found myself at the other end of the bridge and ready for combat against my commander of only a few months before.

* * *

Shall I attempt to account for all of this political confusion? Were I to do so I must examine the policies of Yoritomo. He was already constructing a new order. The Minamoto clan would control everything and he was the unquestioned overlord. Other clansmen, including close relatives, were military vassals who owed allegiance exclusively to Kamakura. They must therefore take orders from no other authority, and this included the imperial court.

The Taira were, to his mind, already a defeated enemy. He was from the outset of this civil war looking quite beyond it to the day of the final battle and the full ascendency of Minamoto rule in Kamakura. What he feared was not a resurgence of the Taira but that his relatives might challenge the authority of Kamakura—possibly with imperial collusion. A history of the later Minamoto would find them more fighting each other than opposing a common adversary.

Consequently, when one of his generals, Yoshinaka, our Lord of Kiso, for example, threatened this grand policy, Yoritomo, regardless of clan and blood relationship, did not hesitate to eliminate him (chastise was the term he preferred) any more than he hesitated to pursue and persecute his own half-brother, Yoshitsune.

When we arrived at the bridge, some twenty-five thousand of us, led by Yoshitsune, we found that Kiso did not want to be chastised. He had torn up the planking, had built barricades of sharpened stakes, had hammered piles into the bed of the river and to them had attached encumbering nets. Thus we were again at the river with no way to get across, particularly now that the melting snows had swelled the waters that rushed by, turbulent as a waterfall.

There would this time be no easy fording. Yoshitsune conferred with his mounted generals there in the early dawn, so dark we could barely see him against the sky. I remember hearing that querulous voice, and in the growing light turned to look at that small, pale young man with his big head, his crooked teeth, his bulging eyes. Now that this same Lord Yoshitsune has been made the beautiful, commanding youth of legend, I derive some pleasure from this memory.

The querulous tones did not, however, imply any lack of resolve. They meant that he wanted as much information as possible. This petulance occurred only when he did not receive satisfactory answers. Right now, on the rushing banks of the river, he wanted to have the present business out of the way so that he could get back to fighting the real enemy, which was, of course, the Taira. Hence the impatience.

I remember him, sitting on his mount in the growing dawn, his helmet just now visible against the winter clouds, pursuing like a true sibling his elder brother's orders, on his way to chastise a cousin. Did he then feel, I have often wondered, that in time he would take the place of his errant cousin and be in his turn hounded by the same brother?

Whatever, he found us a way across. It was not I who made it first into the enemy camp that day. It was Yoshitsune himself, he who cut the ropes that held the nets, which were to entangle our horses' hoofs, and he who then urged his steed on into the flood, followed by five hundred of our number. His beast received an arrow in the forehead, and the brave Lord Yoshitsune jumped from the saddle to the far shore; and thus began the battle, which soon involved us all and which—after much slicing and stabbing, much rolling about and drowning in the violent stream—we eventually won.

As soon as Kiso saw this he seemed to have given up. As well the poor provincial might, for he had confidently brought far too few soldiers with him. Lord Yoshitsune sent a regiment in pursuit and then, in proper diplomatic fashion, announced himself concerned about the much misused retired emperor (now reinstalled in his partially burned-out palace), and set out to present himself.

When Retired Emperor Go-Shirakawa heard that the white banners of the Minamoto were now billowing over a rapidly advancing force, he is said to have wrung his hands in terror, believing us to be the returning forces of Kiso. Finally, someone more composed saw that the insignia were different and eventually the blackened palace gates were thrown open.

We—I was there—made a fine show, since Lord Yoshitsune made us dress up in honor of this imperial presentation. He himself was wearing, over a crimson-brocade battle robe, light armor laced with purple silk cord. His helmet carried gold horns and his sword was studded with the same precious metal. His arrows were smartly black and white and his bow was bound with white rattan. Not at all the sort of thing of which Yoritomo would have approved.

The retired emperor, reassured, approached to greet us and insisted that the names of all the gallant officers be made known to him. These were given the imperial ear and then our lord made a speech about how the lawless conduct of Kiso had angered and surprised Yoritomo, who had thus sent his younger half-brother, your majesty's servant, Yoshitsune, to punish him. As for the villainous Kiso, he was now running to the north and would soon be cut down.

So he was. He who had in the previous year marched into the capital with fifty thousand men was now galloping away from it with only five. At dusk he forced his horse onto a frozen marsh. The tired beast slipped and slid on the ice and Kiso, thrown forward, received an arrow in the neck—at which point his handsome head was struck off and raised high on the point of a sword.

Though he was our enemy, I—perhaps because I too am a provincial—have retained some affection for this bumpkin whose rough country ways led to his death.

* * *

How noisy the blind balladeers are today. This is because they are arguing. And what about? About Yoshinaka, Lord Kiso himself. Apparently they in their labors have already reached the part of my times, which I am at present describing.

The differences in our versions are considerable. Kiso is no longer a rustic. He is no longer even an enemy of the state. Instead, he is a doomed hero and to the very end has along with him—at his very side, I heard with surprise—a woman who is fully his equal in both beauty and bravery.

Attired as a warrior, she—Tomoe Gozen by name—gallops beside her husband, and when he dies she manages to wrestle some mighty Minamoto warrior (name not given) to the ground and chops off *his* head.

Can this be the meek maiden in the palanquin we had glimpsed, the one who was carried about in the train of Kiso during his various Heiankyō parades? If so, she has much changed character. This is what the young musical poets are at present arguing over—her disposition. Should Tomoe enter a nunnery after the death of her brave husband, or should she end up as mistress of one of his illustrious enemies.

I will leave them to their scholarly disputes and merely mention that I do not know what happened because I was at the time guarding the palace of the nervous retired emperor, who would not rest until word had been brought that Kiso's head was off and the disturbance was over. When this occurred we could all go to bed.

And here I will put down my brush and write more another day.

* * *

While these different Minamoto factions were squabbling, the Taira had not been idle. They had won a few small battles and now a large contingent had left for Yashima, on the farther side of the Inland Sea. Here they had made camp and then once more sailed back to Naniwa nearby, where they constructed for themselves—one hundred thousand of them—a mainland stronghold at Ichinotani.

The place seemed perfect for defense, the sea to the south and the mountains to the north. The bay entrance was narrow and the cliffs at the back rose so straight and high that they stood like a screen, protecting the area below from attack.

On the beach, the place the Taira army considered most vulnerable, barricades of stones and lines of sharpened stakes were laid, while in the deeper waters the Taira vessels spread like a shield. In the squat towers of the stronghold were masses of soldiery from Tosa and Tsukushi, bows and arrows at the ready. Below, standing in ranks were horsemen and foot soldiers, swords and halberds in hand. And over it all billowed in the winter wind the red banners of the Taira, roiling like the flames of a great conflagration.

Dislodging this entrenched force was our next task under Yoshitsune. There had been a grand ceremonial departure from Heiankyō, more imperial presents, and an earnest admonition from his retired imperial majesty to be certain that the three sacred treasures—jewel, mirror, and sword (as well as the child Antoku)—all be brought safely home.

We took some time to reach the coast, since Yoshitsune was constantly stopping to ask questions of the inhabitants, and so, by the time we arrived in the area, all of the Taira had crowded themselves into their new stronghold, where they were, they felt, impregnable.

So they appeared to be, and there was consequently an amount of discussion when Lord Yoshitsune decided to split his forces into two. Most were ordered, surprisingly, to the west of Ichinotani. He himself took with him less than a thousand men and began climbing the mountains that protected the rear of the Taira camp. This upset the troops who grumbled a bit and said they wanted to die facing the enemy rather than falling on top of him.

This descent, however, was just what Yoshitsune had planned. And to find the proper way up he tried a country trick we all knew. Taking an old dappled mare, he looped the reins on her neck, slapped her rump and set her up the mountain. He did this because he needed the quickest and safest way to the top, and this the unencumbered animal was certain to find. And so she did. While a scout would have lost himself in the gorges or ended up perched on peaks, the old horse led them through the valleys and up safe slopes.

Following their equine guide, the men observed the snow on the branches and spoke, I am told, of plum blossoms in the spring. The frosted moss grew thicker as they entered the mountain forest, and through the gaps in the trees behind they could see far below the greener hollows through which they had come, while above them were white clouds and whiter peaks.

Eventually, the sage animal led them where they wanted to be, the brink of the precipice. Below them lay the camp of the Taira locked into its little sea-girt valley, the smoke of their fires rising in the still winter air. It rose right past their gaze and some later said they could smell the evening cooking.

Then the men camped in the snow on this height, while Yoshitsune questioned an old hunter he had brought with him as to the possibility of riding down upon the enemy. The aged party is supposed to have shaken a grizzled head and announced impossibility. Then Yoshitune is said to have shown a shrewd expression and asked if perhaps deer ever went down this way. Yes, was the answer, they sometimes did. Yoshitsune then stood in his stirrups and is said to have cried: There we have it. The exercise will be good for the horses.

At this the grizzled hunter was taken aback and said he was too old to be part of such an excursion. Eventually, however, he was prevailed upon to part with his son, a boy who knew the mountains well. It was this eighteen-year-old who led the celebrated descent.

And who proved among the most loyal of all of Yoshitsune's men. I later saw him often—a big, strong boy with thick black eyebrows. His name was Kumao, but after Yoshitsune had adopted him, he was given the grander name of Washio no Saburō Yoshihisa. And when Lord Yoritomo's rage had driven Yoshitsune into the snows of the far north, it was young Kumao who went along and, indeed, died there, defending his lord to the last.

I was not, however, a member of this famous mountaineering party because we were among the throng off to the far west side of the beach stronghold. Along with me rode my son, Naoie, who was then sixteen or so.

I see I have here written little about him. He is very different from me, which is perhaps the reason I haven't. Idealistic, given to all manner of chivalric delusion, deaf even to the slightest suggestion of prudent behavior, he is a most impractical youth. I wonder where he gets it. Certainly not from his mother who all but matches my own concern for improvement of self. Certainly not from myself who have risen this far through prudence and a careful assessment of the world as it actually is.

Anyway, together we now rode through that night, side by side, the imprudent youth and myself, and around midnight the wretched boy, big with the romance of battle, broke away and descended to the beach. Since he was in my charge, I had to go and bring him back to his position in the march.

But he was difficult to contain as he raced over the sand to the western gate of the Taira stronghold. I did not catch up with the delinquent youth until, stirrups clanking, we were all but under the camp gate.

Here he stopped. As did I. We had both heard the same thing. It came from the battlements ahead. The sound soared into the air and echoed among the cliffs.

It was a flute. And beautiful it was—its voice rose and fell, speaking of sorrow and transience, houses falling and men perishing and all things changed. It soared into the dark air, a wordless tongue that told the truth.

* * *

They got that part right, the lute-plunking priests. Just the other day I heard a young blind voice raised in celebration of that flute. It was, they said, played by the young Taira no Atsumori, a person about whom I now know something.

Perhaps it was he I heard. He was certainly inside the compound that evening, and if the melody was his, then this was my second encounter with him. The first was at my wedding when the pregnant Fuji no Kata, round as a melon, had graced our nuptials. Inside her was stirring the person who became this Atsumori. I knew nothing of him in the interim because my wife had no further converse with Fuji no Kata, and I do not go about seeking acquaintance with babies.

If even I could respond to the useless beauty of the flute, however, one may imagine its effect upon my impressionable son. In no time, ears ringing, wild for glory, he had left our somewhat shadowed shelter on the beach and raced to the gate itself.

I had to gallop after him through the dark and it was thus that I was first at the torch-lighted portal of the enemy and added to my belligerent reputation. Once there, there was nothing to do but call out, as was then still the fashion: We are Kumagai Jirō Naozane and Naoie, father and son, from Musashi.

The Taira inside ought to have responded by sending a pair of their own warriors out. When they did not I was relieved because I wanted no part in carving former friends. My son was disappointed, however, because, like most boys, he was interested in cutting people up, and if they were former friends so much the better.

The reason our challenge was declined was that the Taira had over the years become bad horsemen and the recent voyage had left their animals weak. This allowed the boy and myself to canter bravely about in front of the gate. I was fearful of showers of arrows, but the Taira, unlike the Minamoto, were gentlemen. They would never have attacked two warriors going through their beloved and bellicose rituals.

The only thing that occurred was when that fool son of mine raced his horse right up to the gate and tried to stick his arm through the viewing slit. Naturally someone on the other side slashed at it and he was lucky to have come away with but a cut finger. That was the extent of the carnage.

We had apparently, however, served some purpose. While we were capering about in the shadows, Yoshitsune's forces had, all unseen, been forming right over the Taira head. Duty all unwittingly done, my boy and I galloped off into the dawn, then stopped on the sand—I listened for the sound of the flute, but there was none.

* * *

At that moment, dawn of the seventh day of the second month of the third year of Juei (or the first year of Genryaku in the new counting) [1184], Lord Yoshitsune and his thousand men were waiting at the brink of the cliff. And just then two stags and a doe, startled by such numbers of men in that wilderness, turned and started down. Seeing this as a sign, Lord Yoshitsune and his young guide upturned their horses and, followed by all the rest, began this perpendicular descent.

Fast on the bobbing tales of the deer directly beneath them, the horsemen rode down the cliff. It is said that so steep was the way that the stirrups of the man behind struck the helmet of the man in front. Indeed, they perhaps more slid than rode, because the cliff was sand and the horses hysterical: a thousand men sliding straight down, standing in their stirrups, staring ahead over their horses' ears at the rocks below.

It is said that some of the bravest strove to drive out their terror by screaming their battle cry as loudly as they could, while others simply shut their horrified eyes and let their animals do as they could.

By the time the Taira guard, alerted by the crashing deer, had rushed out the back door, the sky was raining horses and men. And though the battle cries had been perhaps howled in terror, they now, amplified by the cliff walls, made a din, it is said, like a hundred thousand descending demons.

Soon these were landing on the roofs of the storehouses backed up against the cliffs. A number of legs were broken, those of both men and horses, but the majority of the troops escaped unscathed and were now leaping off the roofs and grappling with the guards. And just as this was occurring, the other thousands of us had rushed the main gate and were battering at it. The Taira had lost the battle before it began.

This was because it was not the battle they had expected. The antics of my son and myself had seemed to promise a conventional encounter, not this unprecedented attack from the sky, nor the underhanded setting of fires in which Yoshitsune's band now indulged.

The beaten Taira, still half asleep, ran through the smoke as the breeze of sunrise fanned the flames. They tried to reach their boats, but we were everywhere, swords in the air.

So much killing. A woman ran past me, her hair streaming behind. Three of my fellow horsemen turned, circled, closed in, and from the clouds of sand came a thin cry, like the call of a plover.

In the dust the great oxcarts of the Taira bucked and the cattle bellowed. Maddened by the noise and the sand, they rolled their red eyes and tossed their horns. Then one beast suddenly bolted and caught against his curved horn the frantic young groom who had been pulling at his bridle.

The cart lurched forward, cutting through the Taira escort, and from inside the latticed cart came the screams of the women and the cries of the young. A small child dropped from the open back and sat there in the sand crying for a time.

One of our swordsmen rushed up and sliced at the bullock behind the ears. Its neck half-severed, it staggered and fell, the cart turning upon its side. From it a girl scrambled and began to run toward the sea. One of our swordsmen chased after her and had pierced her long before the surf was reached. Then our infantry crowded around the car, lancing its lacquered sides. Blood began to flow, as though the cart itself was wounded.

And on and on. Farther back, our men were cutting off the heads of the fallen. They made a deep slice in the back of the neck, neatly swung the sword around, and the head fell. And, behind them, came our clerks, engaged in the important business of identifying these white and staring faces, keeping track of who had killed which.

The scribes worked, it is said for the space of three days without once putting down their brushes—so vast the labor, so many the fallen. As in those hell-scrolls I earlier mentioned: a whole world of suffering.

* * *

I was sitting here, remembering in the late afternoon sun, when, like an echo, I heard these same memories repeated along the corridor as the ballad singers recreated a time of which they knew nothing.

And they seemed to be getting it right—that part about the battle cry after the descent of the cliff, for example: Though but a thousand men, the echoes made the sound as of a hundred thousand strong.

And where, I wondered, were they getting all of these details? Some they were making up but some were accurate and, for the first time, I was becoming pleasantly disposed to these blind lads and their historical efforts.

Then I heard my own name. At first I thought the cicada's buzzing had confused me but, no, there it came again. And I knew what they were doing. They were repeating that damnable calumny.

The story is that I chased after the young Taira no Atsumori, a sixteen-year-old, and struck by his youth or beauty, or both, I urged him to escape. As this was occurring, however, several of my warriors rode up and so, observed, I was forced to slay the enemy youth myself. Accomplishing this, I was so consumed with remorse that I subsequently turned priest.

Now, none of this is true. I resent this fable because it questions my valor in battle, because it turns my priestly resolve into a sentimental gesture, and because it minimizes my achievement. Also it falsifies what actually happened.

To begin with, killing during a battle is commonplace. I do not know of a single officer who would risk his career by doing what this ignorant fable has me doing—attempting to let the pretty boy escape and then blubbering in the surf after having finally done what is any soldier's duty. I know that if anyone in my command had acted in such a fashion I would have had him flogged.

Yet, there I am, brutal soldier struck by sudden beauty, a figure of fun, which could have been imagined only by romantic adolescence, and by those who have themselves never engaged in battle. These monkish youths, my traducers, were not even born back then. And, further, many are blind—a condition that does not favor accurate reporting. I will therefore write down what actually occurred.

After the sack of the camp, I was riding along the beach away from the battle and I saw this Taira warrior turning his horse into the sea and making for an offshore ship. His uniform proclaimed him an officer and fit subject for a fight. Also, he was smaller than I and his horse seemed weary, and this made the prospect all the more attractive.

So, anxious for a head, I called him back by waving my fan at him and chiding him for cowardice, always a certain ploy to gain the attention of a Taira. And he, sure enough, turned around and we grappled, and I knocked off his helmet.

He was just as young as fiction now has it and just as beautiful. And I will admit that when I saw that fragile face, those perfectly arched eyebrows, the lacquered teeth through the half open lips, I remembered the Emperor Nijō standing in the snow, dressed as a girl but still very much a boy.

But now I was much older, my eyes no longer shone at the sight. And if they lit up, it was because I saw in the youth a sign that I could win the more easily, for he was slight as well. So I launched into the customary address: I am a native of Musashi, Kumagai no Jirō Naozane. And then I asked who he was.

And the youngster had the impertinence to say that he would certainly not declare himself to one so low as myself and that if I desired to know his identity I need only show his head to the proper authorities and—so well born, so favored was he—they would know at once.

The ballad boys got it right up to this point and here made some grand chords and then had Kumagai stop, sword raised, and sink to his knees in the frothing brine and begin to weep in the face of such beauty, such resolve.

Not at all. I did—it is true—stop, sword raised, but this was because the impertinent youngster had stung me. All those years of being taunted for my provincial upbringing, those superior smiles at finding me oafish, those snickers over my presumed rustic qualities—and now this from a mere Taira boy.

It stung the more for it was, after all, I who was being gentlemanly, not he. And then the impolite youth had the further lack of courtesy to turn his back upon me, remount, and proceed to the ship. If I must be ashamed of something, then I am ashamed that I did not run after the pup and lop his head off right then.

Someone else did, however. He ran right past me—some foot soldier I never saw before, someone who certainly had no right to involve himself in a battle between officers, some country youth looking for a fast advance, I suppose.

He ran up to the retreating youth, pulled him off his mount, and hacked off his head. Grinning, holding the trophy under one arm, he turned toward shore and took an arrow from the ship, falling face down in the surf. The head, like a melon, bobbed gently toward the shore.

Of this the blind boys knew nothing. Their Kumagai, over-whelmed by compassion, senses reeling, blinded by tears, slashed away, took the head. And after that, sitting in the water, head in lap, he resolved to become a priest and devote himself to good works.

No, it was too much! Flinging open my door I strode down the corridor and presented myself in their chambers. They were much surprised to see me—those who could see.

And I was surprised as well. The floor of their chambers was covered with old manuscripts, and more paper piles were stacked in the alcove. I recognized some of these manuscripts, having had to do with them myself. They were the ledgers in which was recorded the head harvest. Of great importance back then, they had been well kept. After all, who took which head was important—both advancement and prestige often depend-ed upon this quota.

I had been going to declare myself to the libelous singers and then air my rightful complaints, but the sight of those old papers softened my resolve. The reason was that I knew what was written on that page, which lay open on the floor, right by the knees of the blind lute player, and directly under the gaze of the sighted monk who had been reading it to him when my appear-ance put a stop to the musical activities. It said that Kumagai Naozane had taken the head of Daiyū Taira Atsumori.

And put that way, I had. I took it from the surf where it was bobbing about and tucked it under my arm. With it, I trotted back to headquarters, where it was identified as belonging to the son of Taira Tsunemori, the sixteen-year-old Atsumori. But, I never actually claimed to have myself cut off the head. Never.

* * *

Twenty years of peace have created a whole body of literature that is entirely gossip. Yoritomo was, we are told, really the son of Go-Shirakawa; the infant Antoku yet lives and, now nearly thirty, is gathering troops in the far west; Yoshitsune himself managed to escape to the Asian mainland and is a famous warlord ravaging China itself.

Even my small exploit has been embroidered in this fashion. In a variant of which the musical novices have not as yet availed themselves, I even allowed the youthful Atsumori to escape by cleverly substituting the head of my own seventeen-year-old son, while the beautiful object of my indulgence went to wherever he now is comfortably living, fat and forty.

The truth of the matter will never satisfy those who demand wonders every fifteen minutes. Yet, I much resented being in this fashion falsely imprisoned in the sentimental and whimsical chronicle history these youngsters were compiling.

Still, I did not expostulate, did not confront the poets with their calumny. The reason was that in order to do so effectively I would have to disavow that very piece of paper out of which they were copying their version of what had occurred. And since my own preferment depended upon this paper and the others like it in my file, I would have risked my eventual land settlement had I attempted to catch them at their falsehood.

Therefore I stood in the doorway, drawn up in wrath, and then slowly deflated. The sighted monk politely asked my identity and business—for none have been here long enough to put together the priest Rensei and the warrior Kumagai—and I forced a smile and said I had been attracted by their music.

Politely asked in, I was then forced to sit and for a time endure the caterwauling. In so doing I learned that the doomed youth was on the fatal strand only because he had forgotten his flute and had gone back after it. I also learned that it was I who plucked from the brine this famous flute which, it was fulsomely recalled, I had perhaps heard but the night before. Ah, the transience of all things, sang the bards, sobs in throats.

But at least they guessed that last part right. I had heard it.

* * *

Enough of this. I must get back to my history, my account of myself and the times in which I lived. Know then that on the twelfth day of the second month of the third year of Juie [1184], the heads of the Taira cut off during the Battle of Ichinotani were all sent to the capital. It must have looked like the pumpkin crop, coming in half a year early, all those thousands of heads in baskets and boxes or just bobbing along at shoulder or saddle.

Yoshitsune had wanted to hang them—more like apples than pumpkins—on the trees that lined the Higashi-no-Toin, a wide avenue in the north of the city, but the retired emperor's councilors refused, giving the not unexpected reason of lack of precedent.

So Yoshitsune sent a second petition, saying that these heads had been removed because their owners had dared to menace the retired emperor and that if the Minamoto were not now allowed to parade their trophies, how could they be expected to continue to fight courageously on his highness's behalf.

A precedent was shortly discovered, and the army began decorating the trees while the good folk of the capital looked on—with, I should imagine, strong emotions. Among these many heads were those whose stern glances had terrified this populace. And now these same heads, swaying and bobbing, glanced no more—eyes already pecked out by birds.

My own small contribution was not there. It was in a box, bumping along at the back of my saddle. It was being sent to

Kamakura, Lord Yoritomo's capital. Our number were carrying the more celebrated heads to set up at the great Hachiman Shrine. Since little Atsumori's was considered to be of their number, I was carrying it, though it had begun to turn.

The ceremony began as soon as we arrived. Yoritomo himself was sitting there in full armor, russet with gilt-deer lacings. Holding our boxes aloft we presented them, one after another, while attendents opened them and lined up the contents.

I was ill at ease, because though I was certain that I had been unobserved—that I had seen the actual killer of the boy die— nonetheless, you never know. I could have been glimpsed fishing out the head—like some child retrieving a ball.

My lord looked at the pale features with satisfaction and then stared at me for a moment. After that the scribes gave me a full score for a notable head and my quota rose considerably.

There was then a party, the heads all staring at us as we drank and ate. Then, a few days later we regrouped and marched out in pursuit of the fleeing Taira—those who were left.

* * *

These had fled to sea. Once more the little emperor was thrust aboard the rocking boat, once again the three treasures were floating on the waves. Some of the Taira sailed off to the Kii peninsula; some merely drifted, driven by wind and by tide; but the majority somehow returned to their former retreat at Yashima.

Yoshitsune much wanted to follow the unfortunates and exterminate them, but for two years he was stopped from doing so. The reasons were double. The first was that the Taira had now become a sea-borne people, while the Minamoto had few boats. The second was that Yoritomo, always suspicious, decided to make another brother, Noriyori, the commanding general of the forces of the west. This ineffectual warrior was neither brave nor intelligent but he was obedient, and this quality Yoritomo already prized above all others.

After his experiences with Yoshinaka, Lord Kiso, our master was ready to be doubly suspicious of anyone who presented himself to Retired Emperor Go-Shirakawa, as Yoshitsune shortly did. In addition, Kajiwara no Kagetori—one of Yoritomo's most trusted retainers, recently second in command of the Minamoto forces in Heiankyō—had begun sending reports doubting the loyalty of Yoshitsune. This officer was one of the few who could read and write with any fluency. I sometimes think his flowery and malicious reports were to indulge not only his malevolence but also his vanity.

Thus they procrastinated for eight whole months, and it was not until the tenth day of the first month of the second year of Genryaku [1185] that Yoshitsune finally received permission to search out the enemy, and given the means to do so.

The last seal was finally placed on the orders and Yoshitsune set out on the run. He completed the day's march to the sea in half that time and intended to board their vessels at once, but a gale was blowing and the seamen refused to set out. Yoshitsune, in a hurry, gave orders to kill the sailors unless they obeyed orders, with the result that—the wind behind them—the army made the three-day voyage to Shikoku in just one day.

They arrived at the fortress of Yashima at six on a blustery morning, and even on that overcast day they could see, I am told, the red banners fluttering on the beach. Lord Yoshitsune, once again in the grateful element of battle, laughed and said that he and his men were being welcomed.

Nonetheless, the horses were all safely unloaded while the ships were still offshore. One by one the animals were forced into the deep sea and made to swim, the armored men, up to their necks in the water, holding onto them. When the beasts found their feet in the surf the men mounted at once, and wave after wave emerged as though galloping from the sea itself.

Our men easily took the Taira defense, and Lord Yoshitsune had twenty of their bowmen beheaded so that he could make an offering to Hachiman, the clan god of the Minamoto. Our lord was naturally pious, and, in any event, such a display always goes over well with the men.

They then raced across the strait connecting Yashima with the mainland and set about on their campaign, using many a Minamoto trick. Lord Yoshitsune, like his cousin Yoshinaka, so deployed his men that they seemed many more than they were, troops weaving again and again in and out of the small offshore islets. Also he showed only a few to make them seem less, and when the Taira attacked he revealed his numbers and put them to flight.

Or, something more original, after the skirmishes, he had his men put on white robes of mourning, as though they were Taira searching for their dead. They then killed those bereaved they could catch. This was, I believe, the first time in our history that this particular practice took place.

So successful was Yoshitsune that the panicked Taira again boarded their boats—this time for good. No ports would now have them, and so the entire flotilla floated farther off to the west and to the south, followed by the Minamoto army. Along the way, the pursuers were joined by many remaining family regiments. By the time Tsukushi was sighted, the Minamoto force numbered, it is said, three thousand, while that of the Taira was estimated at under a thousand.

* * *

I was not there but in Kamakura, far from all the excitement. Our regiment had been called back, and it was just as well for me that it was. Service under both Lord Kiso *and* Lord Yoshitsune would not have have looked good on my record. Nonetheless, the details of this famous final confrontation between the two houses are so well known (even the blind bards are getting them more or less correct) that I can with some confidence describe what occurred.

Know then that it was the twenty-fourth day of the third month of the second year of Genryaku [1185]. The Taira fleet

had turned into that narrow strait called Dannoura, between
our main island and Tsukushi. After them closely followed the
Minamoto fleet, but, as it was just a little past midnight, the enemies did not at first discern each other.

It was not until dawn had begun to lighten the late winter sky
that the Minamoto ships saw the Taira bearing down on them
and that the battle could begin. Their ships had turned themselves in the dark and, now moving with the tide, were advancing straight at our fleet, which still had sails down and oars out.

The dawn-filled air was so still that our men could hear the
Taira officers calling out to each other—one of them was saying
that the Minamoto, all coming from the east, might know something about horses but certainly knew nothing about boats.

In the growing light, the advancing Taira flotilla was now
plain: high-prowed vessels, one of them the imperial barge containing the little emperor; around them smaller boats, manned
by rowers and carrying bowmen, their black arrows in their
back-quivers like spines, the red banners hanging over them;
and amid all this, shallower vessels with floating soldiery, their
halberds black against the morning light.

The Minamoto attempted to reverse oars but their impetus
was carrying them against the tide, while the Taira bore down
upon them, grappling hooks at the ready. These two floating
armies then collided.

Where to look in this vast panorama and what first to
describe! The arrows of the Taira struck quivering into the
decks of the Minamoto ships or, with a sudden stroke, like that
of a hand drum, sank deep into flesh. There were so many and
they came so thick that it seemed a downpour of points and
feathers, a barbed rain.

Then large grappling hooks, like the manticles of beetles,
grasped the Minamoto ships and pulled them into close
embrace. The braver Taira leapt across the intervening water—
some officers falling, in their heavy armor, to instantly disap-
pear—and fought on the enemy deck. Floating soldiers were

pushed under with oars and lances, and those who fastened onto prows and gunwales saw their clutching fingers cut away.

As the sun rose higher and warmed the late winter day, the Taira seemed to be winning. They had taken the offensive, they had the emperor and the three treasures, the current was on their side. But, like everything else in this life, tides change.

Lord Yoshitsune knew this. He had his ships stay as they were, oars maintaining their position, because he had seen that if he held out, the waters would shift. And that is what occurred. One does not need the miracles one commonly hears recounted— the massing of anti-Taira dolphins, the sudden appearance of a white banner floating down from heaven, indicating divine preference. Miracle enough is this shifting of the tide.

With this natural advantage—and the favor of a new winter wind behind them—the Minamoto flotilla, sails up, began moving against the Taira ships. These had been pressing the former advantage by using their oarsman, and they could not now reverse in time the impetus of their vessels. Boat crashed against boat, gunwales were broken in, and men leapt from vessel to vessel like boys crossing ponds on stepping stones.

First killed were the Taira helmsmen, spitted on arrows or chopped by swords. Without them the vessels foundered, turning in the trough of the waves. Though officers and their men attempted battle, they were overcome by the sheer weight of soldiery sailing down on them.

In the imperial barge there was a panic. Officers deserted their posts and common soldiers cowered on the decks. In the midst of this the small emperor stood, looking from one grown-up face to another. His grandmother approached, bowed, and then gathered him to her arms, as she doubtless often had when he was an infant.

He, Emperor Antoku, is said to have asked where he was being taken. She fitted his ceremonial robe over him and told him to bid farewell to those about him, since he was going to another capital.

The child, now quite used to moving, bid farewell in a clear voice to those about him, not forgetting Amida Buddha in the west, and the Sun Goddess in the east. Then he looked expectantly up at his grandmother who, holding him close, stepped into the sea.

They fell from the highest deck of the imperial barge, and after the splash nothing more was seen; no officer raced to the spot, no boatman put out a grappling hook. There was a long silence and then the Taira retreat began.

A strange retreat because there was no place to retreat to except into the water itself. The emperor's mother jumped but was taken by a Minamoto boatman who caught her long floating hair with his hook and dragged her in.

By then the sea around was riled with the waves of falling bodies, as the palace ladies followed their mistress, the last one standing by the gunwale, holding in her arms the casket containing one of the sacred treasures—the mirror.

Noting this, a quick Minamoto bowman released an arrow that pinned her skirt to the deck, and as she fell backward another Minamoto man rushed up and caught the precious casket.

At this, all fight ended. The Taira had seen the emperor vanish, the treasure now in the hands of the enemy. Two of the bravest warriors, Norimori and Tsunemori, younger brothers of the dead Kiyomori, tied anchors to their armor and jumped hand in hand, as they might have together, hand in hand, raced and jumped when they were very young.

Thus peaked the wave of self-destruction that overwhelmed the remaining Taira. The ladies slid over the sides like bundles of silk, slipping under the waters with no sound at all. Children were tied to stones and, with a final caress, dropped into the sea, where they were swallowed before they could give a single cry of terror. Officers and men all leaped, most carrying something heavy, pieces of armor, chests, even the ballast stones. These they clutched as they sank through the dark waters. So determined to die, they had the strength to hold, fingers clenched, until they finally loosened, down there.

I think now, twenty years later, of that awful scene, and though I was not there I sense the sadness, and the waste.

* * *

None of this was sensed by Lord Yoshitsune. He was that day triumphant, standing there on the flagship, above him the great white banner whipping in the strong afternoon wind. His victory was complete and he looked with probable satisfaction at the red flags of the Taira lying in defeat upon the strait, which seemed—says one of the histories—like a broad mountain river in autumn when the late gales had torn away the scarlet maple leaves and left them floating on the flood.

Yoshitsune gathered the few survivors, made them captives, and had his scribes complete an imperial report of what had transpired. Though in large part factual, it did report that all three treasures were intact, which was not so—the mirror and jewel were with him but the sword was forever lost and is probably yet at the bottom of that narrow sea.

A further prize that he also now returned was the second son of the late Emperor Takakura, who had been carried off—though this person went peacefully enough—by the bad Taira and was now being brought back by the good Minamoto.

This was very like Yoshitsune—to think of doing this. It must have seemed to legitimize his actions even further in the gaze of imperial Heiankyō. It was also like him that he did not consider that it made him appear the more usurping in the eyes of Kamakura.

And so, on one of the first of the warm days, the Minamoto procession rolled through the southern gate of the capital, victorious officers, proud soldiery, and the captives. These latter were all in carriages, the shades of which had been rolled down, not so that those inside could not look out, but so that those outside could not look in.

The press was great. All the way from the southern gate to the palace in the north, the throng was such that only the continual exertions of the imperial guard kept the way open. Along the route townsfolk and rabble pushed and stared at the carts, trying to discern the captured wretches within.

Some sneered at the sight, but others shed a tear or two at the fate of this proud family. One of these was the lad who led the carriage that contained Munemori, the last of Kiyomori's sons, who had been captured along with his own child. This peasant ox-boy had earnestly asked for this favor, his reason being that, before coming over to the Minamoto, he had been in the employ of Munemori, who had never wronged him. Unable in his former master's misfortune to forget past kindness, he now wished to pull his carriage for one last time as a final service.

This Lord Yoshitune perhaps unwisely allowed. Fond of spectacle, he may have thought a small example of accord amid all of this dissension might quiet the crowd. This it did. The young man, doubtless blinded by his tears, let the animal go where it would, and this was straight along the space opened up in the throng, so everyone got a good glimpse of the patient animal, the weeping servant, and the tragic master.

Though Munemori had been one of the least popular of the Taira, just as excessive as his father and, further, instrumental in having the retired emperor exiled, the people were moved. They stared at the mighty fallen and became quiet.

Munemori was never mighty. It was he who made the tactical error of insisting that the child emperor be taken with them rather than Emperor Go-Shirakawa. If the retired emperor had been carried off, the outcome would have been far different.

But as the people looked at the great man now fallen, so pitiful was the spectacle that for the first time the Taira were perceived as having been somehow wronged. Tears filled eyes and it became apparent that Yoshitsune had indeed been unwise to allow the ox-tender his request. This was because the people of

Heiankyō began to wonder about the Minamoto victors now occupying their city.

Retired Emperor Go-Shirakawa was certainly wondering. He remembered that the last time Munemori had proceeded north it was to visit him in his palace. The Taira general, on his way to confine his imperial majesty, had been accompanied by twelve others of court rank, by sixteen courtiers, by four vice-councilors, three lieutenants-general, and a small army of horsemen.

Now, here, today, he was accompanied by only a handful of his own men, captured like himself. And since they were all bound with ropes to the saddles of their mounts, they could not be of much aid to him. At the same time, here was the victorious Minamoto family, marching north with the same confidence and, perhaps, the same intent.

* * *

Nevertheless, or consequently, Lord Yoshitsune was smothered in honors. And Go-Shirakawa saw that these honors were announced in the midst of the finest ceremony of all—the reinstallation of the sacred mirror. This event occurred at midnight on the twenty-eighth day of the fourth month. Retired Emperor Go-Shirakawa himself appeared, resplendent in his robes, the court orchestra did two rarely heard pieces, there was sacred dancing, and in the midst of this the mirror was welcomed back.

Then the honors accorded Yoshitune were announced—he was made a full lieutenant in the imperial guard, a sinecure that carried considerable revenue, and the privileges of the senior courtiers' chamber, a marked sign of imperial favor. The court applauded this, well pleased at the way things had gone. As well they might have, for this night began a peace that has lasted ever since. With the Taira gone, it would appear that the Minamoto had no more enemies with whom to contend, and could—if they did not sack Heiankyō—devote themselves to restoring peace.

And so they did—at least at first. Of a consequence people

were no longer afraid in the streets or the roads. All could travel freely and go about their business, even by night. After so many months of war, this was luxury indeed, and the grateful people fully credited Yoshitsune for this.

To his discomfiture: Yoritomo was shortly apprised of what was being said—that he had merely lolled in far Kamakura while the industrious half-brother had done everything in Heiankyō. In any event, Yoritomo grew suspicious, and now, quite suddenly, angry.

Even I, who had witnessed several of the late Kiyomori's explosions, was surprised at the vehemence. Yoritomo shouted, ranted on about what an absurdity it was, that he himself had command over the entire army, that it was his own planning that had won the victory.

For a man as seemingly phlegmatic as Yoritomo, the display of anger was impressive. Even I, a master at losing my temper, was impressed. At the time we wondered what it meant. Now I think it meant that he was afraid of Yoshitsune, fearful lest the popular younger brother attempt to usurp his position.

We had, of course, long known of the rivalry between the two. Apparently it had a longer history as well. Among the entries for the new Hōjō history being compiled, there is, I am told, an anecdote from which this enmity is said to have grown.

It began back in the first year of Yōwa [1181], when Yoritomo and Yoshitsune were together in Kamakura. The elder was officiating at the commemoration of the treasure hall of the new Tsurugaoka Hachiman Shrine, during which a pair of horses was to be given the officer in charge of the carpenters as a token of official gratitude. Each animal was to be led on with two men at its reins, and as they seemed one man short, Yoritomo told his half brother to attend.

Yoshitsune said that there was no one to do this with him. Yoritomo asked if these other officers—and he named them— were no one, and what did he mean by this. The younger brother hesitated—it was, after all, a menial task, bringing on the horses. Seeing the hesitation, Yoritomo reprimanded him by asking if he was to understand that the function was thought too low, and that by questioning he was refusing?

Yoritomo's power was being questioned, that is how we would nowadays phrase it. Anything other than unfailing obedience was disloyalty. I know this well because—as will later be described—I was myself in just such a position when I refused to perform a lowly service demanded by him. And I was punished as Yoshitune was punished. That is, I was from then on regarded with suspicion.

As was Yoshitsune. Here he had carried out all commands, won all the victories, and not once had Yoritomo seen fit to recommend him for an appointment. Yet, at the same time, many others—among them Yoriyasu, his brother-in-law, who contributed nothing at all to the war effort—had received many a promotion and official honor. Still, Yoshitsune continued attempting to placate his powerful sibling. He yet strove to please. This he shortly indicated in a manner that did him small credit.

It involved Munemori. Since he was the most high-ranking among the Taira captives, Yoritomo required that he be particularly humiliated and ordered his Yoshitsune to see to it. The manner he settled upon involved Munemori's small son. It was due to this little boy that the father was still alive because, both jumping into the sea at Dannoura, the latter had given himself up only because the former had been dragged on board by the Minamoto boatmen.

Since then the boy had been kept in separate quarters from his father. Now that word of the transfer of prisoners to Kamakura was known, the father asked if he could not see his son, since he did not believe that so young a prisoner—the boy was eight—would be sent on the long, difficult, overland journey to the east.

This Yoshitsune allowed, and a touching scene it apparently was. The child spied its parent from a distance and with a shout of joy ran to meet him. They then sat together for a time and stared at each other and talked. The spectacle was affecting, and those viewing it quite forgot what an unsatisfactory leader Munemori had been.

The father then turned and commended the boy to his captors, saying that he was the youngest, the last, and entirely harmless; that though he himself was certain to die, perhaps this innocent child could be saved.

Tears were, it is said, general—though Yoshitsune probably remained dry-eyed. Perhaps remembering that his own life had been spared by the priest-premier, he was no Kiyomori—not himself about to spare any children who might eventually be in a position to do damage. Further, he had yet to satisfy the commission from Yoritomo that this Taira father be grieviously punished.

Consequently, after father and son had been parted with promises of further meetings, Lord Yoshitsune simply told the attendant in charge to take the child away. This person bowed and asked what he was to do with him. Upon which he was told to do as he liked.

The very next day the child, informed he was again to see his father, was taken off, this time with his unwitting nurse. Instead of his father's rooms, however, the little boy was taken to a dry riverbed and ordered to kneel. This the well-mannered child did. Then he caught a glimpse of the sword and ran to his nurse. She tried to protect him but he was torn from her arms, thrown to the ground, and his little head was chopped off. After which it was carried back for Yoshitsune's inspection.

The faithful sibling then sent word of the deed to Yoritomo and bade him be reassured both as to the defeat of the Taira and the personal fidelity of his loyal youngest brother. Then, he left for Kamakura and the military honors due him, carrying along the bound Munemori.

This military cortege set out at dawn on the seventh day of the fifth month and reached the Koshigoe gate of Kamakura on the twenty-fourth. There Yoshitsune learned how things stood: he was stopped. Though the prisoner was let through, Yoshitsune was—like some delivery boy—kept waiting at the gate. And waiting and waiting.

Eventually he wrote (or had someone write) a letter to his elder brother asking why he was being treated in so suspicious a manner. This did not absolve him in his brother's eyes. To Yoritomo, his even mentioning suspicion made it merited.

While Yoshitsune was kept waiting at the back door, Yoritomo was amusing himself with his captive. Munemori did not know that his son had been beheaded and so he continued in his efforts to have the youngster's life spared. This led him to bow obeisantly to his captor and to attempt other means of ingratiation. Though these actions were later viewed as cowardly—he was called a tiger in a cage, wagging his tail—one ought to remember his reasons.

And though I am myself all for methods that bring results, valuing expediency as much as the next man, I nonetheless feel that some methods, despite their efficacy, should not be used. So, I was sorry for Munemori, though I knew how impractical I was being in this.

Results are what count, not how they are achieved. And yet, even knowing this, I work against myself and my state in the world by refusing those very methods, which by their finality achieve complete success. I sometimes lose patience with these feelings of mine.

Eventually tiring of his game, Yoritomo decided to use the captive as further chastisement for his younger brother. He consequently ordered that Yoshitsune escort the captive back to the capital. This pointless act would indicate how little Taira remnants meant to the victorious Minamoto, and what a complete errand boy Yoshitsune had become. Along with these orders went the strong suggestion that since the victor of Dannoura had already sullied himself with the slaughter of the son, he ought to execute the father as well.

So back the weary way to the capital they went, Munemori in daily dread of the sword. When he was not at once killed, he seems to have reasoned that this was because the weather was unusually hot and his head would have rotted before they got to the capital, and it could not of a consequence be properly inspected—that it was allowed to remain on his shoulders as a kind of preservative measure.

Finally, however, Yoshitsune gave the order and the defeated man kneeled. The sword was already aloft, shining in the sun, when he turned and asked if, then, his little boy was dead. Upon being told that he was, the father bowed his head, exposing his neck. Several days later this head was to be seen on a spike near where Kiyomori's Rokuhara residence had been. But the spike next to it was empty.

It was to have been occupied by the head of the eight-year-old—father and son reunited at last. But the object could not be found. Apparently the nurse had subverted authority and somehow gotten it back. She then united the purloined head with the abandoned body, and the whole was discovered only months later. She had, deep in the forest, killed herself, slitting her throat, and the child was found quietly rotting under her.

* * *

On the ninth day of the seventh month a great earthquake struck Heiankyō. The nine-storey pagoda at Hosshōji fell and the imperial palace itself collapsed. Emperor Go-Toba fled to his palanquin by the edge of the imperial pond and was later found there, crying. The retired emperor, out of the city, came back to spend the next few weeks in a tent, hastily erected.

The earthquake shook mens' spirits as well. It was soon said that the calamity was the doing of the angry ghosts of the Taira. Little Antoku, martyred emperor, was leading their supernatural throng, extracting vengeance upon this faithless capital.

Even Yoshitsune was attacked. An assassin was sent to the capital to do away with him, and though the attempt was foiled and the would-be killer himself killed, the faithful younger brother was shaken, for he now knew how implacably he was hated.

If that is the word. After I came to know Lord Yoritomo, I

began to doubt that he loved and hated as we do. Rather, with him all was expedience. He was a calculating man, not a feeling one. Thus, though he may have been afraid of Yoshitsune and wary of his seeming attempts to wrest power from him, it is equally likely that Lord Yoritomo had decided that the younger brother's period of usefulness was over and that from now on he could be but a dangerous encumbrance. Admirable sentiments, in their way—ones I should learn to emulate.

Consider—Yoritomo was at that time already embarked upon the creation of a new kind of state: the kind that we have now. The Minamoto were to be unquestioned lords, and they would control through this new system of law and order. Since Yoritomo himself was head of the Minamoto and this family was the one in full control, it was necessary that everyone else be vassal to him—and this included close relatives as well. They were to pay allegiance to him not because he was Lord Yoritomo but because he was the leader of the Minamoto clan. Eventually, he was to demand from both military officials and provincial vassals a written oath, and it was to be sealed by a fingerprint made with blood from a pricked finger.

The sentimental now complain that the monster eventually destroyed nearly all of his brothers—that even family members were not safe with him. Well, yes—family members in particular. The success of the larger Minamoto clan was more important to him than the safety of his own family.

Thus any imperial honors were to go to the Minamoto, that is, to himself. Only then could they be distributed. This would assist loyalty in finding its proper object; it would also prevent the imperial presence from dividing the Minamoto as it had divided the Taira.

Yoshitsune was thus disregarding a command when he allowed himself to be covered with honors at Heiankyō. To Lord Yoritomo this seemed a challenge, and a danger too, since those who hated Kamakura could cling to this errant sibling . . . hence the assassin.

In response, the younger brother went to the retired emperor and said that he wished to leave the capital. This was understood to mean that he wished to travel to the western provinces in order to raise troops to attack Kamakura. Emperor Go-Shirakawa put this construction upon it because he had decided that an open conflict between the brothers would be to his advantage. He had perhaps therefore so openly heaped honors upon the younger brother and so openly neglected the older.

His reasons are apparent. The ascendencies of the military houses, first the Taira, now the Minamoto, had undermined the power of the court. With the eclipse of the house of Fujiwara, the retired emperor no longer had military strength of his own, and the imperial coffers were growing empty as well. Go-Shirakawa's hope was to take advantage of rivalries within the victorious clan, hoping to emerge on the winning side. Consequently, he now issued an edict supporting Lord Yoshitsune. If things turned out badly he could say he had been forced into it. This sort of thing he had done successfully often enough before.

He shortly had to do it again, because Yoritomo, learning of the edict, announced that the retired emperor must be once more protected from evil influences, and that he, Yoritomo of the Minamoto, would exert himself to the utmost. This meant that he must have ultimate power: he had himself appointed commander-in-chief of the entire land.

This accomplished, he next sent an official request to the court that he be granted the right to levy taxes in order to supply this army which would protect His Majesty. The retired emperor held a council, saw there was no escaping from the demand, and granted the request. Lord Yoritomo then placed his men in all provinces. Their responsibility was to oversee the imperial officials, and it was thus that in a very few months my master had completed a peaceful military occupation of the country.

As for Yoshitsune, the victorious general was now an outlaw.

He was proscribed by the court as well: Emperor Go-Shirakawa, claiming force, snatched back the imperial edict upon which the ink was scarcely dry.

* * *

This last event occurred at the end of the eleventh month of the first year of Bunji [1185], when I was myself in Kamakura, where indeed I was to spend most of my time until my break with Yoritomo.

As a celebrated warrior—first in the enemy camp—I could feel the tightening discipline, sense the growing power, examine all the new administrative guidance, could be privy to what was now being called policymaking.

There were new rules daily. Henceforth horses will be tethered only on the right side of the official paddocks. Common soldiers are to report to quartermaster stores between the hours of ten and twelve and no other. Halberd tips will not be replaced until requisitions are submitted in writing.

This meant a new need for administrators. Many able warriors were relieved of duties so that they could sit in council. I was myself one of these, and for many a weary hour considered this miniscule point or that.

I was not made councilor because I was well thought of. Just the opposite. Lord Yoritomo never thought well of me. That was why I never received those privileges and honors that may have been my due, why I was never raised in rank. Making me councilor was a way of getting rid of me and, at the same time, a way of keeping track of me.

His low opinion of me was certainly not occasioned by my method of acquiring the head of Atsumori—after all, I was the only one who knew that I had not killed the boy; and in any event, such appropriation of trophies was never rare when, during the height of battle, the rage for collecting one's quota was upon us warriors. No, it was that I was too ambitious for him.

That is, I did not fit easily into this new government, where one entertained a personal loyalty to one's lord. Always looking out for myself, I had been perceived as unstable. This instability had so far, to be sure, served me well. It had, for example, kept me from being associated with the outlaw Yoshitsune. While others, including my son, had gone off to Yashima and Dannoura to pursue the Taira, I had done nothing of the sort. Rather, I had put in for a transfer.

Now, however, as this new consolidation spread over the land, there was less room for maneuvers such as mine. In fact, the military profession was becoming less rewarding than it had been. Still, being stuck in Kamakura with Lord Yoritomo was better than being on the run with Lord Yoshitsune.

* * *

No one knew just where he was. Though he was being pursued, the Lord of Kamakura's guards at every pass, in every border town, the disgraced younger brother was not to be found.

Yoshitsune must have had friends—or else he would have been apprehended—but he did not have enough to make an army. In a country controlled by Yoritomo, no one was foolish enough to flock to the standard of a brother now called rebel and traitor. Once the retired emperor had withdrawn his endorsement, there was no further hope for him.

Thus he fled north, away from Kamakura. There, in the land of the snows, were some families who were not friendly to Lord Yoritomo and had indeed taken the name of Fujiwara. When the hounded brother reached Hiraizumi in Mutsu, he was welcomed by the leader, Hidehira, who even had a fort constructed for the rebel and his retinue. The land was outside the hegemony of Kamakura, and here Yoshitsune perhaps hoped to raise an army, march on Kamakura, and dethrone—the proper term—Lord Yoritomo.

In Kamakura, our commander-in-chief demanded the guilty fugitive be handed over; he even attempted to make the retired emperor issue a direct order to that effect. Now, however, his imperial majesty availed himself of his own bureaucracy, and Lord Yoritomo endured the novel experience of not being able to obtain what he wanted.

He nonetheless was able to turn the hunt for Yoshitsune to his advantage. It allowed him to discover his enemies. Anyone who had supported the rebel was dismissed and often banished. It also gave him a way to extend control. By representing his younger brother as a dangerous threat to the stability of the country, he forced imperial authority to agree upon a national levy, a new rice tax, which was supposed to pay for the search. And in order that the culprit did not slip away, he imposed a system of Minamoto officials in all regions of the land, where they were directed to supervise and thus control the great manorial estates that comprised the wealth of our land.

* * *

In addition, Yoritomo was busy with other things. He had built himself this new capital in Kamakura and now he set about creating the formal pomp of a military court. At the same time, he was securing his hold upon the government: the true one, his own. This meant rounding up and finally getting rid of the last of the vanquished Taira.

To this end he sent a trusted retainer to Heiankyō to proclaim that anyone giving information as to the offspring of the unfortunate clan would receive ample reward. One may imagine that with such incentive an enormous number of Taira children were promptly discovered.

It is said that any child, no matter the parentage, would do. Offspring of even the lowest servants were seized and brought forward, weeping. Understandably so. If the child was very young it was either drowned or buried alive; if older, strangled or stabbed. Whole mounds of slain children grew in the fields, and the air was alive with the wailing of parents.

In among these suspected Taira a real one was discovered— Rokudai, the heir of Koremori and hence of the pure Kiyomori line. Though initially hidden away, he was shortly spied out at a country temple, a handsome twelve-year-old playing with a white puppy.

Apprehended, he behaved in a mature manner, took measured leave of his weeping mother and his sobbing nurse, and climbed into the waiting palanquin. As he disappeared over the mountain, his mother—Taira to the last—said that she hoped he was old enough to be beheaded because that would be a more manly end for him. His nurse, more practical, went to a certain temple and spoke with a certain priest.

His name was Mongaku, a man well known in Kamakura because he had early befriended the young Yoritomo. It was he who had also strengthened that youngster's resolve. Presenting the young Yoritomo with a skull, taken apparently at random from a nearby pile, he told him that it was that of his father, Yoshitomo. The youth received the perhaps paternal relic and then and there swore fidelity to the Minamoto cause.

Now this same priest presented himself before the grown Yoritomo and pleaded the compassion of the Buddha. In this he was successful—though only at the last moment: Rokudai was already kneeling, it is said, the sword raised above him, when Mongaku came galloping up with the pardon that he had extracted from Yoritomo. Thus the handsome boy was put in the charge of the worldly priest. Tears of joy were shed all around, and the child was made an acolyte. A happy ending.

But the story continued. Yoritomo (unlike that other child-pardoner, Kiyomori) did not forget about the young suspect, but kept enquiring about him. Each time Mongaku reassured his lordship that the lad was a spineless coward. This went on for a time and then Yoritomo sent the priest a letter, which said that his reverence seemed to be in the habit of lending support to just anyone raising a rebellion but that this would no longer be tolerated.

Such an accusation was scarcely proper, since it had been, after all, Mongaku who had so assisted the young Yoritomo in his own initial rebellion. But our lord did not want to end up like Kiyomori—bested by the boy he himself had spared.

So young Rokudai—now sixteen—was sent to Mount Kōya and made a monk. Yet even there, with the youth locked up, Yoritomo continued the surveillance and eventually had Rokudai taken out and beheaded.

But this was much later. By this time the handsome youth was thirty years old and handsome no more. So we are not sure who did the beheading or even when. Popular history has no taste for plain-looking, middle-aged priests. When youth can be painted, however, public interest is assured. As with the lacquered teeth and flashing eyes of the young Atsumori. In any event, with the death of Rokudai perished, it is said, the Taira family, since he was the last of that once proud line.

Or so it was popularly thought. In actuality, and Yoritomo certainly knew this, the Taira continued through the Hōjō line, and they continue yet. Indeed, as I write, the Hōjō family (regents, they call themselves, as did the Fujiwara before them) is busy undoing the work of the Minamoto, and what they cannot undo they appropriate.

* * *

I meditate upon this, I who have seen so much promise annihilated and beauty destroyed, who have seen one world sink and another rise in its place. And as I sit and remember, I realize how old I have become.

This has come suddenly, this sense of having aged. Just as our summers, stretching endlessly, one blue day after the other, are followed, suddenly, unreasonably, by a gray, cold morning from which the all joy has fled—so, we discover that we are old.

A bee, its wings ragged, moves stiffly on its brittle legs in the patch of pale sun. And I sit huddled, I who always calculated my time in terms of being half someone else's age, who counted the decades as a man might confidently pat his money pouch. Now I feel suddenly bankrupt.

A warrior does not think he will grow old. He thinks he will die young. He thus sees himself as he always was, hair black, arms strong, permanently youthful. This is how I saw myself until I shaved my graying hair and became a priest. Now I am sixty-five—venerable. And, surprised at my own surprise, I shift about in my patch of pale sun.

I, who rattled my decades like prayer beads, had yesterday all of this time and today have none. And yet I could have seen it coming—a bank of deep but still distant clouds—had I but noticed. There were signs enough: one loses first one's friends, then loses one's generation, finding the young difficult or frivolous, and finally one surrenders one's own time entirely— customs, manners, dress, language, all things are nowhere as they once were.

I look at the old bee and understand. I have finally grown to be as old as I am. But here I am distracted from further meditation by the twangings of the lute down the hall. They are still at it, those blind boys, lying away; but I no longer attempt to understand their lugubrious lyrics.

Apparently they are still at the saga of the Taira and have consequently left the Minamoto, me, alone. Left me sitting there in the surf, looking lovestruck into the dead eyes of a quite ordinary youngster. It is most irritating to be so falsified. Am I doomed to sit forever, bottom in the sand, becoming emblematic of myself?

I am much more than that. These pages are to indicate how much more. It is most irritating. I threw a teacup at a tardy acolyte the other day, and the deacon has already complained about my famously abusive temper. I am growing crotchety in my old age.

* * *

I will give an earlier example of this famous temper. One hot week in the eighth month of the third year of Bunji [1187], our lord, Yoritomo, held a grand archery tournament at Tsurugaoka. All the officers were pressed to participate, and a number of wild animals had been rounded up and were then let loose and slaughtered by the soldiery of Kamakura.

On the fourth day, a group of ten senior officers were to give an exhibition of shooting arrows from horseback. It was a popular spectacle and the stands were full of dignitaries. This pleased Yoritomo because all of these ceremonies were to enhance his family, his court, and himself.

As I have said, it was very hot and heat always seems to shorten my patience. I had watched the ceremony grow from day to day—all the bowing and protocol, all the elevated language, all the sweeping about in courtier suits. And now I discovered that I was chosen to be one of the five who put up the targets and not one of the five who got to shoot at them. Not that I cared about shooting, being an inferior bowsman, but I wanted to feel slighted and so I took this opportunity.

Becoming angry, feeling again the grateful warmth of ire flowing within me, I stomped to the festooned stand where Yoritomo sat and said that though we were all retainers it now seemed that some differentiation was being made, that some were on foot and others were not, that some shot and some got shot at.

This caused whisperings, and Lord Yoritomo turned to stare at me. The master-of-ceremonies, a feisty little man I had long disliked, pattered up and said that there was nothing of victory or defeat about it, that setting up targets was an important commission, even back in ancient history some Chinese emperor or other had asked his own sons to put up targets. And now that I had learned that putting up targets was in its way actually more honorable than shooting at them, I was to go back and do what I had been asked to do.

I refused. Told I was disobeying his lordship's express orders, I still refused. Informed that this was a serious offence, I went right on refusing. Why, I wonder. Perhaps I so disapproved of the motivations behind all this show that I could not conceal my so despising the event.

Lord Yoritomo again turned to look at me and those pale little eyes of his became even colder. Do I flatter myself with the thought that he might have remembered Yoshitsune, who refused his order to play groom at just such an affair as this? If so, the reaction was similar.

Those cold eyes narrowed, and in them I read that I was condemned. Thenceforth, I was no longer one of them, to the extent that I had been. And though everyone continued to be civil to me, I was never included in another staff meeting. Since I had scorned what power my position had brought, I now found myself with none at all.

Everyone knew it. For example, Ōba Kageyoshi, my old commander. He was now high in Lord Yoritomo's cabinet, though his more famous brother, Kagechika, had remained with the Taira and been beheaded for it only five years before. Because of this suspicious fraternal connection, Ōba was assiduous in performing his duties. So, no more drinking, no more monkey dances, no more of anything much except duty. And how gray, how drawn, this once joyous young man had become. He shifted uncomfortably when addressed and bowed low before anyone of higher rank.

When I suffered disgrace, poor Ōba was presented with a problem. I was an old friend as well as a man who had long served under him. Yet, I was now in disfavor. This problem caused him concern. At first, he would smile and nod from a safe distance. Then the distance grew longer and the nods shorter. And finally recognition ceased. Duty had triumphed.

I continued on in Kamakura and now understand that the only one who tried to defend me, the single person who did what he could to keep contained the disgrace, was my son.

I certainly did nothing to merit any such. However, this son of mine is an idealistic sort of person and perhaps even thought I had been a good father to him. To him, Emperor Go-Shirakawa is a good emperor and Lord Yoritomo is a good commander, and it is a good thing that the Taira were taken care of. He is that idealistic.

And he seemed to have been successful in his efforts. Nothing worse befell me, and not two years later he was being mentioned in the dispatches as one of the best of Yoritomo's warriors. And later on, in the accounts of Lord Yoritomo's triumphant entry into Heiankyō in the first year of Kenkyū [1190], my boy is again mentioned, though I am not.

Nor should I have been, since I did not go with them. I was not asked. Indeed, after the affair of the archery targets I was asked nowhere. Though I sat at my customary place, no one spoke to me or even looked at me. It was as if I were not there at all.

I attempted to use what few friends I had left to help myself. But they were one by one taken aside by influential people and told that such activities would not assist me, and might harm them. They did not want, after all, to be treated by Yoritomo in the way he was treating me, did they now? No, they did not, and so, one by one, my friends left me. All except one.

And who was this?—some grizzled warrior, boon companion from times long past? No, it was my wife. She was as tireless in her efforts to clear my name as she had been assiduous throughout the years in attempting to assist my advancement. These efforts she was forced to confine to the ears of the wives of the other officers, but there are worse ways of reaching authority than this.

And she was often successful. A former acquaintance would suddenly greet me after weeks of staring through me. Then I knew that my wife had gotten to his and that she had gotten at him. In every case, however, the suddenly friendly officer was taken aside. Yoritomo was more powerful than my wife.

She was, nonetheless, quite strong. And why, I wondered, did she so expand this strength for my benefit. There was no ostensible reason. I had neglected her, much as other officers neglected their wives, such being the custom. Further, I was forever interested in someone else, and while such dalliance was common enough, mine tended to become too known.

Yet never once did she fling in my face any talk of her being shamed or disgraced or the like, a ploy common among dissatisfied army wives. Indifferent to me from the first, she remained indifferent to the last.

Nonetheless, she had made in me an investment, as it were, and she was determined to see that this investment was made good. It was not, I think, concern for me that made her so assiduous on my behalf, yet indefatigable she was—all but shameless in her attempts to assist me. And though her means—other women—were limited, she used these with great skill. She was, in her way a better warrior than I was, for she was a politician, and this was a capability now called for.

* * *

But I must go back—back to the spring of the fifth and final year of Bunji [1189], just a year before Yoritomo's grand entry into Heiankyō. It was during the long, wet, cold spring that old Hidehira, of the Hiraizumi Fujiwara, had died. His final words to his sons were that they continue to shield and protect Yoshitsune from the wrath of Lord Yoritomo.

When he heard of this death, Yoshitsune galloped at once to the old gentleman's manor and there, it is said, burst into tears. He had, after all, lost his father when he was only one year old, and a possible substitute, his elder brother, had turned implacable enemy. Thus Yoshitsune's tears were sincere.

He followed the funeral procession on foot, dressed in the white of mourning, weeping all the while. Later, people said that he was weeping for himself and for his own predicament. Probably so, and he is not to be blamed the more for that.

Particularly in that Hidehira's three sons shortly decided to no longer shield the fugitive. Messages had come from Kamakura stating that either the miscreant would be returned or the entire Minamoto army would appear and destroy this rebel province.

Seeing no wisdom in continuing to honor their dead father's final wishes, the second son violated this trust by shortly after the funeral himself ordering a full attack on Yoshitsune in his fortified manor house, where, it is now said, on this wet April day the doomed general had only nine followers with him.

They also now say that Yoshitsune, realizing that all was over, retired to an upstairs chamber, where he and his wife and two children piously chanted the scriptures. Broken into upon by harried attendants while completing the eighth book of the Lotus Sutra, the hero is supposed to have told them to go on defending for a time, that he was almost finished, that after he had done so he would kill himself.

Yoshitsune perhaps believed he must do away with himself because orders had been given not to kill him in battle, but to take him so that he could be delivered alive to Kamakura. This he did not want, and so after finishing the sutra he broke out of the defended fortress, killed as many of the enemy as he could, and then retired to an inner chamber, where he took his sword and plunged it into himself just below his left breast. It is said that he did so with such force that it came out of his back. This accomplished, he wiped the sword on the sleeve of his robe and leaned over the armrest.

In this position he watched the dispatching of his wife, his little son, and his ten-day-old daughter. These were attended by the single retainer left—one Kanefusa—and when it was completed, Yoshitsune slumped onto the floor, stretched out a hand and felt a nearby body. He asked who it was—for in dying his sight was gone. Kanefusa told him it was his boy. Then the unhappy general felt the small form, reached for that of his wife, looked up with his sightless eyes and gave orders to burn down the house.

Kanefusa himself met his end in the resulting conflagration, but he dragged in as many of the enemy as he could. Perhaps he also found time to tell someone of the affecting scene in the upstairs apartment, and this is why we have so many details concerning it—there seems no other explanation.

From here the story becomes even more unreliable. It would appear that one of the enemy officers sent soldiers into the burning manor to drag out the general's corpse before it was consumed. This was done for the purpose of hacking off the head so that there would be something to identify. It was put into a black lacquer box that contained saké, intended as a preservative, and taken back to Kamakura.

The head arrived in the middle of the sixth month, at Koshigoe, the very gate where Yoshitsune had been kept waiting by his half brother and from whence he had his pathetic letter penned. Here again he waited until the official inspection party arrived and identified his head as being truly his. I wonder whose head it was. But that made no difference. Yoritomo had need of proof and so it was proof that he received. Now it was all official: the miscreant was punished and Kamakura's power was unchallenged.

Except by rumor. Yoshitsune had, guts trailing, dragged himself out of the conflagration and gotten to Yezu, where he bested the aborigines and made himself their king, where even now he reigns in that land of snow and ice. Or, he took sail to far China, and there even now he heads the massed hordes and fights far beyond the unknown deserts and the nameless mountains.

Rumor remains silent concerning that which I would wish to know. What, for example, happened to Kumao, the black-browed eighteen-year-old whom Yoshitsune adopted, renamed Washio no Saburō Yoshihisa, and took to glory and to death. He too was there in that burning fortress, his strange life having led him far indeed from that cliff above Ichinotani. Perhaps it was this young head that was shown the scowling Yoritomo. When nothing is known, everything is likely.

* * *

The scowling Yoritomo. This was now a permanent expression. Though seven whole years younger than I, he seemed much older. That earnest frown of his deepened through the years, and it was perhaps this which most aged him. This and the endless hours he gave to his administrative tasks.

These comprised his life. It was as though the man had become his duty. He took upon himself the entire weight and dignity of the Minamoto. He became his clan and comported himself with a consequent sobriety, which some found ridiculous initially, but which all eventually decided was fit and proper.

I remember him now, after the death of Yoshitsune, when he had finally brought about the consolidation that, as his admirers say, brought peace to our land. If I close my eyes I can see him yet, sitting on his platform, legs crossed in the military manner, over his robes the light armor he affected. At one side sat his helmet with its dragon headpiece. This military memento he always kept with him even when he was wearing the high, black-lacquered headpiece, which he put on to indicate that he was engaged in civilian duties. But the helmet was always there, a talisman, a reminder of military glories.

Perched on his mat, surrounded by flags whipping in the wind, various plaintiffs kneeling before him, he would bring his eyebrows together, close his eyes, and judiciously purse his lips so that the parts of his moustache met. This indicated that he was deep in thought, and the pose would sometimes continue for so long that the groveling claimants, unable to rise without permission, noses in the dust, would cast worried glances at each other.

Then the small eyes would slowly open, the hand would seek the chin, and judgment would be pronounced in a few terse words. These admitted no appeal, nor, after watching the performance, could one imagine any was possible.

One may call it a performance as I just have, but it was actually not intended merely to impress. Though the effect was impressive, this effect was not sought. It was simply the way the Lord of Kamakura was. Since he knew he was impressive, he need not attempt to seem so.

Now that he is dead, people call him cruel, but this he was not, if that quality presumes a degree of emotional involvement. He simply knew what was right and what was wrong. Yoshitsune was wrong because his aspirations could only disturb the great government his elder brother was creating. After the brief period of military necessity, he must therefore be removed, and the most expedient manner through which absence may be effected is death.

It is difficult to think of the scowling Yoritomo, eyes shut, frown permanent, as a man of vision, yet this was what his creation consisted in—this mighty governmental machine, which I now plainly see, ruling the land and enforcing the peace. This last, peace-enforcement, is necessary if the machine is to continue to work. War, lately so celebrated, must now be banished—like some dangerous relative.

Yet this peace we now have is a military peace. The soldiery will continue, as they have in war, with the difference that skirmishes will be carried on against the civilian population. Spies will still be employed, though they now need report only on the enemy within. The church, independent in our recent wars, is incorporated into this grand military design, which will tolerate not a single battle. And a new child on the throne and a retired emperor kept out of mischief will ensure permanent imperial safety. "Keeping the peace" becomes as victorious a slogan as was ever "winning the war."

Yoritomo was consumed by the great design, which he became. And he became his own memorial as well. It quite resembles him: efficient, powerful, suspicious. This legacy lives after him. As it must, because he himself is no more.

He was riding in state about Kamakura, showing himself, and he fell off his horse. I do not know why he fell, and indeed the official story being now put about is that he did not fall. In any case, the fall killed him.

I, sitting here, a retired sixty-five-year-old, think now of this man, dumped from his animal at fifty-eight; and I remember what we oldsters call the old days. Though we are told that they were no better, that it is simply we who have become worse— still, I remember days when the very mountains seemed more innocent than they do now.

And I suddenly remember perhaps the only time that I saw

Yoritomo smile. He was pleased and proud that his young son, part of an enormous hunt storming the foothills of Mount Fuji, surrounded by beaters and archers, had dispatched a deer with his arrow.

And he had done it unaided! In this time of mass effort, of enforced cooperation, the boy had simply and skillfully shot his own arrow, and this had moved the father—perhaps reminded him of those old and better days he himself had helped to banish.

*   *   *

One of the acolytes has just brought me a letter. Very spruce, very military, obviously from Kamakura. All in Chinese characters, many of which I still cannot read—though the younger officers can, educational standards in Kamakura being quite high. The young acolyte will help me. He is a product of the temple schools.

The letter is from my son. He asks after my health, is worrying about me now that autumn is here and it is turning cold. He wishes that I take good care. Is there anything I need or want? If so, he will send it. It is a filial message from a high-standing officer to his aged father. It makes me feel ashamed of myself.

Letter read, the young acolyte regards me with wary eyes. Ah—he has been listening to the ballad-making down the hall. Also, the connection between present priest and prior soldier has been recently revealed. It is there, in those records they have spread all over the floor.

I am now known as something of a danger to handsome youths. He believes it all—struck by beauty I turned my back upon the field and am now to be found with shaved head and rosary sitting here in this pleasant room writing away at something which some say are copies of the sutras and which others say are not. Since it is believed that I did indeed kill the lad, there is an amount of discrete wariness. Like that of the young acolyte now regarding me.

For a moment I feel tempted to tell him the truth, but then I realize that this would appear to be denial and would not suit my years or my station. Besides, I fear a disclaimer now would not repair the mischief. The rumor is, I am afraid, loose in the world. The bawling boys merely lend it wings. So I kindly thank the suspicious lad and he quickly goes, leaving me alone.

Alone, I become aware of myself. Perhaps my son is right to worry about my health. My fingers hurt, my wrists, elbows, shoulders. The bones seem to grate against each other. And my back—when I bend over. Yes, the body—that poor, faithful mount on which we ride—is getting old and tired. But there is nothing for it. One must ride on to the end.

I do not intend to spare the spur simply because my steed is in its mute fashion complaining. Let it complain. That is its lot. Just as it is mine to gallop through the seasons ahead until a sudden stop throws me headlong. How else to treat that beast, the body?

Well, there is another way. I remember a Minamoto officer during my early years at Kamakura. He was around forty years of age, in no way distinguished, and I noticed him only because of the dispatch with which he did things. And because of the way he treated his body, always tending it, testing it, shooting from the saddle, taking part in mock duels—polishing it as though it were a sword.

While the rest of us lay about, he was galloping in the paddock or striking at straw-wrapped blocks with his practice weapon, or letting loose arrows at targets. And after that he was to be seen at the barracks examining his finely honed body as though looking for imperfections.

He could find none. The rest of us, now growing plump and lax, used to look at that sleek, trim, muscled form with a mixture of envy and disdain. It was handsome enough, but it was after all only a body: a faithful, hard-working mount.

We were right too, because ours carried us right into the future and bear some of us still. His, however, carried him no further than a few seasons. Just a year or two into his forties he killed himself—sat down and cut his throat.

There was some speculation as to why he had done this. Expedients appeared—devotion to the emperor was a common explanation; making some kind of amend to Lord Yoritomo was another, though for what was never ascertained. Yet the explanation was, I think, apparent.

Idle, I used to watch him, and I noticed his exasperation growing. He would look sternly at his sword arm and then repeat the same feint a hundred times as though he was teaching, or encouraging, or punishing. And later he would examine himself carefully, pulling his body this way and that, peering, scrutinizing.

After forty, deterioration is noticible. The breasts sag, if ever so slightly; the stomach protrudes, if but a bit. You are simply not twenty any longer, and the skin ages and there are folds and pouches.

So, I watched this man's exasperation grow. He would hold his breath, then examine his chest; he would stalk about with his stomach pulled in, or when he thought no one else was around he would search his face in the surface of the watering fount. And in this face was despair.

When he killed himself I knew why. He could not tolerate the thought of this body slowly rotting under him—for this is what age consists of. And so rather than stand and stare at this living putrefaction, he killed himself while he was yet almost perfect.

One might say he died of vainglory—and if so, what an enormous vanity it must have been. But I think he died of fear—fear of what would happen when that faithful body of his began its steeper natural decline. This he could not accept.

Accept . . . this is what our Lord Buddha teaches us. You must accept things as they are, you cannot change your life. Rather, you must go where you are led, and when you do, then life's difficulties vanish because you are no longer going against its grain.

True . . . but what sort of life, then, would that be?—so devoid of event that one might as well go directly to the Western Paradise and not bother with this preamble down here at all.

Perhaps this is how the suicide felt. His body disobeyed him by aging and so he cut short the process. If this is so, I can understand. But I am not like that. He did not look after himself in the proper fashion, did not attend to his fortunes in this world; and to do so is, to the best of my calculations, why we are here.

* * *

So, to pick up my neglected story, Yoritomo, before falling off his own faithful steed, decided that an official visit to Heiankyō was called for. This city was the capital, and he was the most powerful man in the country.

He had consolidated his power, as they say, had set up a system of constables to regularize all military affairs in the various provinces, and had his own system of stewards as well, who regulated all private manors and estates; and he also had, of course, the new administrative bureaucracy at Kamakura to handle all legal and governmental affairs.

Though this new government had been imperially sanctioned, Lord Yoritomo perhaps thought that it should now be officially presented. Hence, in the tenth month of the first year of Kenkyū [1190], the triumphal procession to Heiankyō.

It was very grand. On the seventeenth day of the month, Lord Yoritomo and one thousand picked warriors entered the capital. He himself wore an indigo battle dress with light armor of orange fitted with vermilion lacings and a great helmet surmounted by a bronze dragon. One would never have known that this same person once advised sobriety in costume. All the warriors were also fittingly overdressed, and somewhere down the line was my filial son Naoie.

Though the visit did not last long, only a little under a month, it was packed with events: imperial audiences and felicitous visits and dances and concerts and athletic meets. During these weeks all conceivable homage was paid the great Lord Yoritomo, deliverer of his imperial majesty of the great city of Heiankyō, of our very land itself.

Since I was not there, I cannot interest the reader with further description, though I might add that all of these honors did not include the single one that Lord Yoritomo most wanted—the title of Supreme Military Commander. For that he had to wait for the death of the suspicious Retired Emperor Go-Shirakawa and the reign of the trusting Emperor Go-Toba.

This refusal represented all the power that the retired emperor still retained. It was now commonly known that he had been so ill advised as to give authority to that common traitor, Yoshitsune, and that for long decades he had pitted Taira and Minamoto against each other. Though a power was presumed—it was this that Lord Yoritomo and his forces were protecting—the retired emperor was in actuality no longer a force to be wary of.

I wonder what he thought, standing there in his fine robes, little Emperor Go-Toba by his side, being bowed to by a man who now seized everything that had been his. And I wonder what Lord Yoritomo thought, aims realized, back once more in the capital, which he had last left as the thirteen-year-old I had seen in the guardhouse after the Battle of Rokuhara.

Well, whatever it was they both thought, we will not know—yet it is good to wonder. And there is here some consolation to those few of us who do not favor the new military government in recalling that Lord Yoritomo did not then obtain what he most wanted—that title. Perhaps refusing it was Go-Shirakawa's last defiance. Two years later the cloistered emperor died. Of what is uncertain. Old age maybe—he was sixty-six.

Here I—now sixty-five—pause. Was the aged retired emperor only some thirteen years older than myself? Yes, so it appears, and yet I had always thought of his being much the elder—perhaps because powerful folk always seem to us much older. For whatever reason, just my age next year he died.

It was the thirteenth day of the third month of the third year
of Kenkyū [1192], and one may imagine the fuss that the temples made about this chain of threes. The obsequies were extensive and even the great bell at the Shingon temple, where the
dead emperor had prayed, was stilled.

But, I wonder, did anyone truly grieve for him? There was
much official mourning to be sure, but he had, like Yoritomo,
his great enemy, so completely concerned himself with power
that there were few sorry to see him depart. The common people sniffled as they always do when a figure of some consequence passes on, but they do not weep because they are
attached to the person, rather, because they are attached to the
office of that person—they cry because something they had
thought of as certain proves not to have been so.

Yet, now that he is dead, we are hearing more about Go-
Shirakawa—including some small anecdotes which make him
more likeable than we had thought. One such involves the Lady
Kojijū, daughter of the chief priest of the Iwashimizu Hachiman
Shrine.

Not so long ago she was at the palace enjoying a conversation
with Retired Emperor Go-Shirakawa and his courtiers, and he
suggested that each tell a story of some dalliance. When her
turn came, the Lady Kojijū said that once, long before, someone
important had sent for her. She was torn between excitement
and bewilderment, but when enveloped in the embrace of the
interested party she succumbed with trust and pleasure. Then
dawn came, and as the dew slowly disappeared (poetic detail)
they parted, and she was left only with the memory of his evap-
orating fragrance.

The story was well received, particularly by his majesty, who
found it most touching. Then the others pressed her to identify
the mysterious love. When she refused, the retired emperor
himself said that she must—otherwise there was no point to her
confession. So, with a smile, she is supposed to have said that,
very well, if his majesty insisted, then think back. Did he not

remember sending someone for her when he was still on the throne? If he remembered, he would perhaps realize that her story was true. At this all the courtiers began to laugh and the retired emperor was so embarrassed that he all but ran out of the chamber.

His love of music is also remembered—those popular tunes of the day called *imayō*, which he so liked to listen to and to collect. Before he died he is said to have written that he had been faithful to this music all of his life, and that now that most of his life was passed, he should simply hope for paradise. Yet, he wondered, would they allow him in if he entered singing his vulgar *imayō*? But then, he continued: If not, then why not? Even those who love and lust are allowed in, so why not me and my music as well?

Someone here at the temple, scandalized, told me that he had collected whole thousands of these popular songs—that there were over twenty volumes, all annotated with notes on the style of the performance and with musical examples as well. My informant's outraged tone implied that better employment ought to have been found for the imperial staff, but I wonder.

Thanks to Go-Shirakawa we still have what once brought smiles and laughter and what now brings a closeness to those no longer here. Such as, for example, the low-life ditty that was an imperial favorite: That little louse that's playing in my hair, he likes to head for the scruff of my neck; he likes to nibble there.

Yet, during the funeral ceremonies, if one sincere tear ran down a single cheek it was certainly not that of the Emperor Go-Toba—grandpa's choice and now a spoiled brat. This frivolous young person was no sooner on the throne than he began misusing imperial privilege: dressing up, sleeping late, taking endless baths, making constant silly demands upon council and servants alike. As to affairs of state, these were turned over to his beloved nurse, so one may imagine the mess that was made of them. He was also continually playing a game—one consequently much in fashion—where wooden balls were driven about with wooden mallets.

This last occasioned a famous phrase, which went: Oh, damnable youth who loves naught but his wooden balls! And who spoke these well-known words, now used to describe anyone who loves play more than work? It was the priest Mongaku, the same who helped the young Yoritomo in his revolt, and who later saved—for a time—the handsome Rokudai and thus earned Yoritomo's distrust.

Now eighty years old and still at it, Mongaku had been critical of the silly Go-Toba and even tried to sponsor another young prince as second in succession. In the event, the plot was discovered, this lively oldster was apprehended (this occurred much later, after Yoritomo's death) and was sent into exile all the way to the Oki Islands. Hence the famous and furious remark about the damnable youth and his wooden balls.

But now I have raced ahead of myself and have once again failed to recount events in any sober or responsible manner. Let me then return to the third year of Kenkyū [1192]. Retired Emperor Go-Shirakawa died in the third month and, in the seventh, Yoritomo, Lord of Kamakura, finally received his long-desired appointment: he was made Shogun, Commander-in-Chief of all the forces. Just how he managed to obtain this august position I do not know. Perhaps he caught the ear of the emperor's nurse.

Among the many results of this new appointment was a much more affable Yoritomo. The thin smile he now allowed himself would have amounted to a full-toothed grin on the face of anyone else. And he now regarded us with something approaching benevolence. Even me. I thought at the time that my faithful wife had gotten at his faithful wife. Now I think not. We were all simple recipients of these relatively sunny spirits.

These smiles would, I thought, stand me in good stead during the trouble that now descended upon me, but in this I was mistaken—or at the time thought that I was.

* * *

My troubles were occasioned by Hisashita Naomitsu—whom the attentive reader will remember as my relative and my enemy. As I earlier mentioned, Yoritomo had given me back my ancestral lands, as they were called. These were considerable—all of Kumagai township.

And as I have also mentioned, under Yoritomo land became valuable, since preferment and advancement depended upon how much you had and how many people served under you.

Given my land holdings, I might have raised myself higher in the Kamakura government, but there was the affair of the archery tournament and its aftermath, and I let the matter lapse and thus, in my manner, continued to work against my own interests.

Far less supine than myself was Naomitsu, who had only a parcel of land, that of the manor and a few fields beyond. Ambitious, he now brought a suit against me, claiming that my lands were actually a part of his and that the boundary line was in question.

He was too canny to contest Yoritomo's earlier ruling, making the whole parcel mine. Rather, he turned his argument upon this boundary line—a fictitious marking which neither of us had considered for over forty years.

So, one cold day at the end of the eleventh month, we were both summoned to the open court in front of Yoritomo's pavilion—his office, as it was called—and squatted on the gravel while the wind whipped the flags and the gray sky turned dark.

The Lord of Kamakura sat on his dais, on the veranda above us. I had not seen him for a time and, despite his new affability, he looked careworn. Perhaps being commander-in-chief was a bit more stressful, as they now say, than he had thought it would be. And next to him, as always, sat Kajiwara Kagetoki.

I have neglected earlier to write much about this person. Perhaps my error was disinclination. The man was nothing but trouble. And not to myself alone. People said that it was he who so poisoned Lord Yoritomo against Yoshitsune, repeating or inventing calumny until the duped elder brother was ready to misinterpret anything the younger one said or did.

Originally Kagetoki was a Taira, serving under and causing much concern to the good-natured Ōba Kagechika. Then, at the battle of Ishibashi, sent to pursue the fleeing Minamoto, he caught up with them and espoused their cause. Now serving Yoshitomo, he was a member of the campaign to chastise Yoshinaka, and later he accompanied Yoshitsune all the way down to Dannoura, where he had a famous argument with his commander concerning how to use the oars. Yoshitsune's method prevailed, the battle was won, and Kagetoki was discomfited. Perhaps his enmity then expressed itself.

I often used to see him around the government offices. His rank prohibited my knowing him, but I would not in any event have wanted to. Kajiwara was a man with a face like a hatchet and a tongue like a knife. All avoided him—except for Yoritomo.

I suppose that our lord, like most political leaders a very bad judge of men, endorsed him because he thus learned what he wanted to believe. Also, another reason for my dislike—envy this time—was that Kagetoki could read and write. This talent was of great value to Yoritomo who was always receiving reports from him. As a result this learned person was high in government circles and later, after Yoritomo's death, became even member of the council of state where he caused the greatest difficulties. It was only five years ago that someone finally killed him.

This then was the man sitting next to Lord Yoritomo and listening to our evidence. There was not much—simply Hisashita's complaints and my remonstrances. I did not know why our commander was taking up his valuable time with a case as trivial as this. Perhaps, having originally given me the land, he felt some responsibility. Or perhaps in thus formally snatching it back he was finally punishing me for the archery insurrection.

Whatever, I soon relieved him of the obligation or opportunity. I am, as I have perhaps already indicated, never at my best

when confronting authority. Now, however, things took the turn
they did because of Kagetoki. He, bored and irritated from the
beginning, seemed to be siding with Hisashita. He nodded in
agreement upon a number of occasions and then asked leading
questions. Was it not true that this land had been in your family's possession ever since the reign of the emperor so-and-so?
And if this is true, how did Kumagai Naozane come to have any
real title to it? Was it not, rather, the *charity* of my esteemed late
foster father, and so on.

I suppose I could have assisted my cause by dragging out my
maligned grandfather, and then all four of us could have tried
to decide who had been the better Taira. This would not have
seemed strange to the head of the Minamoto, sitting there, listening. Things like this happened all the time.

But I did not. I must have been too angry. Lord Yoritomo
kept raising his hand to his chin in that habitual gesture of his,
and cocking his head this way and that as he thought, and would
then in a judicial manner and in his usual reedy tones ask
absurd questions: Well then, just how old were you when you
were sent to the Hisashita household?

When I smartly replied that this had nothing to do with the
matter of the boundary line, he was taken aback. His lacquer
bonnet wobbled and he stared as though annoyed. And, when I
said further that the proper way to settle the matter was for all
of us to go to the plains of Musashi and measure the land itself,
there was an irritated silence.

Before us, held in place by weights, were the various papers
of the trial. On them were written the offending measurements
and other pertinent manners. They had not once been exam-
ined and were not going to be. Whipping there in the wind, they
became for me the exemplar of the futility of our proceedings.

So I held up my hand, and when Lord Yoritomo looked at
me, I said that Kajiwara Heiza Kagetoki was plainly favoring
Hisashita Gonshū Naomitsu, and that therefore no matter how
truthful and consistent I had shown myself, such testimony

would be of no value. It would seem that it was I who would be questioned and Hisashita who would be cleared of all charges. Therefore these documents here before us, which showed the real truth, were of no further use to us.

So saying, I lifted up the paperweights, and the winter wind lifted the documents into the air like a flock of white birds. While they flapped and soared and Lord Yoritomo stared like a child, I stood up and stamped off.

In our Kamakura, such actions are unheard of. No one stands up without permission, much less stamps off. But I, making a great racket on the board flooring, had lost my famous temper.

Filled with that warmth which only ire brings, no longer divided by quibblings, all now of a piece, I strode down the corridor and then, still in a temper, barged into the west wing, the armory.

There I grasped my short sword, raised it high, and brought it down. But I did not decapitate myself. Rather, catching my topknot with one hand, I sliced through the string, the ribbon, and the hair itself.

＊　＊　＊

Those listening to that silly historical entertainment down the hall, now all but completed, would believe that the warrior Kumagai began the life religious when he brought down his sword on the neck of the stripling, that the lopping of the adolescent head and the blubbering in the brine began the pilgrimage that led him finally to the foot of the lotus throne. Not at all. It began when I brought my weapon down on my own topknot, and then stood, my hair around my shoulders, suddenly sober at what my temper had wrought.

The orderlies gaped, the guards rushed in, and there I stood—reborn, as the good Buddhists say. Dramatically so. There was no precedent for what I had done. There are many stories—and here I have told several—of the severing of the topknot as a signal of disgrace or punishment, or as preamble to execution. But never before, I think, had a warrior committed this act upon himself. After all, military hierarchy is unimaginable without the various symbols of precedence, and among these hairstyles rank high.

My act was thus widely regarded as a kind of suicide. As it was, since it involved leaving one life and entering another. But remorse had nothing to do with it. It was pique, pure, and simple. Pride, not contrition, was what moved me.

The religious life removes one from the military world of power and its attendant strife. Or is supposed to, though both Kiyomori's and Emperor Go-Shirakawa's taking of the cloth did not lessen their interest in worldly matters. I, however, with this single sword stroke removed myself entirely from the concerns of Kamakura.

Not knowing what next to do, standing there, stared at, I called in an attendant who finished the job by completing the tonsure. And then I took a few belongings and simply walked out of the big north gate and did not once look back.

I heard later that my wife took it all rather well and that my son took it all rather badly. As for me, I did not even think of them that cold November morning as, newly shaved head stinging in the winter wind, I walked out of Kamakura.

And as I strode through that winter forest, I saw that a new life was beginning for me, as the pines opened to reveal the first range of high meadows, and then the low hills beyond, whitened with the first snow of the year. I looked at the gray, cloud-swept sky, at the dark green of the pine needles, at the brown of the fallen leaves—and I could really see, for the first time in many years, these things which now lived before my eyes.

I felt as I had long, long before, when I first left my home in Musashi and set out upon the winding road that led to Heiankyō and to my life beyond.

* * *

I was then over fifty, much older than many of my contemporaries, seeing as how most of these were dead. Yet I had survived thanks to my concern for myself. Now, however, in typical fashion, I had flung away my prospects and was back where I started—on the road.

And being pursued. Yoritomo ordered me to return. The first temple at which I stopped, Sōtozan in Izu, sent back a report to Kamakura, and shortly a monk named Senkobō was trying to calm me down. Since I was still angry, I refused to quiet down, and so he wrote me a letter which I still have.

I quite understand, he wrote, that you wish to leave the world and to enter the priesthood. But this does not mean that you should betray the fate given you by heaven. You were born into a warrior family, you have learned the way of the warrior, you know that a real warrior should be able to die for the sake of his master. Yet, you seem to have forgotten this. Indeed, if you now so long to leave behind such worldly affairs, it means that you are going against your own way. You may look like a monk, but you are not one. I advise you to go back to where and what you were.

In employing this unwelcoming tone, Senkobō was merely following orders from Kamakura. When I proved still obdurate, he turned accommodating enough, gave me a robe—dun-colored and too short though it was—and a letter of introduction to a monk in Heiankyō named Seikaku, who introduced me to Hōnen who became my mentor. Thus Buddha won a new convert and virtue accrued to all around.

Why Yoritomo did not have me brought forcibly back was not so easy to understand. I had rebelled against him, had flaunted his authority, and deserved whatever punishments he could devise. Perhaps, I thought, it was because of a tradition of military men taking the cloth. It was customary for those who lapsed, as I had, to show contrition by retiring to a temple. I did not feel the need to exhibit an emotion I did not feel, but I did need a place to go—and, besides, I was already coiffed.

So, off I set. I was, in effect, a new person. The military man was left behind, along with all his concerns. Instead, here was this attractive new person. Thonged straw sandals on his bare feet, shaved head muffled by his hood, white under-robe showing plainly under the outer—a personage of the religious persuasion it would seem.

All day, every day, I happily marched through that crisp winter. At evening in the soft and bluish light of the twelfth month, I would stop in some small hamlet and search out the temple. After a humble repast, I sat on the veranda and watched the smoke from the cooking fires rise to the pale and darkening sky. Then I curled myself on the mat by the hearth and fell into a deep and thoughtless sleep.

I know now how happy I was. It was as though my childhood had returned to me and I was once again a boy, full of my life as I strode that road. My cares, my failures—I was leaving them all behind, and marching toward I knew not what. Actually, I was marching toward Hōnen, founder of that sect which later received me.

Here I wish to say something about him. He was some six years older than myself and much less worldly. Early discouraged by the corruption of Buddhism—both its natural decline and the further decadence imposed upon it by a corrupt clergy—he secluded himself at Kurodani in the foothills of Mount Hiei. There he became convinced that Buddha had lived for all men, did so yet, and that certain early Chinese sages had been correct in affirming that a small prayer, the simple calling of the name—*Namu Amida Butsu*—was enough to ensure one's place in paradise.

I have already mentioned this series of beliefs but here ought to point out what Hōnen's contribution consisted of. The older Pure Land teachings of the Tendai sect, upon which the beliefs are based, state that we are, in fact, already Buddhas and that this troubled land of ours is, actually, nothing other than the Pure Land of Enlightenment itself. This curious belief was doubtless assisted by the spending of so much time meditating that the believer never had time to go out into this Pure Land of ours to discover just how enlightened it was.

Hōnen, however, saw the Pure Land as a place entirely separate, one into which one had to be reborn after death. He then greatly simplified the entrance qualifications. There was but a single practice—this invocation of the name of Amida alone was all that was required to ensure rebirth and ultimate enlightenment.

Such teachings had the advantage of making clear a complicated matter. It took religion from the hands of the priests and offered it, as it were, to ordinary people—those who stood most in need of it.

At the time of my winter journey, Hōnen, already famous, was at Higashiyama in Heiankyō. Though his most important work lay in the future, his teachings were already widespread, and the older, larger Buddhist sects, fearful of his growing influence, were beginning to oppose him.

I cannot say that I was initially attracted to these teachings. They seemed arbitrary. They still do. But, on the other hand, it is obvious that religion does need reform. Thus, if some system of belief is necessary then this one is at least worthy of attention.

Particularly mine. I, a homeless novice, needed somewhere to go. Not that the future life—the proper concern of religion— had until now held many attractions for me. No, for me it had always been the here and the now. And so it was for a large number, the majority certainly, of rough country soldiers, one of whom I had been.

The future world meant little to us. Though it was presumably near, due to our dangerous lives, we were usually too busy to think much about it. Yet, even fools—to paraphrase Hōnen— who have a strong faith in this life here and now have a better chance of understanding than do those who do not doubt a future existence.

I gazed now upon Buddha and my eyes shone, and I remembered the image of him I had seen at the old Toba palace, the expression of contentment upon that face almost smug with accomplishment. This I desired to emulate. If I had failed to climb to the top of my profession as a soldier, perhaps I could as a religious person.

This is what I told Hōnen during our initial conversation. I had searched him out in the small temple where he had apartments. We talked of the Pure Land awaiting and I told him of my heterodox interpretation. He was not offended—merely curious.

– And why then, he asked, are you so of the here and now? And why does the opinion of those about you so move you? They are your companions in life only through accident of birth. They are but pilgrims, the same as you, on their journey to the Pure Land. Why is it that what they think concerning you has such importance? Why are you not already free of this most common of worldly attachments—reputation?

This I thought about. We were sitting in his rooms and it was already early spring—the dim light was tinged with young green from the garden.

– Because, I finally answered, it is all that I have. It is the opinions of others through which I form my opinion of myself, and it is through their regard that I gauge my success.

– Honestly answered, said this good man, in as wry a fashion as was possible for him. You admit to a humanity that most men would deny and I honor you for that. Yet I would seek to try to free you from this attachment to mere earthly reputation.

– Why? I asked.

– Because it is limiting, he answered. You too are capable of being a Buddha. And He, you will remember, did not predicate himself upon the opinion of others.

– I, a Buddha? I wondered, considering that if I could become a Buddha then that would be reckoned success indeed.

– And where did you learn to be so skeptical? asked the good Hōnen. Was it the life of a soldier?

– It was rather, I believe, life itself, said I.

– Skeptical, yet concerned for reputation, dubious, but still following some kind of perhaps posthumous glory. You are much of this world, said the priest.

I nodded in agreement and he continued: But, beware. Those who are obsessed with worldly desire may be doomed to tread the *muryōgo no michi*.

I knew what that was. It was that road, along which discontented spirits followed the living—endlessly, hopelessly. They are forever in pursuit of the living world, which forever evades their grasp.

To tread this endless path, getting nowhere, was the opposite of what I wanted. I wanted to arrive. I looked into the honest eyes of Hōnen and thus began my conversion.

* * *

So here in Higashiyama I have stayed and, except for various excursions—over to Kōmyōji when it became Hōnen's, then back to Komasawa when it became mine—have made my home. It is a pleasant place, a valley in the low hills, one end of which opens near the east upper gate of Heiankyō. It is considerably north of Kiyomizu Temple and the remains of Rokuhara, and it is not too far from the new postroad going on to Ōtsu and to Lake Biwa.

And when I am tired of writing and my fingers cramp and my shoulder pains me in the cold of this early winter, I can go through the grounds to the gate and walk to the bluff where, like any other idle oldster, I can watch the world pass by on this grand new highway.

What was here before, I wonder. I do not remember, did not much come to this part of the suburbs when I was a soldier under the Taira. Perhaps it was not yet even a suburb, for Heiankyō has since then grown much larger. And everything is so changed.

Even the clothes. They seem to have become stiffer. I remember the men's court clothing back in the old days in the capital—how soft and flowing it was, all layers of silk and damask for men and women alike, liquid garments forever rustling and sliding and slipping.

Women's clothing seems to have changed less, as fits that conservative sex. Still, all of those varicolored layers of kimono, one under the other, seem gone. Now the lower body is wrapped into a rather malelike divided skirt and the only color is in the upper kimono—or at least this is what these women I see going about their business on the road wear.

The men's clothing is all points and corners, stiffened with starch and lacquer. It looks faintly dangerous and seems inconvenient but then convenience never determined fashion. All these corners and stiff shoulders and hard footwear and harder hats make me think more of the military, and this is probably the inspiration of these new fashions. These are civilian accommodations to the ideals of Kamakura—they make visible this military regime and, I suppose, signal a kind of popular approbation. And I noticed that now even priests carry swords, or at least daggers. This certainly never occurred before.

Hōnen, of course, carried nothing at all. But then Hōnen was not really of these times. Though he was much concerned with mankind and its salvation, he was not much troubled for those he saw around him everyday. Of a consequence, he had no idea what this life is like. Quite properly so, since he was so exclusively concerned with the next one.

He was, I now see, as unworldly as a child. Hōnen was not to be found hanging around the gate of the temple, as I often am. No, he was in his study with all the doors closed, busy with great thoughts. And if a caller came, someone new, someone from the outside, he barely spared a glance before beginning once again an explication of his great ideas.

This is as appealing in an old person as it would be in someone very young. There is in both a kind of purity. One sees a being uncontaminated by the world and its ways, ignorant of them. Perhaps this is wisdom.

* * *

I have had a dream. In the Pure Land I am on the top of a mountain, obviously occupying the best seat, a spiky golden lotus. It is, however, becoming more and more uncomfortable and I am shifting from buttock to buttock, wondering what to do next. Eventually the pain becomes acute and I want to get down, but there is no way—and the pointed golden petals are cutting into my flesh.

Perhaps this indicates that the religious life does not become me. And yet it is this path that I now tread, and at the end of which I desire to find that reward which has so far eluded me: a good, proud place—if not in this world, then in the next.

I tend to dwell upon my inadequacies, having just now, perhaps thanks to my dream, remembered one of them. It happened one day a year or so after I had been accepted by Hōnen, and had received my priestly name of Rensei. I had heard that the master was going to visit the great Kujō Kanezane and I was determined to go along.

Perhaps I have not mentioned this person. Though ten years younger than myself, he had led a life that in some ways resembled my own. Originally a Fujiwara, he was of some political importance, except that he could not agree with Kiyomori and of a consequence sided with the Minamoto. Here, however, his ambitions were thwarted by Go-Shirakawa, another person of authority with whom he could not get along.

The resemblance to myself is that we have both had difficulties with those in command. And a desire for power is indeed a failing if one does not know how to go about obtaining it.

Once the retired emperor was dead, however, things seemed to go better for him. Since he had been instrumental in having Lord Yoritomo's military title pushed through the imperial bureaucracy, he was officially rewarded. Having been made regent, he was in a position to arrange that, when the time came, his youngest daughter marry Emperor Go-Toba.

Here he was following the precepts of many, including, lately,

Kiyomori, whom he had much disliked, in that he hoped the off-spring would eventually become emperor himself. When this occurred, his position would be impregnable and he would be powerful indeed.

I was curious about this person, and when I learned that Hōnen was going to pay a call I wanted to go along as well. While this probably embarrassed my teacher, since they were going to speak of ways of bringing Lord Yoritomo over to the side of the true faith, he nonetheless, kind man, said I could come.

Lord Kujō's house was very grand, in one of the best districts of the capital, and in the new military style, all walls and embankments. I was not able to view the interior, however, since I was left behind in the inner entry and could see nothing at all—though I could hear.

In any event, I had seen Lord Kujō Kanezane on prior occasions. He was a fine figure of a man. Or so it was thought—he had that small-featured, melon-seed shaped face, typically Fujiwara, which court ladies find attractive and which military gentlemen do not. But I had also seen him surly with authority, disrespectful to those above him, and that is always, to my old-fashioned way of thinking, quite attractive. Now that he had some authority himself I wanted to see—or at least to hear—how he had changed.

Not at all, it would seem. His first words to the priest were: You are rather late in coming to our appointment, and I understand you have brought with you someone who was not invited.

He is a Minamoto, was the answer. He was once a warrior, now a lay priest at our Kurodani temple. I hope for his help in spreading our work throughout the eastern provinces where the good word has yet to take firm root. He wished merely to pay his regards.

This was answered—I saw with pleasure—by a snort. Kujō had not changed at all. The holy Hōnen was being spoken to in this fashion, and Yoritomo himself would perhaps have been met with similar praiseworthy truculence.

Hōnen was going on now about our all being equal in the merciful eyes of Amida Buddha, in whose regard alone could we expect to find contentment in the Pure Land itself. They then got down to business and started talking about Lord Yoritomo and the ways to make our faith even more powerful than it already was.

Perhaps Emperor Go-Toba, now Lord Kujō's son-in-law, could be brought around, and if that happened then Yoritomo, so anxious himself to ape the ways of the court, would make our religion official, and so on.

I was surprised at the simplicity of this. My ear was at the crux of power, and yet they were plotting like two children. Perhaps it is always thus. Maybe the great Kiyomori himself decided policy through such palaver.

But—Lord Kujō was saying—since all are, thanks to the egalitarian nature of this religion, considered equal, this cannot well appeal to our Lord Yoritomo whose system of government is, of course, based on inequalities. At this childishness I could no longer contain myself.

– Yes indeed, I shouted: How vexing this sinful world. But one must remember that it is only in the Pure Land itself that there is no such discrimination.

The nodding guards jerked awake, Hōnen popped a surprised head from behind the screen, and Lord Kujō actually came out onto the veranda where I sat.

How old he looked. He was wasted, and the melon-shaped face had turned long and yellow. We stared at each other. He was looking at a man who had failed in one profession and cut off his topknot and who was now attempting to get ahead in another. I was looking at a powerful man, about to exercise his strength.

Yet, how much more healthy I looked. My skin was still firm, my eyes still bright. This man before me, dry as a husk, yellow, dull-eyed, was old, and probably ill.

Nonetheless, or consequently, he did a curious thing. I—who had intended my remark as angry sarcasm—deserved to be booted out and given a good talking to. Instead, I was invited to enter and sit in the room itself, though safely out of sight, behind a screen. After that Hōnen launched into one of those sermons of his and together they decided the future.

So this was power. I had then perhaps been fortunate in my failing to attain it. Kiyomori on fire, Yoritomo turned to stone, Kanezane here all dried up. This was not, of course, the topic of the sermon. This was merely what I thought, there on the other side of the screen.

Our similiarities, those between Kanezane and myself, continued. In the end, later on, his various efforts all met with failure, he lost the regard of Lord Yoritomo, and he ended up a lay priest just like me. Hōnen gave him a name, Enshō, and now in another part of this temple he sits, I am told, writing away at his memoirs.

* * *

Once back home Hōnen decided I should be talked to. My propensity for losing my temper was known and my tongue was thought sharp. Thus my intemperate remark was misinterpreted. I had meant to remind them that the world was a much more complicated place than they thought, and that inequalities were as much a part of it as the sun that shone.

Thus began the good Hōnen: You know, he said, you think too much.

This rebuke was one the grizzled warrior had not expected. My surprise must have shown, for Hōnen continued with: Ah, that strikes home, I see. You yourself know this. Then listen well. It is thought itself that breeds discord. For without it we would be harmonious.

That was quite true, I agreed, and without thought there would be no need for any dissension at all. For if there were no opinion, there then could be no difference of it.

Hōnen smiled and nodded his head. Then he went on to confide in me his true beliefs. So true, he said, that when it came to the making of his death testament, he intended to phrase them just as he would for me now.

The way of salvation, he said, was nothing but the repetition of the *Namu Amida Butsu,* all the time placing one's trust in Amida Buddha's vow through which one may be reborn into the Land of Perfect Bliss. But this was not, he continued, a method of meditation. Nor was it necessarily a prayer studied and understood in all of its profundity. No, even if I myself held to a more profound doctrine, I would not—you see—profit from the divine mercy because I would remain outside the Vow of the Buddha Amida. Those who would believe must behave like simple, unlettered people, like those ignorant country nuns whose faith is of an absolute simplicity.

While I nodded, not, I hoped, too intelligently, young Shinran, also there, was openly enthusiastic. This man, then in his twenties, nowadays showing every sign of being a true sage, burst out with: How true, how true! If the good are to be reborn in Paradise, how much more then the wicked. If one has faith in the vow of Amida, then there is no necessity for good deeds—for good deeds cannot surpass the vow. One need not fear committing even evil acts, for no evil act can stand in the way of the original vow. Right?

Hōnen nodded gravely—he always did, no matter what was said to him—and shortly after that I was excused. If I repeated my prayer to Amida a number of times, my entrance into the next world would be assured, and my little outburst at Kanezane's would be disregarded. At the same time my implied questioning of the Pure Land—was it indeed as equal in opportunity as I hoped, and would my diligence be rewarded with a better position there?—went not only unanswered but unapprehended. I was merely to understand that with the vow on my lips I would become in the future a much better priest.

So I would. For I now understood that understanding is

precisely that which my religion does not foster. Yet I began to detect a movement in my own depths, and this allowed me to comprehend that by repeating our phrase hundreds, thousands of times, the syllables, like pebbles in the bed of a fast-moving stream, would soon be worn smooth, and that this repetition would itself still all thought.

Which is what Hōnen desired—for he had criticized me for thinking too much—and which, truth be known, I myself desired as well. How often, indeed, had I courted and experienced this blessed stilling of thought—through battle, through making love, through losing my temper—thus becoming one with my faithful brute of a body.

It was this that had interested me in the Jōdo belief, and which still does. It posits something higher than thought. It substitutes, and in so doing it reveals.

Amida triumphant, we are offered entrance to a kind of authenticity: we can decide finally who it is that we are—we are that body that chants the *nembutsu*. Yet, as I lose myself in writing this, I can also see that, behind the satisfied smile of my Buddha, this same belief can benefit several others in a way not dreamed of by such blessed innocents as my Hōnen.

For how convenient to a ruler is a belief that does not stimulate intelligence, but rather seeks to dull it—a truly holy way can lead to a truly dumb incomprehension as well. With a populace concerned only with the future life, a ruler can do what he pleases with the present one.

Remembering what I had overheard, I understood why Kanezane would desire to interest our ruler in this faith. Already Yoritomo was treating his warriors more as subjects than as vassals. He was commanding loyalty, demanding from military officials and provincial governors alike a written oath sealed with their own bloody fingerprints, all carried out before Hachiman, tutelary god of the Minamoto.

He could now cement the alliance further by making official a religion that demanded an absolute faith, and the practice of which required the stilling of all thought. Who then could complain, when the ability to form a complaint was no longer possible.

I remembered one of the last times I had seen Yoritomo. He was praying, hands clasped in front of the great shrine to Hachiman in Kamakura, the one he rebuilt, its high stairs climbing straight up the hill as though right into the beyond.

And as he clapped his hands once and bowed his head in ceremonial obeisance, the sun caught a spark of gold at the topknot. It was the small image of the Goddess Kannon, which, as I have said, he was never without. It had been given him when he was three years old.

Religious, superstitious, careful creature of habit? I do not know. I do know that he once pardoned a condemned man when he discovered that the person daily read the sutras. This argues for an amount of sincerity. On the other hand, he earlier once vowed to recite one thousand times passages from the Lotus Sutra, then discovered that he had to go to battle. So he had the priest in charge reduce the vow, mumbled his way through what was left, and raced off.

So I do not know what impelled the man. I did not understand Lord Yoritomo. And I remained curious. Yet when I had a later opportunity to once again view him, I did not avail myself of it.

He had come to our part of the land in the sixth year of Kenkyū [1195], some three years after I had left Kamakura. The occasion was the reconstruction of the Tōdai Temple and he also wanted to see about the remaking of Rokuhara, which would become the new residence of the shogun's deputy in the capital.

In a roundabout way I was summoned to one of his many audiences and I neglected to go, pleading priestly duties. Yet, I remained curious, and so a month after Lord Yoritomo had left the capital, I—in the heat of the eighth month—set out for Kamakura.

＊　＊　＊

Trudging along the new highway, I could compare my present journey with that of but three years earlier. Now I was wearing proper priestly garb, summer white, with new straw sandals, and a smart ebony rosary, since I was now a proper priest with a name of my own. The Reverend Rensei off to Kamakura to once more meet the great Lord Yoritomo.

Peace is to the affairs of men as the sun is to those of nature. If no one ever before said this, he ought to have. Just as crops grow tall and orchards heavy in the summer sun, so in these newly peaceful times Heiankyō had grown far beyond its old boundaries, and the road, deserted before, was now bordered with new manor houses, barns, huts, and dwellings. There were bridges too, and the mountain passes had steps cut from the rock itself.

Also—lest I forget what kind of peace this was—there were many more grim barrier stations, with wooden-faced soldiers searching the bundles, the parcels, the purses. I had my pass, with an official-looking seal on it, and this allowed me through with an amount of dignity. On the way I passed a wooden-log jail, used for detaining the suspicious. It was filled to the bars.

Then down from the hills and into the summer heat, this time tempered by the still invisible sea, and finally across the fields to the shogun's capital. Approaching, I saw here too new prosperity—the standing forest I remembered was now reduced, and along the road stood new buildings still smelling of fresh-cut lumber.

Lord Yoritomo's house was new as well. House, I say, but it was a palace fashioned in the purest old Heiankyō style, with long, low eaves, rush-blinds, round pillars, and that air of genteel gloom so typical of the old days in the old city. Quite different from the spruce, military, and very up-to-date buildings around it.

This I mentioned to him when, with a surprising lack of fuss, I had been ushered into his presence. We were in one of the low-ceilinged rooms off the main section of the palace, a kind of pavilion opening onto a blindingly white sand garden. The light was reflected onto the chalky features of Lord Yoritomo.

Yes, he answered. He thought it important to maintain the standards of our great past. I, at his feet, kneeling, as befit both priest and subject, bowed politely but privately remembered that recent Kamakura policy had proscribed any of the shogun's samurai from becoming intimate with any of the emperor's aristocracy in the capital—yet here we sat in this lavishly old-fashioned and aristocratic palace, speaking of the standards of our great imperial past.

While he thus perched in royal splendor, Yoritomo nonetheless continued to espouse the true samurai way, which was now said to consist of three virtues. To be of good family and to be a good bowman and horseman were unexceptional and expected. The third, however, was new. The true samurai was to have a modest bearing.

This last has a truly modern sound. In my time I could not have imagined a warrior cultivating a modest bearing. Just the opposite. As I have indicated, we were to be as brash and overbearing as possible. But now obedience is necessary for the new state, and modesty becomes one of its virtues.

That Yoritomo extolled such modest ideals while himself inhabiting such an ostentatious palace would not have struck him as odd. To him incongruity was a stranger. The fact that his august self had decided thus gave this decision a power and a certainty that prevented any doubt as to its worth.

Indeed, no inconsistency could occur because everything was made consistent by this all-important person. He was like a weathered stone—like one of those in my garden here, the main one, the big one there—as entirely and completely itself as he was Lord Yoritomo.

I looked at him, his face livid in the light reflected from the garden, his embroidered robes, his high silk bonnet shining in the shade. He was utterly the shogun that he was; therefore, nothing else.

And I thought back to that thirteen-year-old I had glimpsed so many years back, and that resolute look, the first view of the great lord seated above me, now hardened by the years of power. Having remembered the scene, I remembered the place, and this suggested a further means of converse.

– At Rokuhara, my lord, will the new residence of the shogun's ambassador to the capital also be in the older Heiankyō style of architecture?

– I think not, he said, fingers stroking his chin. It might be within the capital itself more fitting to indicate something of the later styles. Also, since it will be the residence of our representative, a Kamakura man, we must think of his comfort. It will be something more military.

So I observed: It will then much resemble the original Rokuhara will it not?

This might have been interpreted as a forward remark. Rokuhara was, after all, the fortress of the enemy Kiyomori. But Yoritomo merely answered: Yes, it will somewhat resemble that original building. Then he surprised me by asking: Do you remember it—Rokuhara?

– Yes, very well. Though your excellency does not perhaps know, I spent many years there.

– Yes, I know. I remember seeing you there.

– You saw me, sir?

– Yes, I was very young. It was before my period of exile, but I was there before being sent to Izu. Though I was but a child, and a captive one at that, I was already thinking of my future, and I was looking for soldierly qualities.

So that had been the meaning of that gaze, the memory of which I had carried with me so many years. I, an enemy soldier, was being considered by a child who, for all he knew, was about to have his head lopped off.

– Yes, continued his lordship, as though answering my thoughts, I remember you—a fine-looking young soldier.

– Then, sir, when I had the honor to join the Minamoto forces, you knew who I was.

– Not at first, I believe. But later I remembered.

Now, why did this so touch me, I wondered, for I was much moved. I, so accustomed to remembering, had forgotten that others remembered as well. It had not occurred to me that the rocklike Yoritomo was capable of so ordinary an action.

– One has one's memories, said his lordship.

– Then yours of me, my lord, must contain many an unpleasant one.

Those in attendance on either side of his lordship stirred and looked at one another from the corners of their eyes. My comment was far too personal for my station. Yet it was answered.

– Concerning your deed, said Lord Yoritomo, your rights to the land were quite confirmed. They were granted you and we had made no attempt to deprive you of them. The interrogation to which you objected was merely to ensure that your relative would have no ground for further complaint. Those lands are yours still.

– I much displeased you, I said, and the attendants frowned.

Lord Yoritomo looked at me with that appraising gaze I so remembered and said: No, but you were difficult. You had no men, no troops, only your esteemed son. And, further, we needed officers who were capable of being responsible, not those who were interested in being first in the field. Your exploits, you see, we had no further use for. So you were made councilor, but it was difficult to fit you into our table of organization. To that extent, then, displeasure.

– The archery contest, perhaps, my lord?

– The what? No, I refer merely to your actions in this very building: leaving my presence without permission, going to the armory, cutting off your topknot. Were you not aware that this action is reserved for punishment? That I had so used it myself? Your doing so made it appear as though punishment had come from me. And then this self-exile, your affairs here all undecided, your wife bereaved, your son bewildered. That a man could so throw away his life seemed to me incomprehensible.

There he stopped. The lords in attendence were still now,

216 ❖   Memoirs of the Warrior

looking straight ahead, ears wide open. Lord Yoritomo
appeared to be awaiting some reply. It was plain I owed him
one. I made the attempt.

– We, sir, I began, are separated not only by our ages and our
stations, but also by our experiences and our ambitions. Now I
find that I have lingered behind and you have forged ahead. In
this new world, which you yourself have made, I feel I have little
place.

– You would disagree with our policies? he asked, as though
the thought had just occurred.

– I am incapable of appreciating them.

– This I find extraordinary, said Lord Yoritomo. We are victorious in every recent incident, we have unified our land to an
unprecedented degree, we have made possible a lasting peace,
and you cannot appreciate what we have done, and further you
refuse your share in this victory.

I looked at the courtyard and realized that he was correct—
that he had been successful, had made his place in the world. I,
who so professed an admiration for just this, had myself done
nothing of the sort.

– I am, of course, aware of the circumstances, he said, and
regarded me I thought more benevolently.

Since I regarded the circumstances as the courtroom drama
out of which I had walked, I did not understand this new regard
until he added: Your taking of the cloth. Soldier though I myself
am, I can understand a reluctance to waste yet further life. To
form a state, as I have, such is unavoidable and perhaps, even in
religious terms, forgivable. For a person such as yourself, no
such recourse is admissable. I understand your sudden dislike of
the military life.

I stared at him in some perplexity. Never once had I loathed
that life. It had been my profession until my own foolishness
deprived me of it.

He saw my stare and kindly continued: I must admit that
when you left my presence and then impinged my honor by suggesting through your actions in the armory that I had punished

you, I thought you mad. It was only later that I came to realize what had occurred.

He must have interpreted my silence as understanding, for he continued: Sudden conversions are not unusual. In the Chinese classics I believe a number are recorded, but never have I heard of one so sudden as yours—one moment the warrior, the very next the priest. But mysterious are the ways of the Lord Buddha.

I now knew what he was talking about and, seeing intelligence in my gaze, he concluded in an almost kindly manner: And yet I was not amazed. My years have made me astute. I now realize that I felt something unusual when you presented yourself to me with a most estimable trophy. When you delivered to us the person of the most promising of the young Taira. I remember your face then—ambivalent.

Hell and damnation! So, that was it—the calumny again: that devil Atsumori pursuing me still down the *muryō no michi* which is my life. Even Yoritomo had heard about it now. Ambivalence? I was kneeling there shifty-eyed and hoping no one had seen me snatch the bobbing head.

– Youthful beauty, doomed to fade, alas, where now the blossoms of Mount Yoshino? he said, and it was only after a moment or two that I realized that he was in his courtlike fashion quoting something.

I opened my mouth to speak, then shut it again—for what could I say? Not that I had stolen the head. Not that it had been anger that accounted for my stomping off, and mere pique that accounted for my conversion.

– No, no, he said gently, seeing my confusion. I am no stranger to the human heart. Such emotions are known to me, though I cannot in my position indulge them.

I bowed.

Then he stood and, trailing the long-trained trousers of the palace, shuffled out of the room, leaving the black stool sitting there.

I bowed to it and, as etiquette demanded, then backed out of the room.

* * *

Thinking about this, I returned to the apartment allocated me during my visit. And there I found that someone had called upon me and in fact still waited, head bowed, sleeves outspread.

– Please do sit up, I said. Such formality between us is not necessary.

Obeying, my wife sat and stared as though at a stranger.

– You are seeing me for the first time as a priest, I said.

– Yes, your name, reverend sir, is now Rensei, I believe.

– That is the name the Reverend Hōnen has given me.

– Of what characters is it composed? she wanted to know.

That was very like her. Though indifferent to most of the larger things of life, she was addicted to the smaller. Also, like many women nowadays, she knew how to read and so had conceived this enthusiasm for the difficulties of Chinese characters. That I could read these but haltingly had, I believe, long been one of her solaces.

Given life with me she needed every solace she could contrive. So I added to her pleasure by telling her that I was sorry to say that I did not know of which characters my name was composed, but that since I had memorized their form I could, if she so desired, write them for her in my usual execrable hand.

At this she gently waved her fan and asked after my health and the weather in Heiankyō. I, in turn, asked her of her activities since I had deserted her.

She had, as I already knew, entered the train of the Lady Masako, wife to Lord Yoritomo, and there occupied a position. Her life was, as she put it, tolerable.

But did she not perhaps wish to petition for formal separation, I asked, adding that since I had occasioned it I would certainly not dispute it. Also, I said, I had my lands in the east and upon these she was welcome to settle if she so desired.

But she was as indifferent to our divorce as she had been to our marriage. And as for my lands: Oh no, my lord, those are for our son.

I looked at her, looked at her round, sensible, middle-aged face, looked into her round, sensible, incurious eyes. Had I ever, I wondered, touched her, reached her? Had I made any impression upon her at all—other than the purely physical I must have made when we were disinterestedly creating our child.

– Tell me, why did you marry me? was my extraordinary question.

It did not seem so to her, however. She said: Because you asked me, my lord.

– But did not you want, expect, more than you eventually received?

– No, my lord. You have always done me full honor as your wife and certainly given me no public reason for complaint. Your manner of leaving Kamakura was, perhaps, unexpected and indeed caused some comment in official circles, but, once it was understood that you had taken the cloth, the fact was then accepted and speculation ceased.

– Speculation?

– Yes, my lord. The people here did not know why you did as you did.

– And they do now?

– Oh yes, sir. You desired to take the cloth.

– And why did I wish to do that?

She hesitated, an instant only, then said: Because you felt the call of the Great Buddha.

– I see, I said.

And I did. I understood that, for her, life was its surface and nothing more. Things were what they seemed—precisely. There was no delving underneath, no peering behind, no ascribing of motives, no attempt at any understanding. There was nothing to understand in her world because the ostensible was her only reality.

– I had thought myself, she then offered, to go into a nunnery. It seemed a wifely duty, you yourself having become a priest, but the Lady Masako has been good enough to take a kindly interest in me and my position here in the Shogun's capital. Instead, therefore, I have become one of her ladies and as such I am well treated. So, you see, my lord, I am not unhappy.

But not, of course, happy. She had never been either—lacking any interests, she would have had few emotional capabilities. Thinking this I suddenly, perversely desired to reach those distant emotions in her. This was the reason that I asked: You remember the Lady Fuji no Kata?

– How, sir, could I have forgotten? I was her attendant.

– Yes, I too remember, and it was through her that we met. And do you remember that during our courtship she was pregnant?

– I do, sir, and I remember the birth.

– Well, I took that baby's head—once it was grown.

She was silent for a moment, as though for once attempting to assess a motive, then said: Yes, so I heard. Then she added: Such was the will of the Buddha.

At this I became angry. Do you actually believe that? I asked.

– You must not ask me such questions, sir. As a priest, servant to the Lord Buddha, you must well know his will.

I looked at her, at her neutral gaze, the face which seemed, perhaps consequently, featureless.

– You are cold, I said unfairly, feeling the grateful flush of ire, the uniting excitement of temper mounting: Never have you shown me your feelings. You were not pleased to be married; you were not unhappy to be deserted. I do not know you. You are a stranger to me.

Strong words and, of course, unfair. Yet, she did not seem to find them so. She looked at me and said: Yes, my lord, perhaps so, but then you have never honored me by showing me your own feelings.

– That is so, I said, then added, like a warrior: It was not my place to do so.

– That is true, she said and looked down at the polished floor on which we sat—me on a reed mat, she on none.

– So it was, she continued, that for many years I thought that you had none. Not only for myself but for anyone. But when I learned of the true reason for your taking of the tonsure, when I heard the account of the Battle of Ichinotani, I then, sir, realized the depth of your feelings.

Hell and damnation! That accursed Atsumori yet again. Like a vengeful ghost he suddenly appears as though through the floor. When will the boy stop plaguing me?

My sudden ire must have shown, for she added: Do not mistake me, my lord. It was with something like pleasure that I learned of the depths of feeling of which you were capable. I had sometimes thought of you as an able military man whose heart was closed. Now I was so happy to find otherwise.

Her words somehow stilled my mounting temper. Forgive me, I said. We had our understanding, you and I. It was, perhaps, not that which I would have preferred.

– Nor I, my lord, she said in a small voice.

And that was the closest I ever got to my wife. But it was quite close, closer than a long, hushed talk, closer than an embrace.

Then she sat, waiting to be excused.

Waiting. Perhaps she had spent her long married life with me waiting. The lord, the husband, must lead, and the wife must follow. But I had not led, had indicated neither pleasure nor displeasure at anything she said or did—had indeed behaved in the same manner of which I now accused her. She had waited because she had no other recourse. Like now.

So I nodded once, in lordly fashion, and said that she might retire. With a low bow and much rustling, she did so. And that was the last I ever saw of her.

* * *

But not the last I saw of my family. The next visit occurred a day or two later. An orderly came to tell me that an officer was awaiting, had just galloped up to Kamakura for the purpose of meeting me.

This said, Naoie rushed in, still in armor, and threw himself on the floor. Father, he gasped.

He was now thirty-six, a full eight years older than I was when he was born and in much worse condition than I had been at his age. He was overweight, even chubby—perhaps it was this peacetime life.

– My son, I said as cordially as I could to this middle-aged man crouched there, dripping sweat on the floor. Yet I made no move to raise and embrace him, an act now common, as though the generations were brothers.

He had heard, he said, that I was here and had raced to pay his respects. I did not need to ask why—in Naoie's world one did what was expected, and racing through the night to greet an aged and tonsured parent was expected.

– I am happy to see that you are well, he then said. But he could not see me, nose to the floor like that. This fashion for full obeisance from military men is quite ludicrous.

– Oh, do sit up properly, I said. He thanked me and his face appeared, round, like his mother's. In less than ten years he would be my own age at the Battle of Ichinotani, I thought. At the same time—all that groveling—I longed to lose my famous temper.

That I did not was due to my surprise at Naoie's impulsively stating, once he was properly seated opposite, that he had had a most propitious dream the night before and that it was this as much as affection that had sped him on his way to me.

It was again the evening before the Battle of Ichinotani, and he was again sixteen and once more wearing the blue-and-white leather he had worn then, worn it over a light green robe, he remembered. And he was riding Musashi, the cream-colored filly. Didn't I remember her?

And there I was, looking so young and wearing my red armor and my red scarf and riding that chestnut charger, dead these many years. And he and I were capering up and down in front of the Taira gate in the dead of night and I called: We are

Kumagai Jirō Naozane and Naoie, father and son, from Musashi.

I nodded, I remembered.

– And then, he continued, I rushed at the gate and thrust in my hand and someone there sliced my finger with his sword.

– You were fortunate that that was all, I said. It was a foolhardy, not a brave thing to have done.

He looked at the floor: But then they cut off my arm, my right one. They held me there until it was cut through and then I fell back and blood spouted from my shoulder and I looked all around for you and it was all dark and you were not there.

– Did you die? I asked.

– No, I woke up. And then, the surprising part, my orderly came in with the news that you were in Kamakura and so I obtained leave and galloped here as fast as I could. Was it not strange, sir? My dream and then its becoming real?

– You mean my not being there, and my suddenly being here?

– Yes, sir. Was it not strange?

The strange thing was his telling me this without a hint of complaint for a father who had truly not been there—ever. Even stranger was that he was smiling as he told me this, reveling in petty wonder.

– I call that a strange string of events, sir, he said.

– And I call it mere coincidence. But it is good to see you take an interest in the past. And do you remember the flute?

– The flute?

– Yes, before we reached the gate that night. Someone inside was playing the flute.

– Was it a signal, you mean? Like to the enemy?

– No, I mean nothing of the sort. It was someone playing the flute, playing it beautifully.

– I am sorry to say, sir, that I do not remember that. But I do remember one thing.

– And what was that?

– How happy I was, sir. Maybe that was the happiest day of my

life. I was in armor and on a good horse and I was going into battle with my warrior father. I was so happy, sir, that I was almost
wild. And that is perhaps why I was so foolish, as you rightly say,
as to put my hand through the gate slit. I was that wild.

– Well, you have recovered, I said. And you have done well.
Our great lord thinks highly of you, has commended you, and
you will doubtless rise further yet in rank. Already, you see, you
have surpassed me.

He bowed low, perhaps surprised.

– Yes, I said, I am proud of you.

Now he was surprised. But, then, so was I. I had not expected
to say this. Indeed, I had not known until I did so that I believed
it. But why would I not? He had been successful in doing what
he most wanted. Much more so than I myself. That is something, I believe, to be proud of.

After a silence he again spoke. What will you do now, father?

– Your father is now a religious person with the various duties
he has undertaken.

He showed me a surprised face and when I raised my eyebrows, he said, I had thought that the vow of expiation was perhaps satisfied.

Hell! The ghost again! Rarely have I encountered a youngster
more persistent than that Atsumori. Now, however, since there
seemed no getting rid of him, I was becoming accustomed to
the baleful presence.

And so I answered: No, things are more complicated than
that. But, to answer your question, I think, since I now know our
lands are still ours, that I would like, after all of these forty-some
years, to return to Musashi. Not to stay, you understand, but to
see what has occurred in the place where I was born.

– Would you care to be accompanied?

– No, but thank you for the filial thought. You have your
duties here—a young wife, I understand, and a fine child.

– Two.

– And two fine children.

– They are nearby, sir. Would you care to see them?

My grandchildren—already. No, I did not want to see them. But I merely said: Perhaps before my departure tomorrow.

I then hesitated, as I often do at partings, and added, I am pleased that there has been the occasion to see you again, my son.

Then he asked: Will you return, father?

– Perhaps. I am waiting, I said, to see what form my life takes, what shape it has had.

He raised his head to look at me, puzzled—and he suddenly seemed all of sixteen again. And I thought as though for the first time of family, my unseen grandsons, my son here, myself, my father, dead so young, and my distant grandfather, now quite forgot. I saw a correspondence—I, who had lived so much alone.

– Goodbye, my son, I said, rising. He bowed, nose to the floor, and I swept from the room.

* * *

And the next day, early, I left Kamakura, just as I had a number of years before. But this time I traveled north, and in some days I was back in Musashi.

How small everything had become, how petty the distances— this banal thought was my first upon viewing the scenes of my childhood. I had remembered that ditch there as wide as a river, and that grove as a forest some dangerous distance from the manor.

But where was the quince I used to climb? Long dead, I was told. My young informant, a distant cousin, eighteen or so, did not remember it, but a quince is a rare tree, an upland tree not often found in these plains, and so he had been told about it. Remembered it as ancient history, like myself.

The house was much the same but now added to. Hisashita Naomitsu had, when he thought the land his, made some improvements. These were now mine as well. The eighteen-year-old bent his knee when he addressed me and called me master.

So did Naomitsu himself when he appeared the evening of my official welcome. He was still as ill-favored as ever and, seeing him again after these several years, I wondered what it would have been like to have lived through life ugly. Perhaps that alone created his bad character.

Now, however, he was on best behavior. Kamakura had long informed him that the main part of the land was mine and that the lesser part was his. So he bowed low and I politely informed him that as a priest I was no worthy recipient of such respect. At this he bowed even lower.

In the ensuing conversation, I attempted to put his mind at rest. I would found a temple of our sect, and our headquarters would supply a resident priest. No, it would not be myself. I was not ordained. I was merely a lay person, though I bore a priestly name.

They already knew about it. It was Reverend Rensei this and Reverend Rensei that, as we sat about the big open hearth, around which during long winter evenings I had lived my young life and listened to tales of the past.

My father was spoken of. The bear was again brought forth. The martyred ancestor was not, however, mentioned. He had been a Taira and these were not much spoken of.

– Do you remember, sir, asked Naomitsu, back forty years ago when we were youngsters here, and the soldiers used to pass on their way to the capital, and we used to look after them and wish we could go too?

And that was the extent to which those thousands of the dead—the Taira—were spoken of that evening. It was indeed forty years since I, one of them, had seen Heiankyō golden in the afternoon sun, and as I looked about this familiar room, I felt myself becoming younger, as one does upon visiting the places where one was small.

Sitting there, cup in hand, the taste of the raw country liquor in my mouth, I could discover the person I had been. Tomorrow the grove would be larger and the ditch wider.

But at the same time, this dark manor house, this view across the fields became less substantial. It seemed to waver, like a mirage. Its reality—my only reality for those first fifteen years—

had worn thin. It was as though I could see through it, to the dim forms beyond.

And, as I stared, a sudden evening breeze wafted into this low dark room the ripe, full smell of the paddies and the growing rice. And I was ten again, my nostrils filled with the odor of standing water and mud and green stalks. If I closed my eyes I could see again, far away, the late evenings of my youth, see again old Naruki, gruff by the fire, see myself, my rusty sword in my lap.

– His reverence is weary, said a voice. I opened my eyes. It was Naomitsu looking at me. He slapped his nose. The evening breeze had wafted in mosquitos as well.

And the next day, as so often happens in our land, it was autumn. From that ripe summer evening I woke next morning to a cool north wind and some withered insects by my pillow. Outside the sky was as though swept clean, the heaviness of summer was gone, and even the warmth of the sun was of a different quality. It had a sheen to it, the color of autumn.

That morning I again met with Naomitsu and the others and attended to the temple business, then made my deposition concerning the land. It was all written and sealed and I had only to explain. My lands, I told them, upon my death would go to my son and through him to my wife.

This was unexceptionable and so everyone bowed. And in the distance, I remember, a pig squealed. Naomitsu had lately taken to importing and raising these strange creatures. They are said to be edible, though I, as a priest, can know nothing of this.

Then I gave them my blessing as they bowed with folded hands, and I strode along the way I had taken forty years before—then a path, now a road.

* * *

The ghost now accompanied me. And as I trudged along that road it kept pace and directed my thoughts. I hated its presence, but I let it lead me back to Ichinotani.

It was not that much out of our way. From Kamakura to

Heiankyō took about two weeks of walking—though I understand that relay runners now do it in five days—and to detour
onto the Naniwa road took only a few days more. So I found
myself again at the beach at Suma on a bright day in mid-fall,
the gulls screaming and the west wind blowing.

Looking landward from the flat beach, I was surprised at how
low, really, those mountains are. Listening to the poems of the
blind balladers, I had grown to believe that they towered.

So will everyone from now on. Just as they will believe in the
small figure of Kumagai, weeping over the death of the smaller
figure of Atsumori—down there in the left-hand corner, as it
were, of this mighty battle frieze.

I again faced the sea and remembered that day. The tide had
come in on that sandy beach, where I now stood, as it was again
doing, and the Minamoto torrent had flowed down these low
mountains and spread to catch the Taira in between.

Just as one does not see the grains of sand that compose the
beach nor the drops of water that make up the surf, so I now
remembered only the surging movement as those troops to
which I belonged rapidly spread across the strand, their flags billowing like clouds above them.

Here and there in this hoard I remembered a face, turned,
mouth open, hair down, or a gesture, or the way that a halberd
fit into a fleeing back, as though it were homing in, assured at
last of rest.

Our white banners streamed above us as we raced across
the now empty sands and I remembered how my sword handle
squirmed in my half-gloved hand as though alive, but only
because the blood of those I had hacked had made my grip
uncertain.

Racing out of my memory came a fellow officer, sword drawn,
who fell upon a Taira, knocking him down, lying on him in the
surf as he raised his weapon, all unknowing that just behind him
came another Taira soldier, sword drawn, about to fall upon
him, lying in the waves. I saw that strange six-legged, six-armed

creature for but a second, but I had not forgotten. There, now, for another second it lay before me in, for all I know, the precise place that it had fallen.

And where, I wondered, had stood that other Taira, my young guide, my juvenile ghost? Was it here where the wave had just washed in? Or, over there by that piece of flotsam? I closed my eyes in the afternoon autumn sun and saw us again, small, like battling insects, down in the corner of that immensity, our vanished world.

There I was, sword drawn in typical posture, and I savored the consistency. Why, that man is a soldier. That is all he is, but he is a soldier all the way through. All of a piece he is. A fine piece of work.

Like Kiyomori, Yoritomo, those others I had admired because of their cohesion, of their being nothing other than what they were. There I was, small in my corner but real—joining them.

And what was this small but busy figure feeling, I wondered. I remember wondering if Yoritomo ever felt anything. Now I must wonder the same about myself. And I found that I was admiring that blubbering brute who sat in the surf adding salt tears to the salt sea. He was feeling something—he had stepped outside of himself.

He had also stilled his thought, as I had so often attempted—but he had done so by abandoning himself. This was something I had never done. Rather, I had had small patience with these feelings of mine.

I ought to have had more. They are mine; indeed, they are me. And, as the Buddha has said something like, life's difficulties vanish when you are no longer going against your own grain.

To be a true and worthwhile man was all I wanted. And, in so wanting to become that, it was as though I had forgotten to *be* . . . that is, to be myself as authentically as was this figure sitting in the water.

I had thought the choice was between being known as a thief

or a fool, a villain or a sentimental figure of fun. I was wrong. There is a further choice. I can always choose to be what I have become.

Standing there, where I had stood, I slowly began to understand the uses of this legend. There was, after all, a pleasing simplicity to it, and this always appeals. People want to believe in passion. A warrior swept off his feet and landing, smitten, bottom down in the waves, seems to indicate that there is more to life than is actually there.

That I, the most self-seeking and practical of folk, should have been chosen for this romantic role was strange, but as I stood there, whipped by the wind and scolded by the gulls, I became aware that it was to my advantage that I adapt myself to it.

And at once the tale began to have a certain rightness about it, like a habit well cut. Here I was, soldier turned priest, a figure of regard, remembered, even revered, for his sudden access of emotion. It mattered little that none of the emotions, except perhaps anger, had ever played a part in my calculations. What was important was that I be perceived by others to my own advantage.

Also, a further rightness. The soldier sitting in the surf is more real than this haunted priest standing on the shore.

I remembered the words of Hōnen. He wondered why the opinion of the world meant so much to me. He found it limiting. I was capable, like everyone else, of becoming a Buddha, a being who did not predicate himself upon the opinion of others. And this concern of mine had long worked against my better interests, as I recognized.

Where had I learned to be so skeptical, had asked my mentor. Skeptical yet concerned for reputation, dubious but still following some kind of, perhaps posthumous, glory. You are much of this world, said Hōnen.

* * *

So I am, and such is more than my lot: it is my choice. And that is why, looking at the low mountains, at the hanging gulls, the

wind at my back and the sea before my eyes, I called: I, Kumagai
Jirō Naozane, fairly took the head of Taira Atsumori, then feeling remorse at this loss of youth and beauty, I entered the religious life and became the priest Rensei. This I affirm.

The headless ghost turned its head and—headless though it
was—smiled. Though he had died too young to have had followers, he now had me. And I had him. I knew my fellow feeling
would eventually do me in. But I also knew that if I was not
remembered as the remorseful, love-struck warrior, I would not
be remembered at all.

So, I wandered the shore. Where had it occurred, this event
of so many years before? I scraped at the sand with my foot.
Would it not uncover the water-logged flute?

No, it would not, but as I looked at the horizon where had once
floated a flotilla, I saw plainly the face of the young Atsumori. Yes,
he was beautiful and, yes, I am sorry that he is dead.

So, on my way back to Kurodani, I stopped by a wayside
shrine and prayed for the repose of his spirit. I had accepted
what I had become and in so doing had discovered the shape of
my life.

And my next, for I will now lead in the dying, and the memory of Atsumori will be the first.

* * *

I seem now to be at the end of my history. And the lute players
down the hall seem finished with theirs as well. All has been
quiet for several days. Perhaps they are already out in the world,
feeling their way about and entertaining the credulous with
their version of history.

It is quite different from mine. Yet, now that poor Yoritomo's
son is being pushed about by the regents, and now that the
regents are of the widow's family, all of them affiliated with the
former Taira, this new ballad version of the villainous Minamoto
will sit well. I wonder what will happen to these jottings of mine.
I think I will hide them.

I suppose some precautions ought to be taken. Just now I had to throw my sleeve over these sheets when the new acolyte came in. It is thought to be sutras I am copying, but nowadays all the youngsters can read, and a glance would indicate to the prying eye that, whatever else, these stacks of paper are not sutra copies. And though this new boy is a real youngster—he cannot be sixteen yet—he has a knowledgeable way about him and can probably read better than I can.

It was my tea he brought me. It is a solace on these long winter afternoons here in this cold place, where the light from the paper panes is as white as the snow outside. Also, he earlier brought in a brazier, straining and grunting as he trod across the floor, making the boards creak. He is a big boy, though young.

* * *

And intelligent as well, for his years. We have had a little talk. Perhaps I might be able to put him to work, if I can trust him. This manuscript of mine is a great mess, with scribbled additions here and crossed-out deletions there. A clean copy is what is needed. And the lad has a neat hand.

* * *

His name is Jōban. He is a good boy. And honest too. And bright. We have tried out the first several pages, and he realizes that this is no priestly project. He even seems excited by it, as though we were both being bad together.

* * *

Much later. This body of mine has been plaguing me. Pains in the back. In the legs. Old age. It has been several years now since I wrote my deposition—signed it with the impression of both hands, just like those bloody-fingered oaths still required in Kamakura. Glad I did it. Still feel strongly about getting the best place in the highest paradise.

Maybe that is what my dream was about. Last night I went to
the door and there stood a beggar, so I blessed him. And when
I did, I realized that he was the tutelary deity of my house—the
House of Kumagai. He told me that wealth and happiness had
arrived. I was ridiculously happy at this and kept smiling and saying that, oh yes, I had received them.

Have been looking over these pages. Not too bad. Am resisting temptations to add new things. Further collapses in
Kamakura, for example. New shogun, Yoshitoki, eldest son of
Tokimasa, grandson to Yoritomo. Led about by the Hōjōs. The
Minamoto much diminished, playing Fujiwara with their imperial concerns. It seems to be true, that old folk-saying that if
you stay on long enough life makes a full revolution. Then you
may step down.

* * *

Months later, but I have not yet stepped down. Though my
place in the highest paradise is all but awaiting me, I still do not
want to leave this life.

On one of my earlier pages I wrote that I wanted to put my
life in some kind of order and to create a permanence where
none existed. So I have, I now believe, though my method has
in these last pages to embrace and incorporate that which never
in itself existed at all.

Yet, through this lie—Kumagai, the lovesick warrior—I have
become what I wanted to become: a remembered, consistent
person, standing firm against the tides of time.

Life is so pleasant. I look at the dark garden, I feel the warmth
of the brazier, sip my tea, hear the youth turning these pages,
and I am content.

I may have often enough worked against my best interests but
have now, I am happy to say, finally succumbed to them.

I must write more on this interesting subject. Tomorrow, perhaps.

Attached MS.

On the fourteenth day of the ninth month in the second year of the Jōgen era [1208], the priest Rensei, Kumagai Jirō Naozane, passed away.

Above are his final words, just as he left them. After a short illness he expired. Before this he had been in tolerable health, had taken part in the services of this temple, and taken up the chanting of the sutras.

The service was held in the temple grounds and the remains were cremated. Kumagai Naoie, son of the deceased, who had arrived at the temple several days before, took charge of these and will deliver them to Kōmyōji where they will be properly entombed.

In relating the circumstances of the Reverend Rensei's death, I should also report that there is an alternate account. He is said to have forecast his demise and music was heard from the sky, a light came from his mouth, the place was filled with fragrance, and a purple cloud drifted above the temple, paused for a time and then drifted away. Concerning the veracity of any of this, I can have no opinion because, though there, I saw none of it. I can, however, relate what did occur.

On the evening of the thirteenth day, my Master Rensei did not go into the garden as was his nightly habit, but instead took to his pallet. He seemed tired. I spoke of this, and he said that he was sixty-eight years of age and wanted to rest.

I did not report this, as perhaps I ought to have done. The reason I did not was that there was no one to report it to. The deacon was in the city, as he often is, and there was no one else of sufficient rank here in the temple.

It was a year since the Reverend Hōnen was exiled to Sanuki and Master Shinran to Echigo, and since all public sessions for reciting the name of Amida Buddha had been officially banned, the temple was understaffed, as most of the acolytes had left.

Many believers, however, still came; but they are not allowed to pray. It was some of these, I understand, who saw the lights, heard the music, smelled the fragrance, and watched the purple cloud.

It was consequently left to me to put my Master Rensei's effects in order. And looking at his last words, I feel that he so empowered me. I had spent half a year in making a fair copy of his manuscript. The deposition I left as it was; the rest I transcribed into proper script.

This manuscript was, I must say, in a sorry state. Not only was the calligraphy most badly formed but the pages were full of deletions and amendments, and in addition some were out of order. Nonetheless, I have done my best to ensure that my master's intentions are observed.

Signed: Acolyte Jōban

Attached MS.

It has now been some years since the death of Priest Rensei, and I have again reread the manuscript. My work—as the master said of his own—was not so bad as I expected. The reason is, I believe, that—young though I was—I felt the importance of retaining my master's conversational style, one with which I was familiar. Though the result may be of small literary elegance, it is an account, I hope and believe, true to the writer's intentions.

My reason for now disinterring this manuscript is that I long pondered how properly to dispose of it and to ensure that it is kept from harm.

During the recent disturbances, I have kept it among my effects, but now the times seem less dangerous. The Hōjō Regent is in full command of Heiankyō and His Majesty, the Emperor Juntoku, is on the throne.

Therefore I can now place this manuscript, plus the deposition and these final notes of mine, into the temple archives, hoping they will rest undisturbed until such time as they may be read as their author intended.

The seventeenth day of the fourth month
of the first year of Jōkyū [1219]

Lay-Priest Jōban
Seiryōji

The Memoirs of Kumagai: Bibliographical Notes

There are a number of sources for the life of Kumagai, and there are also some remains. To begin with the latter, there are several extant examples of his writing. The Buddhist prayer, *Namu Amida Butsu,* said to have been written by him (in *kanji*) is in the collection of the Renchi-in at Kurodani in Kyoto. Another (in *kana*) is owned by the Kōmyōji, also in Kyoto. His statement: *Kumagai Naozane no Jōbon Jōsho Ōjo ritsugan ni tsuite,* (again in *kana*) is in the Saga Shaka-dō of the Seiryōji, Kyoto.

This is all that remains of the man himself, but there are some pictorial representations, which are either of his period or later. These include: a wooden portrait statue at Renchi-in, Kurodani; a polychrome statue at Kōmyōji; a picture scroll *Kumagai Naozane Ichidai Jiseki* (The Life of Kumagai Naozane), at the Renchi-in; and the *Hōnen Shōnin Eden* (Saint Hōnen's Illustrated Life Story), owned by the Chion-in in Kyoto, some pages of which are devoted to the relationship between Hōnen and Kumagai. There is also a picture scroll, the *Atsumori Ekotobagaki,* which illustrates the life of Atsumori and his death, and is owned by the Suma Temple in Kobe. There are many other pictorial representations as well, but these are from later periods. Among them is the *Kōmyōji Engi* (A History of Kōmyōji), a scroll illustrating the history of this temple, said to have been for a time Kumagai's residence. A portrait is included, and both are owned by the Kōmyōji itself.

There are numerous historical and literary sources. For the life as a whole, two versions are found in the very late *Zoku Gunsho ruiju* (Classified Collation of Japanese Classics—Part II). These differ substantially from each other—one says Kumagai died at sixty-eight, the other that he died at eighty-four—but both give some reliable indications as to his genealogy.

Kumagai's first mention in the histories is in the *Azuma Kagami* (Mirror of the East), the fifty-two chapters of which cover the eighty-six years from 1180 to 1266, the account itself having been written sometime between 1266 and 1301. Though the manuscript is incomplete and the early entries are obviously influenced by the war romances, it is usually accepted as the earliest reliable history of the period.

Kumagai is mentioned in the entry for 1180. After the names of Ōba Kagechika and thirteen others comes "and Kumagai Jirō Naozane and other *hikan* warriors." The title refers to those soldiers who directly served officers, something like sub-lieutenants or warrant officers. He appears again in the 1182 section, which records that Yoritomo awarded Naozane his lands in Musashi, in the account of the battle of Ichinotani, and in later pages as well.

A fuller rendering of the battle is found in the *Gempei Seisuiki* (The Rise and Fall of the Genji and Heike), a chronicle written at least a century after the events described. This is often considered a later variant of the more famous account in the *Heike Monogatari* (The Tale of the Heike), but it contains more detail—particularly concerning early events, such as the Ichinotani battle, where Kumagai's part is given in full.

The *Heike Monogatari* is the most important and most famous of the military chronicles. It is now believed that the first version was written in the early thirteenth century, some fifty years after the events themselves. It is also thought that this account is based upon earlier versions, ballads intended to be sung, a form of entertainment which much later became the *kowaka-mai*.

There is some evidence that the *biwa-hōshi* singers were at work shortly after the events with which they concerned themselves. It is of this which I have taken advantage in my account. There is in addition some scholarly agreement that the *Gempei Seisuiki* was meant to be read, but that the *Heike Monogatari* was created to be listened to.

In the latter chronicle, Kumagai first appears in Chapter X of Book 9, and his story forms several chapters thereafter. Following the death of Atsumori (Chapter XVI), we hear no more of him. Both the *Gempei* and the *Heike* conclude their accounts with

Kumagai's resolve to make amends by entering the priesthood and never again fighting in battle.

The *Azuma Kagami*, however, gives the circumstances that actually led to Kumagai's resolve, including the 1187 argument at the archery meet. Three years later, when Yoritomo paid his first official visit to the capital, the *Azuma Kagami* does not list Kumagai among the accompanying warriors, though his son, Naoie, is listed. Later, under the events for 1192, the argument between Kumagai and Hisashita Naomitsu in the presence of Yoritomo is chronicled. This took place in November, and by December Kumagai appears again, his head now shaved in priestly style. We last see him in the 1195 section. This includes a visit to Yoritomo and an announced decision to return to Musashi. The 1208 section tells of Naoie visiting the capital because of his father's approaching death.

Kumagai is also briefly to be glimpsed in the pages of the *Ichigon Hōdan*, that collection of sayings of the pupils of Hōnen. He is diligently practicing the *nembutsu* and piously attempting not to turn his back on the divine west—the Pure Land—during his daily activities. He also states that worrying about salvation is of little use, since it is assured anyway.

Among the historical writings, the final glimpses of Kumagai are to be found in the *Hōnen Shōnin Kojo Gazu*, a chronicle written in the thirteenth century, at some distance from the events themselves. In Section 27 we see Kumagai being stubborn again and are later given an account of this. Finally, in the same section, we have a description of his death, one quite different from that in the *Azuma Kagami*. The first recounts the music, fragrance, and purple cloud. The second does not.

This then is all that remains of Kumagai and his history. Everything else is even more conjectural than these chronicles have been.

* * *

All later material devoted to Kumagai concerns itself with the battle of Ichinotani and the meeting with Atsumori. Much of it takes the form of drama based upon the version of the encounter given in the *Heike Monogatari.*

The Noh play, *Atsumori,* was written by Zeami during the fourteenth century, and *Ikuta,* a Noh written by Zembō Motoyasu, was composed during the fifteenth. There are also two more Noh on the subject, *Katami Atsumori* and *Koya Atsumori,* both no longer performed. The *kowaka* ballad-text, *Atsumori,* was only transcribed in the sixteenth century but was certainly composed much earlier. There is also the Kabuki play, *Ichinotani Futabagunki* (The Chronicle of the Battle of Ichinotani), written in the eighteenth century by Namiki Sōsuke and his assistants.

All of this drama offers varying literary interest and no historical value at all—except perhaps as an indication of changing attitudes toward the Kumagai-Atsumori episode. Details and motivations vary, but all agree that Kumagai is sorry for having had to kill the handsome youth and shortly thereafter embraces the faith. In the Noh plays, a generation has passed. In *Ikuta* the son of Atsumori meets the ghost of his father, while in *Atsumori,* the ghost meets the aged and holy Kumagai himself. In the *kōwaka* ballad, Kumagai burns the head and places the ashes in an amulet, which he thereafter wears. In the Kabuki, his anxiety to save Atsumori finds him slicing off the head of his own son instead.

Supporting these interpretations of the encounter is a vast amount of illustration, from such extraordinary works as the "Gempei Gassen-zu" *byōbu,* an early screen in the collection of Yabumoto Hagijirō of Amagasaki, to such popularizations as the Kumagai/Atsumori prints by Utamaro, Hokusai, Hiroshige, Kuniyoshi, and others.

All of this then constitutes the extent of early source material for work on the life of Kumagai. There are also several excellent modern compilations: the "Kumagai Naozane Nyūdō" by Karaki Junzō, which was originally published in *Rekishi to Jimbutsu*

(Tokyo: *Chūo Kōron,* April 1973); the same author's later article on Kumagai's deposition; and "Religious Life of the Kamakura Bushi: Kumagai Naozane and His Descendants" by Miyazaki Fumiko (Tokyo: *Monumenta Nipponica,* Vol. 47, No. 4, winter 1992). To these I am much indebted. I also want to thank the staff of the Cultural Program Division of the Nippon Hōsō Kyōkai, who allowed me access to the materials used in a television program devoted to the life of Kumagai (April 21, 1973).

* * *

There are a number of sources for the period itself: the *Hōgen Monogatari* (The Tale of the Hōgen War), and the *Heiji Monogatari* (The Tale of the Heiji War), authorship unknown, originally chanted by the *biwa hōshi,* generally attributed to the early Kamakura period; the later *Gempei Seisuiki* (An Account of the Gempei War), already mentioned, and the very late *Gikeiki* (The Story of Yoshitsune). There are a number of secondary sources as well, among the most useful being the relevant sections of Paul Varley's *Warriors in Japan: As Portrayed in the War Tales* (Honolulu: University of Hawaii Press, 1994), Satō Hiroaki's *Legends of the Samurai* (Woodstock: 1995), and Louis Frederic's *La Vie quotidienne au Japon* (Paris: Hachette, 1968).

Among writings of the period, there are a number available. The *Kenrei Mon'in Ukyō no Daibu-Shū* (or, as it has been translated, The Poetic Memoirs of Lady Daibu) begins in 1174 and ends around 1213, probably having been written after the latter date, though the postscript is dateable as 1231. A number of famous figures appear, including the Emperor Takakura and Sukemori (the Lady Daibu's lover), as well as others.

In addition, the *Hōjōki* of Kamo no Chōmei, was written in 1212 by a man who was roughly contemporary (1156–1216) with Kumagai and was, like him, a disciple of Hōnen and also a priestly recluse. *An Account of My Hut,* as his work is often translated, offers a contemporary insight into the period.

A major poetry collection of the times is the 1205

Shinkokinshū, and another such is the *Ryōjin-hishō,* put together by the Emperor Go-Shirakawa and containing a selection of popular songs and poems of the day. There are in addition the extant diaries of the period: the *Gyokuyō* of Fujiwara no Kanezane, the *Meigetsuki* of Fujiwara no Sadaie. There is also the diary of Minamoto Ienaga, Minamoto Michichika's account of the Emperor Takakura's voyage to Itsukushima *(Takakura-in Itsukushima Gokōki),* a later account (same author) of the emperor's ascent to heaven *(Takakura-in Shōkaki),* Fujiwara Sadaie's account of the visit of the Emperor Go-Toba to Kumano *(Go-Toba-in Kumano Gokōki),* and the anonymous journal, the *Kaidōki.* There is also the *Kokon Chomanjū* of Tachibana Narisue, which, though late (1254), is devoted to tales from earlier times and includes at least one about Go-Shirakawa.

I also want to list among my sources those reconstructions that influenced mine: Ibuse Masuji's *Sazanami Gunki* is the imagined diary of a real Taira warrior, Tomoakira; Inoue Yasushi's multi-part *Go-Shirakawa-in,* an imagined biography of the emperor as seen from fictional accounts purportedly written by those near him; and Umehara Takeshi's account of the last days of Kumagai in his *Chūsei Shōsetsu-Shū* ("Hasu").

In addition, I am indebted to two books that solved (for themselves at any rate) stylistic problems involved in approximating the language of one time (Latin) to those of another: Hermann Broch's *Der Tod des Virgil,* and Marguerite Yourcenar's *Memoirs d'Hadrien.*

Finally, I am indebted to the art of the period, and to later picturizations of the major events. This material is so scattered in various collections that it would not have been available except for a special issue of the *Taiyō* magazine devoted to picture scrolls of the *Heike Monogatari* (No. 13, winter 1975).

* * *

In conclusion, I (like Kumagai, not a fluent reader of *kanji*) want to mention the translations used: *The Founding of the*

Kamakura Shogunate: 1180–85, by Shinoda Minoru (Columbia University Press, 1960), which contains selected portions of the *Azuma Kagami;* the *Heike Monogatari: The Tale of the Heike,* an annotated translation by Kitagawa Hiroshi and Bruce Tsuchida (University of Tokyo Press, 1975); in addition Helen Craig McCullough's more recent translation (Stanford University Press, 1988), as well as her translation of the *Gikeiki—Yoshitsune: A Fifteenth-Century Japanese Chronicle* (Stanford, 1966); and the *Ichigon Hodan,* translated as *Plain Words on the Pure Land Way: Sayings of the Wandering Monks of Medieval Japan,* by Dennis Hirota, (Kyoto: Ryūkoku University Press, 1989).

Also, the *Hōgen Monogatari: A Tale of the Disorder in the Hōgen,* an annotated translation by William R. Wilson (Sophia University Press, Tokyo 1971); the *Heiji Monogatari,* a partial translation in *Translations from Early Japanese Literature,* by E. O. Reischauer and J. K. Yamagiwa (Harvard University Press, 1951); *The Poetic Memoirs of the Lady Daibu,* translated by Phillip Tudor Harries (Stanford, 1980); the *Hōjōki,* translated by Helen Craig McCullough as *An Account of My Hermitage,* in *Classical Japanese Prose* (Stanford, 1990); the *Ryōjin-hishō,* translated by Moriguchi Yasuhiko and David Jenkins as *The Dance of the Dust on the Rafters* (Broken Moon Press, 1990); Donald Keene's partial translations of the *Meigetsuki* (Chronicle of the Bright Moon), *the Diary of Minamoto Ienaga, The Visit of the Emperor Takakura to Itsukushima, The Ascension to Heaven of the Late Emperor Takakura*—all in *Travelers of a Hundred Ages* (Holt, 1989); Yoshiko Dykstra's partial translation of the *Kokon Chomanju,* "Notable Tales Old and New" (*Monumenta Nipponica,* Vol. 47, No. 4, Winter, 1992); *Waves,* the David Aylard and Anthony Liman translation of Ibuse's *Sazanami Gunki* (Kodansha International, 1986); Paul McCarthy's translation of Umehara's "Hasu" in *Lotus and Other Tales of Medieval Japan* (Tuttle, 1996), and G. Cameron Hurst's unpublished translation of Inoue's *Go-Shirakawa-in.*

* * *

"A reconstruction of an historical figure and of the world of his time written in the first person borders on the domain of fiction . . . it can therefore dispense with formal statements of evidence for the historical facts concerned. Its human significance, however, is greatly enriched by close adherence to those facts." Thus writes Marguerite Yourcenar in her bibliographical note for the *Memoirs of Hadrian,* and I have here followed her precept.

The general outline of Kumagai's memoirs follows the chronology found in the *Heike Monogatari,* with many additions from the other histories listed above. The sources for the major sections of my reconstruction are:

Early Years	*Zoku Gunshoruiju*
Early Battles	*Azuma Kagami*
Joins Minamoto	*Azuma Kagami*
Mandala at Toba	*Hōnen Shōnin Kojo Gazu*
Battle of Ichinotani	*Heike Monogatari/Gempei Seisuiki*
Archery Contest	*Azuma Kagami*
Legal Argument	*Azuma Kagami*
Meeting with Yoritomo	*Azuma Kagami*
Meeting with Kujō	*Hōnen Shōnin Kojo Gazu*
Meeting with Hōnen	*Hōnen Shōnin Kojo*
Kumagai's Death	*Kumagai Naozane no Jobon Josho Ojo ritsugan ni tsuite*

Much material has been left out either because I did not believe in it (Yoshitsune's bodyguard, Benkei) or because Kumagai could not have known about it (Kiyomori's goings on when not in Kyoto). Very little has been added, however. Most of what occurs can be found somewhere in these chronicles, though many of the details are transposed.

More free are those sections during which there are no indications as to Kumagai's whereabouts. Most free is the assumption that Kumagai did not in fact kill Atsumori. But the evidence that he did not is at least as strong as any that he did, since we have no proof of the matter at all.

Also, I have modeled the style of Kumagai—what I imagine it would be had he been writing in English—upon that in Daniel Defoe's impersonation of diction from nearly a century before in *Memoirs of a Cavalier*—old-fashioned phraseology wed to the modern colloquial.

Finally, I would like to thank those friends who over this decade have read and criticized this book in its several versions: Alan Brown, the late Earle Ernst, Richard Hayes, Leza Lowitz, Paul McCarthy, Jonathan Rauch, Mary Richie-Smith, Hiroaki Sato, and Edward Seidensticker.

—DONALD RICHIE

March–October, 1985; August–November, 1990;
April–July, 1993; March–June, 1994; May–June,
1996; March–June, 1998

Other Books by Donald Richie

ON FILM

The Japanese Films: Art and Industry, with Joseph L. Anderson, 1959

Japanese Movies, 1961

The Japanese Movie: An Illustrated History, 1965

The Films of Akira Kurosawa, 1965

Japanese Cinema, 1971

Ozu, 1976

Viewing Film, 1986

Japanese Cinema: An Introduction, 1990

The Japanese Film: Cinema and National Character, 1999

ON JAPAN

This Scorching Earth, 1956

Companions of the Holiday, 1968

The Inland Sea, 1971

The Japanese Tattoo, 1980

A Lateral View: Essays, 1987

Public People, Private People, 1987

Tokyo Nights, 1988

The Honorable Visitors, 1994

Partial Views, Essays, 1995

The Temples of Kyoto, 1995

Lafcadio Hearn's Japan, 1997